Capital punishment is a legal penalty in the U.S. state of Arizona. After the execution of Joseph Wood in 2014 executions were temporarily suspended but resumed in 2022. On January 23$^{rd}$, 2023, newly inaugurated Governor Katie Hobbs ordered a review of death penalty protocols and in the light of that, newly inaugurated Attorney General Kris Mayes issued a hold on any executions in the state.

# TONATIHU AGUILAR

Born February 11$^{th}$ 1980 – sentenced to death June 19$^{th}$, 2003

Aguilar had no reason to shoot up a Nissan Truck in the West Rose Garden area of Arizona on 21$^{st}$ September 1996, but he did. The truck was driven by its owner David Nguyen, in the back were his friends Jonathan Bria, David Glover, Steve Thorstensen and Wesley Ray. They had been to an ASU football party and were on their way to a restaurant for a meal.

The first police new about the incident was a call from Phoenix General Hospital alerting them that several gunshot victims had arrived in the emergency care department that evening at about 11pm.

The first shots fired at the Nissan were in the area of West Deer Valley taking the driver David Nguyen by surprise, he had told the others to hit the floor and tried to get away from the shooter who kept up driving alongside and shooting before leaving the truck at 2700 Block of West Rose Garden Lane in Phoenix. When

Nguyen realised some of his friends were shot he drove straight to the hospital. David Glover had a wound to the right thigh and Steve Thorstensen a graze wound to the head, Jonathan Bria had been shot in the chest and was in a bad way and transported by air ambulance to The Good Samaritan Hospital where he was not expected to survive and sadly died during surgery. The other two slowly recovered in time.

Witnesses to the event couldn't be of much help as it all happened very fast with cars racing by but slowly evidence was pieced together with informant's statements that pointed to a Hispanic male known as 'Dopey' who they identified as Tony Aguilar who drove a 1979 Chevrolet El Camino.

Aguilar sold the Chevrolet to Hector Imperial, 28, and when Imperial was slow coming up with the money he started to threaten him and his wife Sandra, 29, until on October 15th. 1996 he went to the Imperial's home in block 1600, North 62nd Drive in Phoenix and shot and killed both Hector and Sandra in front of their 5 year old son before fleeing.

Aguilar must have got wind that the police were coming for him as he disappeared until July 23rd the next year, 1997 when he was taken into custody by the El Paso Police department at the Mexican border after checking him and finding outstanding warrants for Homicide, Parole Absconding and Fraud. He was interviewed by the Phoenix Police and extradited back to Phoenix on charges of homicide and 6 counts of assault with a deadly weapon for the drive-by shootings and murder of Jonathan Bria plus 2 charges of murder for the Imperial's killings.

On January 4$^{th}$, 2002, Aguilar was sentenced to life in prison for the drive-by plus 35 years for the double murder.

After the trial and sentencing it became evident that none of it should have happened. On April 25$^{th}$, 1995, Aguilar had been sent to a juvenile detention centre for assaulting a police officer where he should have been kept until the age of 18. Mistakes with the paperwork meant he was released after 18 days. The families of the victims of the drive-by sued the police and got a settlement in excess of $1m.

# FRANK WINFIELD ANDERSON

Born April 4th, 1948 – sentenced to death June 2nd 1998.

This is a peculiar case and a bit light on information.

It appears that on August 13th, 1996 Frank Anderson,48, and Kimberley Lane, 15, were hitchhiking in a remote area in Mohave County when they arrived at the mobile home of Leta Kagen,39, Robert Delahunt, 15 ( Leta's son), Roland Wear ,50, and Bobby Poyson, 21, a drifter.

Anderson asked Kagen if he and Lane could spend the night there in an empty travel trailer on the property and she agreed. Why 15 year old Lane was with Anderson, 48, is not known or recorded.

The next day Anderson and Lane decided to go onto Kingman to find work but it was 17 miles away. Sometime during that day after drinking moonshine Anderson and Lane together with Poyson hatched a plan to kill the others and steal Roland Wear's truck and with it anything else they might be able to sell later. Lane enticed Delahunt into the trailer early that evening on the pretext of having sex where Anderson set upon him and cut his throat with a bread knife and held him down whilst Poyson crushed his skull with a rock. The three then had dinner before entering Kagen's mobile home where Poyson shot her in the head with a hunting rifle whilst Anderson held a lantern. This awoke Wear and Poyson shot him in the face but didn't kill him and he fought back with all three tumbling into the yard where Wear was finally bludgeoned to death with the same rock used to kill Delahunt.

All three were picked up in Illinois within days as they started selling the stolen goods.

It transpired that Anderson was a trailer park manager in Antelope valley with a disabled wife. He met Lane when she was 14, the product of a broken marriage living with her father and brother in the same park he managed. He started having illegal sex with her before persuading her to run away with him to Las Vegas where he told her he was a Mafia Member and they would live in luxury. Both were reported as missing soon after leaving the trailer park.

Anderson was sentenced to death in 1998 which was overturned on appeal. He was re-tried in 2002 and sentenced to death again. Robert Poyson received the death sentence which a Federal appeals court overturned. Kimberley Lane pleaded guilty and being a minor served 8 years and was released. The long road of Anderson's appeals reached the Arizona Supreme Court in 2021 with Anderson then 70 years old and in a wheelchair. The defence argued that if the sentence is upheld he might not live long enough to face the execution. The verdict is not in as at this time.

# DAVID LAMAR ANTHONY.

Born May 29th, 1948 - sentenced to death March 10th, 2004

David Anthony married Donna Romero in 1997. He had been living with her and her two children, Danielle and Richard, from her previous marriage to Samuel Romero. On 7th July, 2001 Donna and the two children were declared missing by the Phoenix Police who suspected Anthony of abducting and killing them based on his statements to others that he was going to 'get rid of Donna' and 'those fucking kids' and was known to have violently assaulted Donna who had reported the assault to the police. It was also noted that he had transferred a large amount of money from their joint account into his private account just prior to the three disappearing. The day before they went missing they were supposed to travel by air to Ohio to visit Donna's parents but they never arrived. The police found that they never checked in for the flight although they had bought tickets a week before. David Anthony told police the three had left the house to go to the airport that day and he had noticed nothing unusual. He insisted he and Donna had a very good and loving marriage, and he was faithful to her and thought of the children as he would his own. In truth, he had had quite a few ex-marital affairs, fiddled their joint business finances to his benefit and ridiculed Donna behind her back.

Under interview caution Anthony repeated he was innocent and had no idea where the three were and expressed fake concern. Despite this he was charged on three charges of first-degree murder and found guilty of all three on April 1ˢᵗ 2002. He was sentenced to death on March 10ᵗʰ, 2004 and his appeals began by citing the lack of hard evidence in the case although bloodstains of Donna's blood were found around the house which he could not explain.

The breakthrough came on October 18ᵗʰ, 2005 when construction of a Walmart Store in Buckeye area, 40 miles away, unearthed two hidden metal drums with skeletal remains inside both. DNA testing confirmed they were the remains of Donna and her daughter, Danielle, 14 at the time she went missing. A police examination of the area found a third drum with the bones of Richard inside. He was 12 when he disappeared.

After the breakthrough discovery David Anthony's second murder trial began in June 2012 and the jury handed down the death penalty on all three counts. David Lamar Anthony died aged 67 in prison in July 2017.

# SHAD DANIEL ARMSTRONG

Born June 14th 1973 – sentenced to life in prison.

In August 1996 Shad Armstrong, his sister Farrah and one other robbed a home in Texas. In 1998 he, his sister Farrah and his girlfriend moved to Tucson. Farrah started a relationship with Frank Williams and wanted to start over with a clean sheet and marry him. She had a criminal record and wanted to clear it and was thinking of handing herself in for the 1996 Texas robbery. Unfortunately she told Shad's girlfriend, Rusty Medina, of her plan and Medina told Shad.

Her relationship with her brother Shad hit rock bottom over this as he stood get a very long prison sentence, because of his past criminal record, if the Texas robbery was pinned on him so he made a plan with a friend, David Doogan and Rusty Medina. They decided to kill Farrah and steal her money to go on the run. In the weeks before the planned murder he stole money from Farrah's bank account using her credit card.

On February 19th, 1998 Shad lured Farrah and Williams to Doogan's trailer and shot them both in the torso and the head. Both were killed. Shad and Doogan then tied them up in sheets and rubbish bags and buried them in a pre-dug grave in the ground outside Doogan's trailer. They then fled to California and Mexico together with Rusty Medina trying to use Farrah's bank card but she had changed the number and it registered at ATMs but would not dispense any cash. The police were able to follow them by those ATM registrations and arrested them in Texas. The prosecution needed to prove Shad had killed his sister and Williams for money in order to ask for the death penalty and knowing this legal requirement Doogan and Medina did not once mention money as the reason for the murders. They always said it was to stop Farrah and Williams turning Shad in to the police for the Texas robbery, not a capital crime.

However on March 10th, 2000 the jury returned guilty verdicts of first degree murder on the two murder charges. On December 7th Shad Armstrong was sentenced to death on both charges. The Arizona Supreme Court upheld the convictions on July 16th 2004 but overturned the death sentence and remanded him in prison where he is now pending further appeals. Doogan is serving 22 years with no parole and Rusty Medina served 12 years and is out.

# FRANK JARVIS ATWOOD

Born December 9th, 1956 – executed by lethal injection June 8th, 2022

Vicki Hoskinson was an 8 year old who disappeared on September 17th, 1984 when riding her bike to the post box to post a birthday card to her aunt. When she had not returned home after 20 minutes, her mother sent Vicki's 11-year-old sister Stephanie to look for her; Stephanie found Vicki's bicycle lying on the side of the road a few blocks away, one block from the elementary school. Her mother placed Vicki's bicycle in her car boot and called the Pima County Sheriff's Department, Gary Dhaemers responded, and a few hours later a command centre was set up.

After interviews with possible witnesses, Sam Hall, a coach at the elementary school, told the police that he saw a driver parked in a vehicle in an alley beside the school on the day Vicki disappeared. According to Hall, the driver was making strange gestures and was struggling with the manual gearshift lever. He memorized the license plate, ran to his car to get a notepad and wrote it down. He later gave it to the police after hearing Vicki was missing. A little girl said the same driver made an obscene gesture to her as he cruised by her house. Another saw the driver back his car into a telephone pole.

The trace on the license plate led to a 28-year-old Los Angeles man named Frank Jarvis Atwood. Atwood had past kidnapping and child molestation charges and was out on parole in California halfway

11

through a sentence for sexual abuse of an 8-year old boy. The address where Atwood's vehicle was registered was the home of Atwood's parents, Frank Jarvis Atwood Sr., a retired army brigadier general, and his wife. She was very protective of their son. A few hours after the police had spoken to them, Atwood phoned his parents stating his car had broken down in Texas and he needed money wired to Ken Stoepel Ford, a garage in Kerrville, to get it fixed. His mother wrote down the address of the garage in Kerrville, Texas, where Atwood was waiting for the money transfer. His father copied the information and drove to a nearby payphone and reported the address to the FBI. FBI agents in Texas detained Atwood and his travelling companion, James McDonald, at the garage on September 20th and impounded the car.

During questioning, Atwood told detectives he was in Vicki's neighbourhood on September 17th, the day she disappeared, staying in a nearby De Anza trailer park. About 3:00 pm, he left to buy drugs and returned to the park about 5:00 pm, but did not say where he was during the two-hour period between. McDonald corroborated Atwood's story and told investigators that he and Atwood had an argument in the park about 3:00pm. After that, Atwood left for two hours and returned with bloodstains on his hands and clothing. Atwood had told McDonald he got into a fight with a drug dealer and stabbed him. Investigators found two men who claimed Atwood spent two nights in their trailer at the park before leaving for New Orleans. One of them, known as Mad Dog, claimed Atwood's clothes and hands were bloodstained, and that they had suggested Atwood get rid of his clothes when Atwood told them that he stabbed a drug dealer who had ripped him off..

While no physical evidence in Atwood's car could be linked to Vicki, pink paint on the car's front bumper matched the colour of the paint on Vicki's bike, and traces of nickel plating from the bumper were also found on the bike. At the site where the bike was found, investigators discovered damage to the mailbox post about 12 inches above ground, consistent with the height of Atwood's sports car, and believed this to be the spot where the car allegedly struck Vicki's bike at a slow speed.

Ten days after Vicki's disappearance, Atwood was arrested and charged with one count of kidnapping. A month later he was extradited from Texas to Arizona to answer the charge. On December 3rd, 1984, Atwood pleaded not guilty to kidnapping charges. Because of the publicity of the case in Tucson, the trial was moved to Phoenix. Jury selection took almost 6 weeks.

On April 12th, 1985, a hiker found a small human skull in the Sonoran Desert near Tucson, about 20 miles from where the bike had been found. The rest of the skeleton had been scattered by animals. Due to the state of the remains, the cause of death could not be determined. Dental records confirmed they were Vicki's remains. Analysis of some traces of adipocere , a body fat that breaks down after death, found on the skull fixed the time that the body had been placed in the desert to within 48 hours of Vicki's disappearance.

Atwood's trial began in January 1987. He was found guilty of first degree murder on March 26th, and was sentenced to death on May 8th, 1987 and the long appeals procedure started.

During his years on death row, Atwood got married, was baptized in the Greek Orthodox Christian church, obtained two associate degrees, a bachelor's degree in English pre-law and a master's degree in literature, wrote six books, five of which have been published. He claimed that police tampered with the evidence found on his car, and that no physical evidence had been found placing Vicki inside his car. His appeals for judicial re-review of his case were denied.

In April 2021, Atwood was one of twenty Arizona death row inmates who had exhausted all their appeals. On April 6th, 2021, Attorney General Mark Brnovich announced that his office was seeking to file an execution warrant for Atwood. As he was convicted of his crime before November 26th, 1992, he would be allowed to choose either lethal injection or gas inhalation as his preferred method to die. Atwood did not elect a method, so it defaulted to lethal injection.

On May 3rd, 2022, the Arizona Supreme Court set an execution date for Atwood of June 8th, 2022. Clemency was unanimously rejected on May 24th 2022.

Atwood was executed by lethal injection at the state prison in Florence, Arizona, on June 8th, 2022. In his last statement, Atwood maintained his innocence and did not apologize to the family of Vicki Hoskinson. He was pronounced dead at 10:16 a.m. Atwood was then 66 years old and the murder was 8 years before.

# LESTER BARTHOLOMEW

Born October 6th, 1926 – executed in Arizona on August 31st, 1955.

The reason Lester Bartholomew, 28, shot and killed his wife and two of his children is still unknown.

On 28th May 1955 he took a .22 semi-automatic rifle and at 2133 East Monroe Street, Phoenix, Arizona the truck driver killed his wife, Marie, his 3 year old son Rickie and his 2 year old daughter Pamela. His other child was saved by his wife shielding her.

Bartholomew had previously been arrested many times on charges of petty theft, bogus cheques, common assault, assault with a deadly weapon and aggravated assault. He had served a 2 year prison term for the latter in 1953.

The interviews with police after the shootings revealed that he had planned the shooting for some time but gave no actual reason or could state any provocation that caused him to do it.

He entered a guilty plea to three counts of first degree murder and on 22nd June 1955 was found guilty and sentenced to death at the Superior Court of Maricopa County, Arizona. No appeals were posted. The court fixed the time of execution to be 31st August, 1955 in the Arizona State Prison at Florence, Arizona.

Psychiatrists were appointed by the court to assess his mental condition and reported back that he was legally sane and knew the difference between right and wrong.

Bartholomew was executed, age 28, by lethal gas asphyxiation on the prescribed date, 31$^{st}$ August 1955 and buried by his family at the City of Mesa Cemetery, Maricopa County. Plot 0496-1-6.

# PATRICK WADE BEARUP

Born April 2nd 1977 – sentenced to death February 5th, 2007.

In February 2002, Jessica Nelson discovered that money was missing from her room in a lodging house in Maricopa County. She suspected that Mark Mathes, another resident of the home, had taken it and sought to confront him but he was out. She called her friend, Sean Gaines, and told him of her suspicion of Mathes. Gaines told her to call back when Mathes returned home and he would come with two friends, Jeremy Johnson and Patrick Bearup, and *'sort him out'*.

When Mathes returned home that evening, Nelson called Gaines and told him. After receiving Nelson's call, Gaines and Johnson armed themselves and left for Nelson's house. According to Johnson, they brought weapons because they *'knew there was going to be a confrontation'* and they were going *'to take care of business.'*

On the way, Gaines and Johnson stopped at a convenience store to meet Bearup. At the house the three men got out of their vehicles and were joined by Jessica Nelson and went looking for Mathes who was on the back patio. Gaines had a folding knife with a nine- or ten-inch blade. Bearup carried a loaded shotgun, Johnson had an aluminium baseball bat.

Bearup, Johnson, and Gaines surrounded Mathes. Johnson attacked him with the baseball bat, striking him in the head and upper torso as many as twenty-five times. Bearup stood at the doorway throughout the assault, preventing Mathes from leaving.

The assailants disagreed about whether Mathes was alive following the beating. Nelson was certain that Mathes was dead on the patio, while Johnson claimed that Mathes was still conscious and groaning. After the attack, Johnson and Bearup dragged Mathes to one of the cars and stuffed him in the trunk. Bearup stamped on Mathes's head to make him fit into the trunk.

The four got into two vehicles – Bearup and Nelson in Bearup's car and Johnson and Gaines in the vehicle containing Mathes's body – and all drove to an isolated area near Crown King. Johnson testified later that he heard Mathes mumbling and moaning in the trunk during the drive.

When the cars stopped on Crown King Road in a parking space above a ravine Bearup pulled Mathes from the trunk and finding him still alive shot him in the chest with the shotgun. Gaines and Nelson then stripped his clothes off to make the body difficult to identify. Nelson was unsuccessfully trying to remove Mathe's gold ring when Bearup approached and cut off the ring finger with a pair of wire clippers and removed the ring for her. Mathe's body was then thrown over the guardrail and, as he lay in the ravine below, Gaines shot him twice.

The four then returned to their vehicles and departed for Phoenix. Bearup stopped at a gas station and then drove Nelson home.

Later that February 2002, Bearup told his ex-wife, Sheena Ramsey, that he had gone with friends to beat up a man who had stolen a ring, but the person was killed and he helped dispose of the body. Bearup also told an ex-girlfriend about the killing who recognised the details as those of a body found in Crown King Ravine and told the police.

The three killers were arrested and sent to trial individually. Bearup was found guilty of first degree murder and kidnapping. His appeals are ongoing. Johnson and Nelson pleaded guilty to second-degree murder and kidnapping and sentenced to life in prison with parole. Gaines is awaiting trial.

# DONALD EDWARD BEATY

Born February 7th, 1955 - executed by lethal injection May 25th, 2011.

Christy Fornoff, a 13 year old disappeared whilst on her paper round at Tempe, Arizona on May 9th 1984. A full police search was made but it was two days later on the 11th that a neighbour, Joseph Knapp, encountered Donald Beaty, the maintenance person of Christy's apartment block, looking at a girl's body behind a dumpster. Beaty told the neighbour that he had called the police. No police arrived until the neighbour also made a 911 call. It later transpired that no previous call had been made. The body was identified as Christy's. Medical examination showed that she had been asphyxiated by smothering and sexually assaulted.

The police concentrated on Beaty as the main suspect and found vomit from Christy in his work closet plus Beaty's blood and semen on her clothes. Her hair strands were found on his apartment carpet and bed covering. They also found hairs from a ferret on Christy's clothes and body. Detectives found that the previous tenant in Beaty's apartment kept ferrets. Joseph Knapp told police the body was in view beside the dumpster when he encountered Beaty but another neighbour, Robert Jark, had driven by the dumpster at 4.50am that morning and was sure that no body was in view at that time.

Beaty was taken in for questioning and told police that he was with another tenant, George Lorenz, at the time Christy had disappeared and also named

Teresa Harder as a witness who had seen them together. Both Lorenz and Harder disputed Beauty's account and denied seeing him. Beaty also asked why he was being questioned as officers had searched his apartment on the night Christy had disappeared. This was not so, they had not been to his apartment until he was in custody. They also found it suspicious that Beaty had asked to borrow a friend's car late that evening at 11.30pm the night after Christy had disappeared and not yet been found. The loan was not given. Police  assumed he wanted to use it to move the body away from the area.

With the forensic evidence and destruction of his alibi Beaty was charged with Christy's murder and sexual assault on May 21st, 1984 and remanded in custody. Two months later he was moved to the jail's psychiatric facility as he was becoming very depressed and taking a lot of death threats from other inmates. Whilst in there he confessed to a doctor that he had accidentally killed Christy when he put his hand over her mouth after she had started to scream. Being patient doctor privilege the doctor didn't tell the prosecution.

On March 18th, 1985 Beaty went to trial for murder and the jury came out 10-2 in favour of a guilty verdict which meant a second trial with a new jury on May 8th. In the period between the trials the doctor who Christy had confessed to told a prison officer who alerted the police and the trial court ordered him to testify.

In the second trial with the addition of the confession to the doctor the jury gave a  unanimous guilty verdict and the judge handed Beaty a death sentence as he stated the murderer '*had committed the murder in an especially cruel, heinous, or depraved manner,'* He also gave a consecutive 28 year sentence for sexual assault.

Twenty seven years after the murder of Christy Fornoff on May 25th, 2011, when the appeals had finished and no clemency was given, Donald Edward Beaty was executed at ASPC Florence by lethal injection.

# RICHARD LYNN BIBLE

Born January 23rd, 1962 - executed by lethal injection in Arizona on June 30th, 2011.

Richard Bible was already known to police. In late May 1987, he was released from prison after serving a sentence imposed in 1981 for kidnapping and sexual assault. Bible lived in Flagstaff, Arizona. In April 1988, the Coconino County Sheriff seized a dark green and white GMC Jimmy vehicle in Sedona, Arizona for traffic violations. The GMC had been used to deliver newspapers. A deputy who drove it to Flagstaff noticed rubber bands in the GMC, as well as damage to the left rear quarter panel. Another officer noticed the damaged quarter panel and saw bags of rubber bands in the vehicle. The Sheriff stored the vehicle in a fenced impound lot near Flagstaff, close to Sheep Hill. On June 5, 1988, Bible stole the GMC from the impound lot.

The next day, June 6th, 1988, shortly after 10:30 am., nine year-old Jennifer Wilson, began bicycling from where her family was staying in Flagstaff to a ranch a mile away. Jennifer's family passed her on the road whilst also driving to the ranch. When the child did not arrive at the ranch, her family began to search and found her bicycle by the side of the road. Unable to locate the girl, Jennifer's mother called the police at 11:21 am. The police arrived within minutes, called in a helicopter, set up roadblocks, and alerted the Federal Bureau of Investigation.

Jennifer's mother told the police that she saw two vehicles on the road on her way to the ranch. One was a royal blue Blazer-type vehicle that she saw later going in the opposite direction at high speed. She described the driver as a dark haired, dark-complexion Caucasian male, mid-to-late twenties, possibly wearing a white T-shirt.

That same day, Bible's brother was at his home near Sheep Hill when Bible arrived there around 1:00 pm., driving a dark-green or dark-silver, white-top Chevy Blazer-type vehicle with a dented left bumper, it was the vehicle Bible had stolen from the police pound. Bible was wearing Levi pants, a plaid shirt, a camouflage baseball-type cap, and boots. He told his brother that the Blazer belonged to a friend. After Bible left, his brother called the police and described the vehicle. There was no love lost between them and Bible's brother was convinced Bible had stolen money from him. A detective realized the description that Jennifer's mother had given of the Blazer-type vehicle and its driver fitted Bible and the GMC Jimmy. At about 5:00 pm, the GMC was discovered missing from the police pound. At 6:20 pm, police officers saw Bible driving the GMC which had been painted a different colour. The officers attempted to stop him, and a high-speed chase began. When finally cornered, Bible ran from the vehicle and hid. Police called in a dog and found him hiding under a ledge, self-camouflaged with twigs, leaves, and branches. When arrested, Bible was wearing a levi-type jacket, jeans, a plaid shirt, boots, but no underwear. Bible also had wool gloves, and police found a baseball-type cap nearby. They also found a large folding knife near to where he was hiding and another knife in one of his pockets.

Within hours after his arrest, Bible confessed to stealing the GMC from the pound the previous day and painting the vehicle by hand two hours before his arrest, but he denied being in the area of the abduction. When Bible was booked, the police confiscated his clothing and remanded him in custody.

Searching the GMC, police found a green blanket and numerous rubber bands but no rubber band bags. The steering column had been cut open and one piece of metal had fallen to the floorboard. The GMC contained a case of twenty 50-milliliter bottles of "Suntory" vodka with two bottles missing. In the console was a wrapped cigar broken in two places, a Dutchmaster brand cigar wrapper and band were in the ashtray, and Carnation Rich hot chocolate packets were in the vehicle. Investigators found blood smeared inside and under the GMC, although testing did not reveal whether the blood was human.

Three weeks later hikers came on Jennifer's naked body under a tree near Sheep Hill covered with branches. Her hands were tied behind her back with a shoelace. Police found one of Jennifer's sneakers, without a shoelace, near the body. Jennifer's panties were hanging in a tree nearby.

An un-wrapped, un-smoked cigar with two distinctive breaks in the middle was on the ground near the body. The cigars near the body and in the GMC looked very similar, they had consistent breaks and identical seals. Microscopic forensic analysis showed that the cigars had similar thresh cuts and tobacco mixtures. They also had similar sieve test results and pH values. The cigars were similar to, and consistent with, tobacco residue found in Bible's shirt pockets. An empty ten-pack box of Carnation Rich hot chocolate packs that matched those in the GMC was on the ground near the body as were two empty 50-milliliter Suntory vodka bottles identical to the full bottles found in the GMC. Rubber bands were on a path near the body as well as under the body and in the tree where the panties were hanging. One of Jennifer's shoes was found. Visual observation as well as testing revealed that the rubber bands in the GMC were round rather than oblong and were identical to those found near the body. A rubber band bag containing a few rubber bands was found beside the body.

A patch of blood-matted grass was near the body. Testing revealed that this blood was human and was subtype 2+, the same subtype as Jennifer's blood. Luminol spraying revealed a faint blood trail leading from the blood-matted grass to the body. Testing also showed blood on the top of the branches covering the body. Near the body, police found a piece of metal that fitted the GMC's broken steering column. In Flagstaff, police found another piece of metal from the vehicle's steering column. The three metal pieces, one from inside the GMC, one near the body, and one where the GMC had been in Flagstaff fitted together like a jigsaw and were part of the GMC's steering column.

An autopsy on Jennifer revealed that portions of the body (including the head and genital area) were severely decomposed, consistent with having been on Sheep Hill for approximately three weeks. Jennifer's death had been caused by multiple skull fractures and a broken jawbone indicated that blows to the head had been made. The blood-matted grass near the body was consistent with the blows being inflicted there. Although the body was naked with the hands tied, suggesting sexual molestation, no sperm or semen was found. The physician performing the autopsy took pubic hair and muscle samples. Near the body were several clusters of golden brown hair approximately six to ten inches long. Although the hair found at the scene appeared to be lighter in colour, it was microscopically similar to Jennifer's hair and could have come from her having faded over time. Entangled in one of the locks of hair was a pubic-type hair similar to Bible's pubic hair samples. Long brown hair found on Bible's jacket, shirt, and in his wallet were similar to Jennifer's hair. Investigators found hair similar to Bible's on a sheet used to wrap the body, and hair found on Jennifer's T-shirt was similar to Bible's. Hair on a blanket in the GMC was similar to Jennifer's, a total of fifty-seven hairs in the GMC were similar to Jennifer's hair. Some of the hair found near the body, as well as the hair on Bible's shirt and in his wallet, was cut on one side and torn on the other. The investigator had never before seen such a cut/tear pattern but was able to duplicate the pattern by using the knives Bible possessed when arrested as well as other sharp knives. Twenty-one of the twenty-two hairs on Bible's jacket had similar cut/tears.

Fibres found at Sheep Hill were identical to the GMC's seat covers, and similar to fibres from Bible's jacket lining and the green blanket in the GMC. A blue or purple fibre found on the shoelace tying Jennifer's hands was similar to the lining in Bible's jacket.

Blood found on Bible's shirt, pants, and boots had a spatter pattern consistent with beating something with force. Testing could not determine whether the blood on his boots was human but revealed that the blood on Bible's shirt was human and PGM 2+ subtype, the same subtype as Jennifer's blood. Less than three percent of the population has PGM 2+ subtype. Because Bible is PGM 1+ subtype, the blood could not have been his.

While still in jail for stealing the GMC, Bible was charged with first degree murder, kidnapping, and molestation of a child under the age of fifteen. In April 1990, a jury convicted Bible on all charges and he was sentenced to death on the murder conviction. It took 23 years from the date of the murder for all the appeals to wind through the court system until finally the U.S. Supreme Court denied a stay of execution, justice was done and Richard Lynn Bible was executed by lethal injection on 30th June, 2011 at Florence prison.

# MICHAEL GENE BLAKLEY

Born October 24th, 1977 – sentenced to life in prison July 11th, 2003.

Michael Blakley, 21, was babysitting his girlfriend's 16 month old daughter Shelby at his girlfriend's rooms in the Arizona Clearwater Hotel in Bullhead City on July 18th, 1998. He had met his girlfriend, Melissa Behunn just the April before and moved in with her after he lost his job at a local fast food restaurant and he looked after Shelby when her mother was working in a care home.

On the 18th a 911 call was received by the local police from the Hotel manager who told them that a resident had reported that a baby in their care was not breathing. The dispatcher asked to be put through to the baby's room and instructed Blakley on CPR as the medics were on their way to the hotel.

When they arrived they immediately rushed Shelby to the Sunrise Hospital in Las Vegas, Nevada by helicopter. The child died a few hours later from lack of oxygen to her brain. During the autopsy the medical examiner noticed bruises to her face that he believed were consistent with her being suffocated and injuries to her vagina and rectum. He passed this information to local detectives who asked Blakley and Melissa Behunn to come in for a voluntary interview which they did. Blakley told them that after Behunn left for work he gave Shelby a bath, put her on the bed and had a sleep himself. When he awoke later he realised Shelby was not breathing and called the Hotel manager. That left the three hours between Behunn leaving for work and the time of the call to the manager unaccounted for.

The detectives presented him with the trauma evidence and he admitted sexual assault by penetration of the child's vagina and rectum. He said he laid her on the bed afterwards and she wouldn't stop crying so he put a hand over her mouth for some time and then noticed she was not breathing.

Blakley was sent to trial and charged with two counts of sexual assault and one count of first degree murder. On February 17th, 2000 he was found guilty on all counts and sentenced to two terms of life in prison to be served consecutively without parole until after 35 years.

# STEVE ALAN BOGGS

Born December 1<sup>st</sup> 1978 – sentenced to death February 21<sup>st</sup>, 2006.

Steve Boggs and his friend Christopher Hargrave were the founders of a white supremacist organisation they called The Imperial Royal Guard.

Hargrave was dating Gayle Driver the daughter of the owners of a pawn shop and living in a trailer on their property. In the April of 2002 Hargrave began work at fast food store Jack-in-the-Box on Main and Lindsat in Mesa. This employment didn't last long after he was reported for stealing money by an assistant manager and he was dismissed. When the Driver's heard about the crime they asked him to leave their property.

On May 19<sup>th</sup>, 2002, Boggs and Hargraves went to the Jack-in-the-Box store around 11pm. Only the drive through window was open as the restaurant part of the store had closed for the night. Hargraves was wearing his store uniform which he had not returned and told the other employees he had been re-instated and come to work. He was let in and immediately let in Boggs who had a gun.

The three employees, Beatrix Alvarado, 31, Kenneth Brown, 27, and Fausto Jimenez, 30, were herded into the walk–in freezer and all three shot in the back of the head. Brown fell dead in the freezer, Jimenez managed to dial 911 before dying but didn't talk on the phone and Alvarado crawled to the store's back door. At around 11.30pm a customer, Luis Vargas, pulled up to the drive through window and when nobody came to serve him he got out of his car and looked in. He could see Alvarado at the back door and hear her moaning loudly. Vargas called 911 and went round to help Alvarado who mumbled that two people were in the store before she too died. When the police arrived Vargas told them about the two others and they found Brown and Jimenez's bodies.

Examination of the scene during the night and the next morning revealed shell casings in the freezer which pointed to all three victims being shot inside it plus cash registers that had been forced open. The till receipts showed less that $300 had been stolen. No attempt had been made to open the safe.

Hargrave came under suspicion as he had been reported twice by Jimenez for the stealing episodes which had resulted in his being told to leave the Driver's trailer home and stop seeing their daughter.

But it was Boggs who made the big mistake by pawning the hand gun used to kill the three workers at the Driver's pawn shop. Mrs Drivers was suspicious and called the sheriff who took the gun for forensic tests. When Boggs called at the shop to buy back the gun Mrs Drivers phone the police and took a long time pretending she couldn't find it until the sheriff arrived and took Boggs to the police station to be interviewed in connection with the three murders.

The gun was found to be the one used in the murders and on June 5th, 2002 Boggs was interviewed which led to Christopher Hargrave also being taken into custody. Boggs told the interviewing officers, *'All I did was get rid of a few illegals, I don't feel sorry at all.'*

Boggs was found guilty on three charges of first degree murder and sentenced to death on February 21st, 2006. Hargraves was found guilty of three counts of first degree felony and premeditated murder plus lesser charges and also received the death sentence. Both sit on Death Row in the Arizona State Prison Complex.

# DAREN LEE BOLTON

Born September 9th, 1966 - executed by lethal injection in Arizona June 19th, 1996.

Bolton was the offspring of two unhappy and unstable parents who divorced when he was a child. By the time he was 16 he had already amassed a string of assault charges and served a prison term in 1990 for unrelated offences of assault, kidnapping and sexual abuse. He was a near alcoholic and addicted to both cocaine and marijuana that followed in his father's footsteps. He was listed as 'suicidal' in his teens by a court psychiatrist but was not referred anywhere for help.

On the night of June 27th, 1986, Bolton, 20, kidnapped two and half year old Zosha Pickett from her bedroom at her family home in Tucson and took her to an abandoned vehicle on waste land where he stripped her, stabbed her in the chest, re-dressed her and left her to bleed to death. No evidence of a sexual assault was found. Her body was not found until July 1st when some boys playing in the area came across it.

Bolton was the prime suspect when fingerprints on the vehicle and on the window sill of Zosha's bedroom were identified as his matching those on the Illinois card index system put there after Bolton was convicted of assault in 1984 and 1985 in Champaign. Arizona had no system at this time.

After he had been charged with Zosha's murder a re-examination of the evidence in the 1982 sexual assault and murder of 7 year old Cathy Fritz in Tucson linked him to that crime and he was charged with her murder too.

Bolton was found guilty of Zozha's murder and sentenced to death. He was refused a stay of execution by the U.S. Supreme Court and refused clemency by the governor. He was executed by lethal injection on June 19th 1996. At that time his trial for the murder of Cathy Fritz had not been heard.

# WILLIAM BRACY

Born August 23rd, 1941 – Died in prison whilst waiting on Death Row.

This case is one of those where you have to pick bits of information out of many different places and even then it isn't complete. The main reason for that being that the killings were said to be connected to local Mafia. And naturally, nobody knows anything. So this is my thinking on the case.

On the evening of December 31st, 1980, William Bracy and Murray Hooper, both from the Chicago area and known to be paid enforcers for the Mob and suspected of also being hit men members of the 'Royal Family' street gang, were with Edward McCall, a disgraced ex Phoenix police officer who had been sacked for taking bribes and informing criminals of impending police actions. The three of them went to the Phoenix home of businessman Patrick Redmond who was at home with his wife and mother-in-law Helen Phelps preparing for a New Year's party.

The reason for their visit was to kill the Redmonds who had refused to sell their printing business to the mob. Bracy had been offered a considerable sum to do the job and had been paid some in advance telling Hooper that they would get $50,000 for the hit. The money had been arranged and given to him, it is alleged, by McCall and one Robert Cruz, a go-between to the Chicago mob and McCall.

The three of them entered the house and forced the Redmonds and Mrs Phelps into the master bedroom and bound and gagged them before ransacking the place and stealing jewellery and money to give the impression of a robbery gone wrong. They then shot all three killing the Redmonds but Mrs Phelps survived and was later able to identify all three from mug shots and they were arrested and charged.

Bracy and Hooper were convicted of the murders after a joint trial as were McCall and Robert Cruz. Cruz won a new trial on appeal and was found not guilty. He was later found dead in a field in Chicago. Bracy, Hooper and McCall were all sentenced to death for first degree murder in February 1983. It took 42 years of appeals before Hooper was executed by lethal injection in 2022 age 76. Bracy died in prison during his appeals process.

# JOHN GEORGE BREWER

Born November 8$^{th}$ 1965 – executed by lethal injection in Arizona on March 3rd, 1993.

The only interesting part of this case is the fact that Brewer was the first Arizona inmate on Death Row to be executed by lethal injection.

On November 11$^{th}$, 1987 Brewer's girlfriend, Rita Brier, had had enough of him. She was over 5 months pregnant with their child and Brewer had no job, no money, lived in her apartment in Flagstaff and had showed no intention of doing anything to improve their way of life. The argument swelled during the day until Brier told Brewer she was leaving him and he ought to sort out his life if he wanted her to come back.

Brewer lost his temper and locked the pair of them into the bedroom where he beat and strangled Brier with a tie killing her. He then slept for a short while, took a shower and had sexual intercourse with the corpse before walking to a nearby bowling alley and calling the police.

He was arrested for first degree murder and kept on remand. He admitted to the crime and necrophilia and at his trial dismissed his attorney and pleaded guilty to all charges. He was found guilty and sentenced to death refusing his right to appeal. He repeatedly declared that he '*deserved to die*' and refused to work with civil liberty organisations working against the death penalty in the State. Brewer's mother filed a 'next friend' habeas petition challenging his competency to defend himself and the validity of the sentence in that circumstance. It was dismissed. Then Brewer may well have had second thoughts about his death sentence as he next invented extra terrestrial friends from a planet he called Terracia visiting him at night to try for a dismissal of the sentence or it being reduced to imprisonment due to his mental state. That didn't work and he was executed, aged 28, by lethal injection in Arizona on March 3rd, 1993 roughly 6 years after the killing of Rita Brier and their unborn child.

One thing we do know is that Brewer died with a full stomach. His last meal consisted of 3 grilled pork chops with gravy, ¼lb of pacon, 6 fried breaded shrimp, Beef Rice-a-Roni, 3 slices of French bread with butter, apple sauce, 2 cans Canada Dry Ginger Ale with ice, slice of Coconut Cream Pie, 1 pint of orange juice, 1 can of Chicken Noodle soup with crackers, I can of Pear Halves with syrup and a Maxwell House Coffee with cream and sugar.

# ANTHONY BROPST

Born 1953 – sentence to two consecutive sentences of 40 years.

Robert May left his home in Phoenix on September 7$^{th}$ 1986 to go to work on a construction site in Houston, Texas and disappeared. He never made it to Houston and his car was found abandoned the next day in Bowie, Arizona. Two days later his dead body was found in the desert outside of Bowie. He had been shot twice in the face. His bank and I.D. cards were recovered dumped in the waste bin at a local motel. The room the waste bin came from had been booked in the name 'B.R.Mills'.

Later that week on the 12$^{th}$ September the frozen body of Steven Myllo, a travelling salesman from New Mexico, was discovered outside Castle Rock, Colorado, Steven had last been seen two days previously on the 10$^{th}$. He had been shot at close range and his van was missing. The van turned up a week later burnt out on waste land in Overland, Missouri. The owner of the land was known to the police and after questioning admitted to helping a friend to incinerate the van. That friend was Tony Bropst from Arizona, a man with a criminal record.

Detectives picked up Bropst, 33, in Phoenix and he confessed to killing both May and Myllo to rob them of their vehicles. Bropst was sent to trial for May's murder in Arizona on March 12$^{th}$, 1987 and received a sentence of 40 years in prison with no parole until after 25 years. He was then sent to Douglas County,

Colorado and received a consecutive 40 year sentence for the murder of Myllo.

# ROBERT MARCUS BURGUNDER

Born January 10<sup>th</sup>, 1917 – executed by asphyxiation-gas in Arizona August 9<sup>th</sup>, 1940.

The perfect crime that wasn't so perfect after all.

Robert Burgunder was the son of a prominent criminal lawyer in Seattle and took great interest in his father's work and took pride in examining each case and spotting where the criminal made errors that led to conviction.

Burgunder was known as a well mannered and polite young man, a Boy Scout and helper at charity events. So when 19 years old he put on his Scout uniform in 1936 and robbed a drugstore of just $14 everybody was surprised. He was caught and spent two years in a youth detention centre. A crack in his personality had opened. He was a gambler with debts to pay.

After he was paroled he enlisted at a teacher training college at Tempe, Arizona and seemed to have put the past behind him but unknown to others he was still gambling hard on slot machines. His peers were envious of how he continually attained high marks without much study. One of the modules he took part in was 'public speaking' and he surprised his tutor when he handed in an outline for a speech on committing The Perfect Murder. He then moved out of the college dormitory and took a room at a hotel.

On May 1<sup>st</sup> 1939 it seems Burgunder tried to enact his *'perfect murder'*. He walked into a car showroom and told the two salesmen, Jack Peterson, 35, and Ellis Koury, 24, that he was interested in a particular car, a Ford Deluxe Sedan and would be paying in cash if a demonstration of the vehicle was to his liking. The two salesmen sensed a sale and all three went off on a demonstration drive on little used roads west of Guadalupe near South Mountain. They never returned. The two salesmen were found shot dead a week later in the Arizona desert. The witness descriptions of the prospective buyer soon had the police looking for Burgunder who had disappeared with the car.

A few days later in Johnson City, Tennessee, staff at the East Tennessee State Teacher's College became suspicious when a lad turned up and asked to enrol. They were aware of Burgunder having been at the Tempe Teacher College and that he was being sort by the police. At the same time the family he had rented a room with had read about the murders and noticed the names Koury and Peterson, the two dead salesmen, on a piece of paper in Burgunder's room. The police were called and identified Burgunder who was driving the stolen Phoenix car. Inside was an automatic pistol of the same calibre that killed the two salesmen.

Burgunder was sent to trial within 90 days of his arrest, convicted of the murders and sentenced to death. His father was one of the defence team. Burgunder appealed his conviction up to the Arizona Supreme court which dismissed it. He was executed by asphyxiation-gas on August 9th, 1940. It was reported that the witness area of the gas chamber was extremely crowded and peopled filed by the body afterwards to get a glimpse of a real murderer.

# ALBERT MARTINEZ CARREON

Born February 4$^{th}$, 1962 – sentenced to death May 1$^{st}$, 2003

Albert Carreon walked into the home of Armando Hernandez in the evening of January 23$^{rd}$, 2001 and shot dead Hernandez whilst also shooting and wounding Christina Aragon, the girlfriend of Hernandez who shared the property at 3175 North Price Road in Chandler, Arizona. The three were known to each other and all had criminal records. Aragon, although severely wounded recovered in Scottsdale Memorial Hospital and gave Carreon's name to the police as the shooter. Her two small sons were sleeping in the premises at the time but were unhurt.

Aragon, now clearly worried about her and her two son's lives gave testimony to the police that prior to the shooting she had been approached by Robert Palofax and Richard Trujillo, who had ties to the New Mexico Mafia, who took her to Trujillo's home and told her that Hernandez was a police informer and his information had led to the arrest and jailing of Trujillo's brother Frank. She agreed to set Hernandez up for the murder by telling them when he would be at home on the understanding she would not be involved.

Albert Carreon was the Mafia hitman given the job as he had become friends with Hernandez when they served time previously in adjoining cells at the same Florence Maximum Security Prison and therefore Hernandez would not be suspicious of him turning up at his house.

Indeed Hernandez was pleased to see his 'old friend' and invited him inside. Carreon made an excuse to visit the bathroom and came back with his gun drawn and fired the fatal shots at Hernandez and then at Aragon. The plan was obviously to kill both so she could not tell the police anything. However, Carreon didn't do a good job and Aragon survived and called the police when he had left. When she described a web tattoo on Carreon's left hand the police immediately knew it was him and showed Aragon a photo of Carreon who she identified as the killer.

Carreon was arrested the day after the killing at Richard Trujillo's home and charged with the first degree murder of Hernandez plus attempted first degree murder of Christina Aragon plus supplementary charges of weapon possession and burglary. He went to trial at Maricopa County Superior Court, was found guilty and sentenced to death by lethal injection on May 2nd, 2003. The Supreme Court of Arizona dismissed an appeal in August, 2005.

Carreon is still in prison now aged 62 and since being incarcerated has been charged with the first degree murder of Jose Gonzalez who was found dead in a parked car on December 20th, 2000 at the Fiesta Village Townhouse Complex in Tempe.

At the time of writing Carreon is still involved in his appeals process.

# JOSE JESUS CEJA

Born October 24th, 1955 – executed by lethal injection in Arizona January 21st, 1998.

Jose Ceja was 19 when he decided to expand his one man drug dealing enterprise by robbing his suppliers, Randy and Linda Leon of a large shipment of marijuana that he knew they had recently received. On June 30th, 1974 he went to the Leon's home carrying an empty suitcase. Linda was alone and after a short scuffle he shot her twice in the chest with a .22 calibre pistol and then used a bed pillow to muffle the sound as he fired a further 4 shots into her head. He then rifled through the couple's belongings and found Randy's pistol in a drawer in the bedroom. When Randy arrived home he shot him four times with his own gun killing him. Ceja then filled the suitcase with twelve one kilo bags of marijuana before he took the phone off the hook and turned the television on loudly to make it seem somebody was at home. He then left and went back to his own home and distributed the marijuana amongst his family members who were all small time dealers. It took 11 days before the police arrested Ceja and charged him with two counts of first degree murder. During that time he even attended the Leon's funeral and helped relatives remove furniture from their house. At his trial the jury returned guilty verdicts on both counts and Ceja was sentenced to death. The automatic appeal resulted in the verdict being overturned on a technical fault by the Arizona Supreme Court and second trial on May 12<sup>th</sup> 1976 found him guilty again with the same death penalty. Appeals followed with Ceja's attorney submitting that the court erred by not taking into account mitigating circumstances. Those circumstances being that Ceja was under unusual and substantial duress at the time of the murders, coping with marital problems and lack of employment. Witnesses were also produced to testify that Ceja was not a violent man. The appeals wound their slow way through the court system being dismissed at each one until Ceja's string of courts ran out and he was executed by lethal injection on January 21$^{st}$. 1998 after spending 23 years on Death Row. He went to the chamber with a request that no family members were to witness his execution and after a meal of red chili beef burritos, 2 cans of Coke and a slice of cherry pie.

# ANTHONY LEE CHANEY

Born April 4th, 1954 – executed by lethal injection in Arizona on February 16th, 2000.

In September 1982, Anthony Lee Chaney and his 'wife' Deanna Jo Saunders-Coleman, (Chaney was already married when he married Deanna), had already committed several burglaries in Texas and Colorado, before bringing their crime spree to Arizona.

At one burglary they had stolen several guns and rifles. In a burglary in New Mexico they stole a black Ford pick-up truck and dumped their own vehicle after changing the pick-up's number plate. It was the Labor Day holiday weekend when the couple crossed the border into Arizona, driving the stolen pick-up truck and carrying 11 stolen guns.

They heard on the radio that the Arizona Highway Patrol was setting up their usual holiday weekend DUI roadblocks to catch drunk drivers and not wanting to be caught, they found a place to camp outside Flagstaff until the roadblocks were taken down.

Coconino County Sheriff's Deputy Robert Cline happened to see the couple camping in an unusual area and went to investigate. Deputy Cline asked Chaney for his ID, and as Chaney went to the truck to retrieve it, Deputy Cline talked with Chaney's girlfriend, Saunders-Coleman. Chaney soon emerged from the truck with a gun pointed directly at the deputy. Saunders-Coleman took Deputy Cline's gun and they handcuffed him to a tree.

Little did they know that a dispatcher was trying to get a hold of Deputy Cline on the radio and when he failed to answer, the dispatcher sent another deputy to investigate he was reserve Deputy Dr John Jamison, a doctor working as a part time deputy.

As Chaney and his girlfriend were leaving the area in the stolen truck, they crossed paths with reserve Deputy, Dr. John Jamison who pulled up near to their vehicle and called the dispatcher to check it.

Chaney jumped out of the truck, firing off more than 30 shots from an AR-15 at the deputy's vehicle and the deputy. Using the screen of bullets as a shield, he pinned down Jamison and moved closer and closer to his target. Chaney fired 3 more shots at point black range; so close that gun powder residue was found on Jamison. He was hit with over 200 pieces of flying glass and metal. The officer was pinned down, unable to unbuckle his seat belt and use his weapon.

Chaney returned to the pick-up truck telling Saunders-Coleman, *"Murder one, reload."*

As the couple left in the truck, Saunders-Coleman told the police later that she saw that reserve Deputy Jamison was still alive and trying to drive away. He was still conscious when the medics arrived, telling them, *"I'm dying and I can't breathe."*

Chaney wanted to change vehicles, and soon came on two boys in a truck pulled in a lay-by beside a forest. He sent his girlfriend to talk to the boys on the passenger side of their truck while he crept up on the driver's side and told them at gunpoint to get out and run, which they did, into the forest.

Once Chaney was gone, the boys came out of the forest and called police with a description of the stolen truck.

Thanks to their quick action, the truck was quickly spotted in Flagstaff where Chaney had gone to get gas and police surrounded it and took Chaney and Saunders-Coleman into custody without anyone else being hurt.

Chaney was indicted for first degree murder, kidnapping, aggravated assault, two counts of armed robbery and one count each for burglary and theft. The jury found him guilty on all charges. The judge sentenced him to 28 years for kidnapping, 21 years for aggravated assault, 28 years for each armed robbery, 20 years for burglary and twelve years for theft. All were the maximum sentence for each crime and to run consecutively. They really didn't matter as he was sentenced to death for first degree murder.

Defence attorneys argued that Chaney suffered from a mental disorder that caused him to react violently when he saw reserve Deputy Jamison arrive in his patrol car that day in the forest.

They also said, Chaney wasn't given enough time to be properly tested for the mental disorder during his criminal trial. Prosecutors rebutted this, saying Chaney's attorneys were given adequate time to examine the possible mental disorder, and six experts had testified over five days during the trial.

Over the next 12 years, Chaney filed multiple appeal claims, but on December 28th, 1995, a federal district court rejected all the claims.

On June 17th, 1999, the state requested that the Arizona Supreme Court issue a warrant of execution.

Deanna Saunders-Coleman testified against Chaney in the trials and herself pleaded guilty to second degree murder, receiving a 21-year prison sentence for which she served 14 years. She was released from prison on January 31st, 1999.

Chaney was executed on February 16th, 2000, eighteen years after the murder of Deputy Jamison. When asked if he had any last words he simply said, *'no.'*

# JAMES DEAN CLARK

Born October 18th, 1957 – executed by lethal injection in Arizona April 4th, 1993

James Clark was convicted on four counts of first degree murder. He worked as a wrangler at the Cochise Lodge and Guest Ranch owned by Charles and Mildred Thumm near Elfrida in Cochise County, Arizona.

On December 3rd, 1977, Clark, 20, had dinner at the lodge with Mr. and Mrs. Rush Allen, guests at the lodge, and with George Martin and Gerry McFerron, two wranglers at the ranch. After dinner, the Allens went to Tombstone with Martin. McFerron and Clark called Janie Hendrickson, a friend, who met them at the lodge. The three of them went to the Elfrida Tavern and then onto a disco lounge in Douglas. Hendrickson and Clark went into the disco lounge. McFerron had drunk too much already and was ill. He vomited and stayed outside.

Later on the three returned to the lodge between 1:00 and 1:30 a.m., and Hendrickson left in her car. Clark did not appear to be intoxicated. During the evening, McFerron told Hendrickson that Clark was dangerous when he was drunk. Clark overheard the statement, but he simply chuckled and made no comment. Clark had been playing with a .357 Magnum pistol at one point during the evening.

After McFerron went to bed, Clark entered the wranglers' quarters and stabbed to death George Martin, an older wrangler who was passed out drunk in his bed. Clark then fatally shot McFerron in his sleeping bag. He then picked up a .357 Magnum from McFerron's room, walked from the wranglers' quarters to the Thumms' house and shot to death both Charles and Mildred Thumm.

A pathologist later testified that Martin died of seven stab wounds to the chest, which penetrated the heart and lungs. McFerron died of three gunshot wounds to the head, one in the temple, one in the ear, and one to the top of the head. Charles Thumm was shot three times, once in the chest, once in the left shoulder and once, from a distance of three to four inches, in the head. Mildred Thumm died of a gunshot wound near the left earlobe, fired from a distance of approximately two to six inches.

After the killings Clark slashed all the tires on the vehicles at the ranch and fled the area in the Thumms' station wagon taking with him rings and credit cards belonging to the Thumms, plus guns, including those used in the murders, and a saddle. He drove to El Paso, Texas, where he sold Mildred Thumm's engagement and dinner rings to a jeweller. Clark was hunted by the police who circulated a picture and information. He was caught a few days later in El Paso, Texas.

Clark volunteered the statement to the El Paso police that he had been given permission by the Thumms to use the car and some credit cards to pick up his girlfriend and take her back to Arizona to get married. A spent lead bullet, which appeared to have organic matter on it, was removed from the pocket of a jacket in Clark's hotel room. When accused of killing the Thumms, Martin and McFerron, Clark stated that he might have killed them, but he did not remember as his memory of that night was blurred.

The prosecution witness was a Drug Enforcement Agency informant who was allowed to testify using the name 'John Doe' he said he had met Clark at a bar in El Paso, Texas on the evening of December 4th and had bought heroin from him and arranged to sell four guns that Clark had in his possession. He stated that Clark told him he had shot three people in Elvira, Arizona. Clark tried to turn the scenario round saying 'John Doe' was the killer and had asked him, Clark, to sell the guns.

The jury at his trial in Arizona would have none of it and convicted Clark of four counts of first degree murder with the death sentence attached to each one. Requests for leniency were dismissed.

James Clark was executed by lethal injection in Arizona on April 14th, 1993 aged 36, sixteen years after the murders.

Whilst in prison in 1985 he met Adele Schoterman a psychiatric nurse and they were married there in 1988.

# ROLAND H COCHRANE

Born March 2nd 1908 – executed by asphyxiation-gas in Arizona on October 2nd, 1935.

Hold on tight! This crime plays out like a Marx Brother's film!

On the evening of January 2nd 1935, Otis Phillips and Horace Hunter made their way to the Royal Apartments in Phoenix to take part in a poker game with a rich player who they were going to rip off with a cold deck. Cold deck is the name given to a deck of cards that has been doctored. They had been told this rich player would be gambling at least a $100, a considerable sum in 1935.

When the pair reached the apartment they learnt that two other men had persuaded their intended victim to go to another card game elsewhere. They called up Roland Cochrane and Harold Burk, two other card cheats and discussed what to do and whether to find where their mark had been taken and go and hijack that game. Hunter told them he was aware of another game that night at Chandler, Arizona run by a wealthy player called Dick Giles where a few rich Chandler residents would be playing for considerable amounts of cash.

All four agreed to hijack that game and they split into pairs to find out where the game was to take place. Phillips and Hunter found Giles at the Avalon Club in Phoenix and Cochrane joined them, Burke had gone off elsewhere. The three planned to rob Giles at Hunter's home as he knew Giles. The robber would be

Cochrane who Giles did not know. Hunter joined in with Giles party of people and later on left the club in Giles's car and made for Hunter's house at 1722 East Adams Street with Giles, Harold McDaniels and Lorain Garvin, two friends of Giles. Phillips and Cochrane followed in another car and parked away from Hunter's house as the others went inside. Cochrane left the car and walked to the Hunter's house to rob Giles. As he approached the house Giles and Mrs Hunter left it and got into Giles car. Cochrane went to the driver's side and pointed a gun at Giles and demanded money. Giles gave him $2.45 from his jacket pocket and Cochrane demanded his bill fold that Hunter had told him Giles carried in his back pocket.

Giles told Cochrane he would have to get out of the car seat to reach the pocket and Cochrane ordered him out of the car. When he had left the car Giles reached into his back pocket and took out the bill fold and threw it over a nearby fence into the Hunter's back yard before turning on Cochrane who shot him in the face killing him instantly. Cochrane then ran back to Phillips in the car and they drove off with Cochrane getting out of the car at The Royal Apartments. Later that night Phillips returned and took the gun that Cochrane had used off him to hide it as it belonged to him. He hid it in a car lot nearby and it was found a few days later. With witnesses seeing the group together throughout the evening in the Avalon club and elsewhere and Mrs Hunter identifying Cochrane as the killer all three were picked up quickly on January 8th.

Cochrane admitted his part and Phillips and Hunter denied anything to do with it until Cochrane's statement involving them was made known to them, then they admitted their part.

Cochrane was tried, convicted and given the death penalty. His appeal to the Arizona Supreme Court was dismissed. Phillips was offered life imprisonment if he would testify to against Hunter which he did. Both got life sentences.

Cochrane was executed by asphyxiation-gas in Arizona on October 2nd, 1935.

# LEONARD COEY

Born July 7th, 1898 – executed by asphyxiation-gas in Arizona on May 22nd, 1957.

On January 27th, 1955 the Sheriff's Office at the back of the Maricopa County Courthouse in Phoenix, Arizona had a surprise delivery. Leonard Coey, 57, drove up and deposited his wife's dead body on the pavement outside the door shouting *'there she is the son-of-a-bitch. She tried once too often to kill me and my kids.'*

It transpired that over a fifteen year period Coey had abused and beaten his wife, who was half his age, and she had finally had enough of being the working bread winner whilst he lounged at home, purporting to be looking after their children, whilst gambling and drinking, and she had engaged a divorce attorney.

The first Coey knew about this was when a process server came to the house and issued him with a restraining order from the court that demanded he leave the house and not make contact with his wife or children.

Later that same day he pushed his wife inside a small shed in the backyard of their home and shot her dead with a .45 calibre pistol he later told the court he had bought to protect his children from assaults by his wife. No evidence was given that she had ever assaulted their children. He then loaded her body into his vehicle and drove it to the Sheriff's Office.

At his trial for first degree murder Coey claimed that whilst he and his wife were in the shed talking about the divorce she attacked him with a hammer and he shot her in self defence. He insisted his attorney's put forward 'self defence' as his defence although they presented a defence of insanity to the court which Coey violently opposed. The judge rejected both defences and the jury returned a verdict of guilty to first degree murder. Coey's appeal was dismissed and he was executed by asphyxiation-gas in Arizona on May 22$^{nd}$, 1957.

# GRADY B. COLE

Born Xmas Day 1914 – executed by asphyxiation-gas in Arizona January 8th, 1943.

In early January 1942 the Texas police discovered a vehicle with the inside covered in blood parked up behind a bus station. A check on the registration gave the owner as Coy Collier Qualls from Fry, Arizona. Qualls was a taxi driver and both he and his taxi had been listed as missing for a few days.

The Arizona authorities were also aware that three soldiers had been missing from the Fort Huachuca Army base, also for a few days, and were known to have been picked up at the base gate by a taxi on January 7th and left without securing permits to leave the base. They were Grady B. Cole, Charles Sanders and A.C.Levice. All three had home addresses in Texas and were quickly arrested there and gave confessions and the following tale of events.

They secured the services of Coy Collier Qualls and his taxi on the night of January 7th, 1942, to take them to Maco, Arizona, without their having secured permits to leave the Base.

They returned to Fort Huachuca early on the morning of January 8th, 1942. They then determined to take the day off and go to Douglas, Arizona, to do some more drinking and dancing. Grady B. Cole had given Qualls his watch to hold as security for money to be paid to him later to cover the fare.

Qualls was waiting for them at the Base gate after they had secured a loan of further monies in the Fort from friends. Before they left the Base and got into the automobile it was stated by Charles Sanders that they discussed the matter of killing and robbing Coy C. Qualls. Grady B. Cole had picked up a rock near the Base entrance which fitted into his hand neatly for the purpose of using it as a club.

On the way into town Coy C. Qualls purchased some gin with the money off the defendants which the four of them, including Qualls, were drinking. According to their statements they told Qualls on the road to Douglas that they had to answer a call to nature. This was a pre-arranged plan and once Qualls had stopped the vehicle Cole hit him from behind with the rock and Sanders hit him with the empty gin bottle. Qualls managed to get out of the car but Cole and Sanders caught him and beat him to death with the rock and bottle as well as kicking him when he fell to the ground.

The body was loaded back into the car and Cole and Sanders made sure Qualls was dead by repeatedly kicking it where it lay on the floor in the back of the car with Cole using a pocket knife to cut Qualls's throat whilst Levice drove. They took any money they could find and drove on to about nine miles the other side of Douglas where they hid the body inside some bushes where it remained for four days until the three were arrested and told the police where it was.

All three were sent directly to the Arizona Superior Court where they all entered a plea of guilty to first degree murder throwing themselves on the mercy of the court. Bad move. The court held a hearing and determined there were no mitigating circumstances in a pre-meditated murder and passed the death sentence on all three defendants on 21st January 1942.

Grady B. Cole, Charles Sander and J.C. Levice were executed separately by asphyxiation-gas on January 8th 1943.

# ROBERT CHARLES COMER

Born December 14th 1956 – executed by lethal injection in Arizona on May 23rd, 2007.

On February 3rd 1987 Comer, 31, and his girlfriend, Juneva Willis together with her two young children, were at the Burnt Corral camp site near Apache lake. They had met Larry Pritchard who was at another local camp site and invited him over for dinner and drinks. At about 9pm that evening Comer shot Pritchard in the head killing him and together with Willis hid the body under a heap of wood. They then drove to Pritchard's camp site and stole anything of value from his tent including his dog.

They then went onto yet another campsite and posing as Drug Enforcement Officers entered the tent of Jane Jones and Richard Smith who they tied up with duct tape and wire. After stealing anything of value from the tent they put Jones and Smith into their pick-up truck and Comer drove off in it with Willis following behind in their truck. Willis separated to go back to their original camp site where her two children were.

Jones had Comer stop the truck by some woods so she could relieve herself. Comer accompanied her and raped her. He then threatened to shoot Smith but was persuaded not to by Jones and told Smith to run off into the woods and stay there or he would shoot Jones. Smith ran off and Comer raped Jones again in the truck. Comer drove off again but the truck ran out of gas and Comer and Jones walked back to the Burnt Corral campsite and together with Willis and her two children drove in Willis's car back to the truck with a can of gas. Comer then shot Pritchard's dog and raped Jones in front of Willis.

Comer went to pour in the gas and Jones ran off into the woods and escaped. She later flagged down a passing motorist and was taken to the Sheriff's Office. Smith had managed to walk back to the Burnt Corral site and had also reported what had happened to the Department of Public Safety.

Comer and Willis were quickly caught and charged in Maicopa County with first degree murder, armed robbery, kidnapping and aggravated assault. In addition, Comer was charged with two counts of rape and three of sexual assault of Jones. Willis agreed to testify against Comer and plead guilty to one charge of kidnapping if other charges against her were dropped, which they were.

Comer refused to attend his trial. He tried not to go to his sentencing and tried to stab his prison guards with a handmade knife. He was flushed out of his windowless cell by a high power hose and attended the hearing tied into a wheelchair naked except for a vanity cloth on his lap.

Comer was found guilty of all charges and sentenced to death in April 1988.

Comer's history of violence and crime is told in thousands of pages of legal documents, psychiatric reports and other paperwork that have become public record over the years. It still remains something of a puzzle how Comer evolved from a personable kid who finished one badge short of being an Eagle Scout into a stone-cold killer.

He was raised in a middle-class family, the oldest of Patricia and Charles Comer's four children, all boys. His father was an engineer for a technology firm, and his mother worked as a quality-control inspector in Silicon Valley. Photos of a youthful Comer depict a good-looking kid with an impish -- some might say devilish -- grin. He loved to fish and was a member of the school safety patrol, and played football for a time.

Comer's journey to death row started when he was detained as a juvenile in the early 1970s on charges of assault, burglary and trespassing. He quit high school during his senior year, and enlisted in the U.S. Army in January 1975. He was training to become a military policeman when his past caught up with him. In July 1975, Army officials issued the 18-year-old an honourable discharge after learning of his juvenile record. Comer reverted to crime and the next year served four months in a California youth facility on a burglary rap, during which he became a member of an offshoot of the Aryan Brotherhood.

After that, his crimes escalated. In December 1978, police arrested Comer on charges of kidnapping, rape, assault with a deadly weapon, and other counts. He plea-bargained to a relatively soft prison term of seven years, and was sent for the first time to an adult prison.

Comer later admitted to having been involved in several stabbings during his prison stint, some as perpetrator and others as recipient. In his early 20s, he spent months in solitary confinement at the prison in Folsom, California, a profoundly violent institution.

Years later, Comer wrote about Folsom from Maricopa County Jail while awaiting this trial: '*I remember feeling my mind shut down, one piece at a time. I used to mess with the rats. I never could figure how they got in. At night, they would crawl on you. At first, it bugged you. But just like love, or the girl you left behind, you turned them all off. You live like a robot. . . . I used to talk to the rats at first. After four months, they talked back. You think you're going crazy, so you don't talk with the rats no more. . . . After 6 or 7 months, all your mind could say was, Fuck you.*'

Comer was released in August 1984 after he'd served less than six years, and found sporadic work as a carpenter. He used methamphetamines heavily during his 30 months of freedom after being paroled, and became increasingly determined to seek revenge against society for evils perpetrated against him at Folsom. That revenge started at the Burnt Corral campsite on February 2nd, 1987. It ended 20 years later with his execution in Florence Jail.

# DANIEL WAYNE COOK

Born July 23rd, 1961 – executed by lethal injection in Arizona August 8th, 2012.

Daniel Cook, John Matzke and Carlos Cruz-Ramos shared an apartment and worked together in a restaurant in Lake Havasu City. On July 19th, 1987, Cook stole $90 from Cruz-Ramos, 26, an illegal immigrant from Guatemala. When Cruz-Ramos began to search their apartment for the stolen money Cook and Matzke beat him with a metal pipe, cut him with a knife and tied him to a chair face down where Cook sodomised him, used a staple gun on his foreskin and burnt his genitals with cigarettes. They then killed him by crushing his windpipe with the metal pipe until he was dead and threw him inside a closet.

Another worker at the restaurant, Kevin Swaney, 16, turned up at the apartment to go to work with Cruz-Ramos. Cook forced him into the apartment and showed him what they had done to Cruz-Ramos. Cook and Matzke then tied Swaney to another chair and whilst Matzke took a nap in another room Cook sodomised Swaney before the two of them strangled him with a bed sheet. Matzke then went to work and later that evening whilst out at a bar confided in another worker what had happened. That worker told him to go to the police and confess or he would. Matzke did go and confess and Cook was arrested at the apartment when officers went there and found the awful scene.

Cook told police that it was a drug party that got out of hand. Matzke was persuaded to testify against

Cook in exchange for a second degree murder charge which didn't carry the death penalty. He agreed to that and was found guilty of second degree murder and sentenced to 20 years in prison. He has served his time and was released in 2007.

Cook was charged with two cases of first degree murder plus additional assault charges and was found guilty and sentenced to death. Appeals citing his mental capacity and poor upbringing as mitigating circumstances cut no ice with the appeal judges and were dismissed all the way up to the Supreme Court.

He was executed by lethal injection on August 8th, 2012, aged 51.

# MICHAEL EMERSON CORRELL

Born January 8<sup>th</sup>, 1960 – sentenced to death November 23<sup>rd</sup>, 1984.

At about half an hour past midnight on April 12<sup>th</sup>, 1984 Guy Snelling and his girlfriend Debra Rosen returned to Snelling's mobile home after attending a concert. Both had consumed alcohol and taken cocaine and marijuana. Not long after they had gone to bed a co-worker of Snelling, John Nabors knocked at the door saying he had to talk to Snelling. When Snelling opened the door he found Nabors and another man standing outside. Nabors introduced the man as his friend 'Rick'. That friend was Michael Correll.

After Snelling let them in Nabors pulled out a gun and said *'I know you have money.'* Nabors told Snelling to call Rosen from the bedroom which he did telling her that they were being robbed. Both then had their hands tied behind them with duct tape. As their ankles were being tied a car pulled up outside the mobile home and Nabors dragged Rosen into the bedroom leaving Correll with Snelling.

In the car were Robin Cady who rented a room from Snelling and her boyfriend Shawn D'Brito. When they entered Nabors came from the bedroom and held the gun to Snelling's head whilst Correll taped Cady and D'Brito's hands and feet. Then Nabors and Correll took Snelling through the home's rooms collecting packs of marijuana and roughly $5,000 in cash.

Then Nabors and Correll forced Snelling, Cady and D'Brito into Snelling's car with Correll sitting in the car covering them with the gun. Nabors went back into the mobile home to tie Rosen to a chair. When he came back they drove the car to where Nabors' truck was parked. Nabors then drove his truck followed by Correll in the car to a desert area north of Phoenix. There they took the three prisoners out of the car and laid them on the ground. Correll told Snelling he was going to have to knock him out and shot him in the head. Miraculously Snelling survived and remained conscious. He saw Nabors take the gun and kill D'Brito, it then misfired as he aimed at Cady and pulled the trigger. He tried several times to fire it until he was successful and killed her as well. Then Nabors and Correll left and Snelling was able to free his feet and run to a nearby house to phone the police who went to the mobile home only to find that Nabor's had strangled Cady when he had gone back into the home prior to the car journey.

Snelling was taken to hospital for his head injury to be seen to and shown two photographic line-ups of suspects. He identified Nabors as one of the killers. A week later another photo of a line up was shown to him which had Snelling in it who he identified as the second killer.

On April 20th 1984 Correll was arrested at his father's house in Las Vegas, Nevada. In addition to the positive identification by Snelling his boot prints were found at the crime scene. He was known to associate with Nabors and the police persuaded Correll's brother to phone Nabors and tell him an untruth that Correll had been shot by police as a ruse to get him to admit the crime, which he did and he was arrested.

Correll was charged with three counts of first degree murder, one of attempted first degree murder, armed robbery and four counts of kidnapping. The trial began on October 16th. 1984 and lasted 3 days with the jury finding  him guilty on all counts. At his sentencing hearing the judge found no mitigating circumstances and passed the death sentence on each of the murder counts. Correll's appeals are still slowly moving through the system being dismissed at each court so far.

Nabors committed suicide with a gun when police went to arrest him.

# LONNIE CRAFT

Born April 6th, 1917 – executed by asphyxiation-gas in Arizona March 7th, 1959.

Vernice Lonnie Craft AKA 'Battling Blackjack' an African American was a lifelong Arizona citizen who had a career as an undercard boxer.

After only 13 months of marriage Craft and his wife Virginia Cook got divorced. Craft was not happy with this and put the blame for the break of his marriage on his father-in-law's continued interference. They had never got on at all well or seen eye to eye.

On the morning of March 6th, 1957 Craft, 40, collected his pay check, left his work place where he was a scaffolder and labourer and went to a pawn shop where he bought a gun and ammunition. He then made his way to Virginia's place of work at the Dispatch Laundry at 1600 East Washington and asked her to have lunch with him.

He went to Sublet's Cafe a short walk away and Virginia joined him and they ordered lunch and sat at a table. Craft asked Virginia to reconsider their relationship and come back to live with him. He didn't expect her answer which was *'no'* and that she was making arrangements to leave Phoenix altogether and not see him again.

Craft pulled the gun from his pocket and as Virginia stood and ran off he shot her twice in the back and she fell to the floor on her face. Craft stood and fired two more shots into her back before turning the gun on himself and shooting himself twice in the chest before firing off the rest of the magazine into Virginia. He then buckled to the floor and re-loaded the gun firing once more into himself.

Craft, who had 40 previous felony convictions on his criminal file, was taken to hospital and made a full recovery from his wounds. Virginia died at the scene. He was sent to trial on first degree murder and entered a plea of not guilty. The jury returned a split verdict and were given instructions by the judge to return to the jury room and come to a majority verdict. They did this and came back with a verdict of guilty on 20th August, 1957. Craft was sentenced to death. Unusually the appeals moved fast through the court system until the Arizona Supreme Court upheld the sentence on December 31st, 1958. Craft was executed on 7th March 1959 at Florence prison by asphyxiation-gas. Just two years after the murder.

# ROBERT LOUIS CROMWELL

Born February 20th, 1964 –sentenced to death March 7th, 2003.

*This is the Maricopa Court's Facts transcript which details the crime in full.*

Stephanie Short lived with her mother, Ella Speaks, and two younger sisters, Amanda and Heather, in a one-bedroom apartment located on 3208 East Flower Street, near the intersection of 32nd Street and Osborn Road in Phoenix. ☐

Ella met the defendant, Robert Cromwell, in the early evening hours of October 7th, 2001 while walking from her apartment to a nearby convenience store to purchase transmission fluid for her car. Ella passed a building where she saw Cromwell sitting on a bench. He called out to her, *"Hey, are you a prostitute or a police officer?"* Ella continued walking and replied, *"I'm neither one. I'm a mother and I'm having a bad day. Leave me alone."* ☐Cromwell then got on his bike and rode toward Ella. Upon reaching her, he said, *"I just want to apologize to you. That was a very rude thing I said. In this area, there's a lot of prostitutes. I can't believe that I disrespected you that way and I want to give you my fullest apology."* Ella told Cromwell, *"It's okay. I'm just having a bad day. I don't mean to lash out at you, but I'm not in the mood for those kind of comments."* Cromwell then told Ella he would escort her to the store because *"this is a bad area and it's now dark."* Ella saw some men in a group off to her left and was *"almost relieved"* that Cromwell was going to walk with her to the store.

Ella went into the store alone where she purchased transmission fluid. □ When she emerged, she found Cromwell waiting for her. The two walked back to her apartment and according to Ella's testimony, Cromwell seemed *"kind"* and *"caring."*

At her apartment, Cromwell helped Ella put the transmission fluid into her vehicle. Ella then asked Cromwell if he would like to accompany her and her three daughters to a nearby fast-food restaurant. Cromwell agreed to go, but wanted first to take the bicycle back to his apartment. Ella and the children followed Cromwell and parked the car to wait for him outside the apartment. □ Cromwell parked his bike, changed his clothes and then drove with Ella and her three girls to the restaurant.

On the way, Cromwell and the children sang songs. At the drive-through window, Ella offered to buy Cromwell a hamburger. He declined. They obtained food for Ella and the children and went back to Ella's apartment. □ While the children ate, Ella and Cromwell went into her bedroom where the two talked and Ella smoked methamphetamine. After spending about an hour in the bedroom, Cromwell agreed to accompany Ella to a number of local bars where she filled out job applications and played a few games of pool. They left the children in the apartment.

Cromwell had just one drink during the bar visits, and Ella had none. □ At one bar location, Cromwell leaned over a pool table and tried to kiss Ella on the mouth, but she turned her cheek. Cromwell said,

*"I can tell you didn't like it, but I will do it again."* Ella replied, *"I don't think you will,"* at which time Ella noticed that Cromwell smiled as if he understood, and he apologized once again.

When Ella and Cromwell returned to her apartment around 1:00 a.m., the children were on a mattress in the living room, still awake. Ella told the girls to go to sleep, and Ella and Cromwell went into the bedroom where they played cards for about an hour.

At some point, with Cromwell still in the apartment, Ella received a phone call from a friend, Kelly Lancaster, asking that she come to his house to help resolve a disturbance being caused by a mutual acquaintance, Kim Jensen. ☐Ella agreed and decided it would be all right to leave her children with Cromwell because *"he seemed so nice."* Cromwell told Ella he would just stay in her room while she was gone. Ella was gone from the house for a little more than an hour.

During Ella's absence, Stephanie's nine-year-old sister Amanda says she was awakened by the sound of Stephanie making a noise as if *"she was really hurt."* Amanda then saw Stephanie standing in the bathtub, unclothed, while Cromwell, with socks on both of his hands, washed her with soap. Amanda got out of bed on several occasions while Ella was gone, but Cromwell angrily told her to get back to bed each time. Eventually, Amanda saw Stephanie follow Cromwell into Ella's bedroom. Although Stephanie remained in Ella's bedroom, Amanda saw Cromwell move from the bedroom to the kitchen several times. ☐During one such trip, Amanda heard a noise like *"silverware shatter'*, and while Cromwell and Stephanie were in the bedroom, she heard noises that made her think Stephanie was hurt. She then heard a *"big bang"* that sounded like a television dropping to the floor. Amanda finally fell asleep while Stephanie was still in the bedroom with Cromwell.

When Ella returned to the apartment, accompanied by Kim Jensen, Cromwell immediately attacked both of them with a pool cue, resulting in injuries to each. Cromwell ran out of the apartment after the attack and Ella quickly followed convinced Cromwell had taken Stephanie with him. She called 9-1-1 from her car

Cromwell's attack on Ella and Kim woke up Amanda. She saw her mother chase Cromwell out of the apartment. Kim Jensen was lying on the floor with a head injury. □Amanda and Heather, the youngest sister, then got up and went to the bedroom to look for Stephanie.□ Amanda reached into the bed, felt Stephanie's legs and saw that the television set was resting on Stephanie's head. □She and Heather removed it, then ran downstairs and asked the landlord to call 9-1-1, which he did.□After the call, Amanda and Heather went back upstairs and into the bedroom. They observed blood stains on the bedding and saw Stephanie's body, bruised and bloody.

Police Officer Tallon Busby responded to the 9-1-1 call. When he arrived, the door was open and Kim Jensen was laying on the floor. Officer Busby described the scene: *"Laying inside the doorway was a white female. □ From the waist down she was outside the apartment, from the waist up, she was laying face down in the apartment. □ There was a blood smear on the door."* ☐ He asked Kim, who was semi-conscious, if anyone else was in the apartment. ☐ She replied that the baby was in the bedroom. He then asked Kim where she was injured, and she replied that she had been hit on the back of the head. ☐ Officer Busby observed that the hair on the back left side of Kim's head was *"matted in blood."*

The officer then went into the dark apartment and observed a light in the bedroom. He walked toward the doorway and saw Stephanie lying face up on the bed. A blanket covered her unclothed body from the waist down. She had *"visible wounds on her face and blood coming out of her nose, lips and out of her mouth."* ☐ There was a *"huge pool of blood"* under her head and shoulders. ☐ Officer Busby checked to see if Stephanie was breathing and if she had a pulse. ☐ He felt a *"slight pulse"* at her neck. ☐ He placed his hand on Stephanie's chest and *"felt a slight rise and fall."* Visible evidence of severe vaginal trauma indicated that Stephanie also had been sexually abused.

By the time Gary Ford, a Phoenix Fire Department paramedic, arrived, Stephanie no longer had a pulse and had stopped breathing. While performing cardiac pulmonary resuscitation, Ford observed that Stephanie had suffered a head wound and multiple stab wounds to her back. Ford also observed the vaginal injuries. After attempting CPR and other life-saving procedures, the paramedics rushed Stephanie to the Good Samaritan Hospital.

Dr. Wendy Lucid was on duty at the Good Samaritan emergency room when Stephanie arrived. Stephanie had no heartbeat and was not breathing. ☐

Initially, Dr. Lucid did a full body assessment. She found a large laceration on Stephanie's forehead. Closer inspection revealed a skull fracture. Due to the severity of Stephanie's head injuries, Dr. Lucid stopped all life support efforts and pronounced her dead. Dr. Lucid then turned Stephanie onto her side and observed eleven stab wounds on her back. Further examination also revealed the vaginal injuries.

The medical examiner performed an autopsy on Stephanie's body. ☐Based on the injuries, he determined Stephanie had received a minimum of five blows to the head and thirteen stab wounds to the back. The stabbing punctured her right lung, causing it to collapse. In the opinion of the examiner, Stephanie was alive at the time she suffered the vaginal trauma and at the time she was stabbed. The cause of death was multiple blunt force and stabbing injuries inflicted on her head and back.

Cromwell was apprehended at his apartment, 9, 3329 East Osborn Road, Phoenix and arrested. He was charged and sent for trial.

The grand jury indicted Cromwell on October 16th, 2001 on one count of first degree murder, one count of sexual assault and two counts of aggravated assault. On November 9th, 2001, the State filed a notice of intent to seek the death penalty for the murder and on August 9th, 2002, filed its notice of aggravating factors. ☐ Trial began February 3rd, 2003, resulting in conviction by the jury on all counts in the indictment. Cromwell's appeals are continuing.

# ROBERT WAYNE DANIELSON Jr.

Born 1947 – sentenced to death in California 1986. Committed suicide at San Quentin State prison in September 1995.

On June 23rd, 1970, Danielson ,23, got into an argument with 21-year-old Thomas Elroy Davis after a roadside encounter near Marcola, Oregon. After some time, Danielson pulled out a gun and fatally shot Davis. He was charged with first-degree murder not long after, but after an initial mistrial, which resulted from the prosecution presenting improper evidence, that charge was dismissed. Instead, in November 1970, Danielson pleaded guilty to voluntary manslaughter and several other charges, persisting in his defence that he shot Davis only because Davis pulled a gun on him first. He received a sentence of 25 years in prison.

In 1981, after serving eleven years of his sentence at Oregan State Penitentiary, Danielson was granted parole, and released from prison. On December 9th, 1981, just weeks after his release, Danielson confronted 60-year-old Harold and 55-year-old Betty Pratt at a desert campsite in Arizona. He bound their hands with a rope, and shot both of them in the head before stealing their pick-up truck. The next day, their bodies were discovered, and their truck was found abandoned in Yuma. Investigators put out a reward of $5,000 for information leading to the arrest and conviction of the killer.

In the following months Danielson was residing in Springfield Oregon, and became friends with 14-

year-old Lenora Hart Johnson and the two sparked a relationship with Johnson later stating it was 'like a common-law marriage'. On June 25th, 1982, Danielson and Johnson bound 62-year-old Arthur Gray at a park in Eugene, Oregon, and Danielson shot him in the back of the head for no reason.

In July, Danielson, accompanied again by Johnson, stumbled into 69-year-old Benjamin Shaffer and his 62-year-old wife Edith at a park in Manchester, California. Johnson tied the Shaffer's hands with twine, and Danielson told her to walk their dog away from the scene. When she was a good distance away, Danielson shot the couple to death. In November, Danielson murdered 38-year-old Ernest Corral in a similar fashion in Apache Junction, Arizona.

They made one mistake. In March 1982 they made friends with Edwin and Ida Davis, both age 64, near El Cajon, California and left them for dead after injecting both with a powerful horse tranquilizer. Luckily for the Davis's they were found in time and their lives saved. After recuperating in hospital both were able to identify Danielson from mug shots as one of the pair who attacked them.

In December 1983, the Shaffer's bodies were unearthed buried inside a ravine off Mountain View Road. During the investigation, detectives identified Johnson as being involved in the killings and interviewed her. She confessed to being involved but said the murderer was Robert Wayne Danielson, a 37-year-old who was on parole for a 1970 murder at the time of the Shaffer's murders. She also told the investigators about the murder of Arthur Gray, and other murders which Danielson had confessed to her.

Following this, Danielson was charged in absence with two counts of murder and a wanted notice circulated. He was considered a fugitive as he had broken his parole on the Thomas Davis case by not contacting his parole officer regularly, in fact not at all. On April 6th, 1984, Danielson was located in Odessa, Texas, by the FBI and arrested at his job at a travelling circus.

Danielson was listed to stand trial for the California murders first. During one day of his trial, his mother, Mary Ann Bishop, attempted to pass her son a loaded revolver as he entered the Mendocino Courthouse. The attempt was noticed, Bishop was arrested, and was given a 3-year prison term.

In July 1986 Danielson was found guilty of the Shaffers's murders and sentenced to death. He was then extradited to Oregon in February 1987 to stand trial for the murder of Arthur Gray in 1982. He was again found guilty but escaped the death penalty as Oregon's capital punishment statute was not in effect at the time Gray was murdered in 1982. The jury imposed a sentence of life in prison. Danielson was sent to San Quentin State Prison to await his execution for the Shaffers's murders and on September 7th, 1995 used his socks to hang himself in his cell.

# BRIAN JEFFREY DANN

Born, date unknown – sentenced to death January 24th, 2002.

Brian Dann went to the home of his former girlfriend, Tina Pace-Morrell on the evening of April 3rd, 1999 to borrow a gun. He told her that Andrew Parks, the brother of his ex-girlfriend, Shelley Parks, had fired a gun at him earlier in the day as a warning to stay away from his sister. Dann told Tina he just wanted to go to Andrew's apartment to pick up his belongings. Tina loaned him her father's .38 calibre pistol.

With the gun in his pocket Dann went to the Double K bar in Phoenix and stayed there until closing time. People who knew him said he didn't want to talk. When the bar closed Dann went to the parking lot and asked a friend, George Thomas, if he could provide an untraceable gun. Thomas could not and asked why would Dann want one and was told of his plan to kill Andrew Parks. They talked for some time until Thomas was convinced he had talked Dann out of such a deed and they parted at about 1.30am on what was now Sunday April 4th.

Sometime in the early hours of that Easter Sunday Dann phoned Tina and told her he had killed three people with the gun and what should he do? She told him to go to the police but instead he turned up at her home and told her he had shot both Andrew and Shelley because they had laughed at him. Their friend Eddie Payan was there and Dann shot him because he was a witness and could identify him. He asked Tina to

tell the police he was with her all night, return
gun, washed and changed his clothes and went back
Andrew's apartment at around 7am and called the police
saying he had just found the three bodies in the
apartment.

The police conducted extensive enquiries and
recovered the pistol from Tina which forensic scientists
matched to the bullets in the three bodies. The
apartment had a surveillance camera but the tape was
missing. Andrew Parks brother, Michael, insisted it
would have been in situ as Andrew was paranoid about
burglars in the area. The tape was never found.

On Wednesday April 7th, 1999 Dann was arrested
and charged with the three first degree murders. On
October 1st, 2001 at his trial the jury returned a guilty
verdict on three counts of premeditated murder, three
counts of felony murder and one count of first degree
burglary. He was sentenced to death on January 1st
2002. The Supreme Court of Arizona reversed the
convictions for premeditated murder of Shelly Parks
and Eddie Payan but affirmed his conviction for
premeditated murder of Andrew Parks. The State of
Arizona affirmed it would retry Dann on the two
reversed convictions. The appeals are still active.

# D SCOTT DETRICH

20th, 1959 – sentenced to death, 1991, tion.

Clear your brain for this one, probably one of the best examples of attorneys using the USA appeals system to keep the client alive.

In September 2013, the 9th Circuit Appeals Court ordered a new hearing for a man   sat on death row since 1991who claims that he was found guilty for a murder committed in 1989 because of ineffective assistance from his counsel.

Prosecutors had shown that on November 4th, 1989, David Scott Detrich and his co-worker, Alan Charlton, picked up Elizabeth Souter after a night of drinking heavily in Tucson, Arizona,. They bought drugs from a bar and went back to Souter's house, but Detrich became angry and threatened Souter with a small knife because the drugs were bad and couldn't be injected.

The three left Souter's house together, and Souter's body was found two days later with a slit throat and about 40 cut and stab wounds.

Charlton pleaded guilty to kidnapping and agreed to testify against Detrich in return for a 10 year sentence. He claimed at the first trial that he merely sat behind the wheel while Detrich forced Souter into a car by knifepoint, raped her, slit her throat, and dumped her body in the desert.

Detrich's first trial ended in a mistrial, and a defective jury instruction led the Arizona Supreme Court to reverse the conviction that resulted from a second trial. The court refused to reverse the next convictions for kidnapping and murder handed down by a third jury in 1997.

In a petition for post-conviction relief, however, Detrich claimed that counsel at his third trial had been ineffective for many reasons, including failing to present live testimony from an exculpatory witness.

That witness, Phillip Shell had testified in one of the earlier trials that Charlton confessed to him in jail that he had stabbed Souter not Detrich. Rather than call Shell to the court again at the third trial, Detrich's attorney had presented the recorded testimony on paper.

Shell said Charlton had told him he had become enraged at seeing Detrich kiss Souter because she was black. Unlike most jailhouse snitches, Shell testified against the interest of the prosecution and received no benefit from doing so.

Supporting Shell's testimony, the woman who was divorcing Charlton at the time testified about his long time prejudice against black people.

A Pima County judge found that the ineffective assistance claims were not strong enough, and Detrich then sought habeas relief in a petition that raised some new ineffective assistance of counsel claims for the first time.

Before the federal judge ruled, Detrich raised those new claims in a second petition with the state court. Both the state and federal courts then found the claims barred, but a three-judge panel of the 9th Circuit reversed and vacated Detrich's death sentence in 2010.

The Supreme Court directed the panel to reconsider in light of its finding in the Cullen v. Pinholster case that defendants should be banned from introducing new mitigating evidence in federal court for a claim previously exhausted before a state court.

Unmoved, the appellate panel nevertheless again vacated Detrich's death sentence on remand.

In the meantime, the Supreme Court decided on another case about ineffective assistance, Martinez v. Ryan. This ruling found that substantial ineffective assistance of counsel, such as that which Detrich described, could establish cause for the default of a claim of ineffective assistance of the trial counsel.

Detrich moved for remand to the District Court under Martinez, and the 9th Circuit convened an en ban hearing on the issue.

The court ruled 6-5 in September 2013 that the appeal should indeed be remanded.

'We need look no further than the jury verdict to get a general sense of the strength of the evidence,' was the opinion of Judge William Fletcher. 'Three out of the 12 jurors refused to convict Detrich of premeditated murder. They were willing to convict Detrich of only felony murder.'

Fletcher said Detrich's claims are 'sufficiently plausible to warrant remanding to the district court.'

The testimony of two witnesses 'would have suggested that other witnesses were not testifying truthfully' after one claimed police instructed her to lie, and another claimed Charlton had ties to the Aryan

Brotherhood, which would have 'strengthened the evidence of Charlton's motive for the killing,' according to the ruling.

Fletcher also noted that certain pieces of evidence - Souter's fingernail, Charlton's fingerprints, blood on the driver's side of the car and a lack of semen – 'were consistent with Charlton having killed Souter.'

Charlton admitted to driving the car, suffered scratches from Souter, and claimed to have watched Detrich raping Souter, the judges noted.

The failure by Detrich's counsel to cross-examine a witness also failed to undermine testimony from a co-worker that Detrich had told him that he killed Souter by slitting her throat with a knife.

In fact that witness had said in a pre-trial interview that Detrich 'didn't say that he killed the girl.'

Judge Susan Graber, on behalf of four other dissenting colleagues, said Detrich's 'counsel had effectively presented to the judge and jury much of the evidence that the majority cites in support of the view that petitioner's co-defendant may have been the killer.' She added that the evidence against Detrich 'was powerful,' and the 'jury's verdict and the sentencing court's determinations appear to reflect their reasonable assessments of the evidence at trial, not any ineffectiveness on the part of counsel.'

So, although sentenced to death on February 7th, 1991 Detrich is still there sitting on Death Row as his appeals of various kinds wind on through the legal system.

# GREGORY SCOTT DICKENS

Born April 7th, 1965 –committed suicide in prison on January 27th, 2014.

In 1990, Dickens was working in a young offender's placement centre in Temecula, California when he met 14-year-old Travis Amaral. Dickens was a paedophile who enjoyed sexual services from his young friends in return for gifts.

Dickens's relationship with Amaral grew a year later when in 1991 Amaral contacted Dickens in Yuma, Arizona, and told him he was going AWOL from the centre. Dickens bought Amaral a bus ticket to Yuma, and the pair discussed their financial woes and how to alleviate them.

They decided the best way, according to Amaral's subsequent testimony, was to plan and commit robberies. They flipped a coin to decide who would commit the first crime and Amaral 'won'. He opted to commit the robbery at a highway rest stop.

The two robbers headed east out of town on Interstate 8 in Dickens truck and stopped on the east-bound rest stop outside of town. Once there, they waited three hours until the opportunity was right.

It was shortly after 9 p.m. when Bryan and Laura Bernstein pulled into the west-bound rest area opposite.

Taking a .38-calibre revolver and a walkie-talkie from Dickens, Amaral sprinted across the freeway while Dickens kept in contact with him from his truck.

The twenty-something couple had pulled into the rest area to get a little sleep, and were surprised when

Amaral approached them and asked the time before he produced the gun and demanded Bryan's wallet, which Bryan handed over. Turning to Laura, he asked for her wallet, but she said she didn't have one.

Amaral and Dickens disagree as to what happened next. According to Amaral, Dickens, through the walkie-talkie, said *'No witnesses.'*

*'What?'* replied Amaral. *'What do you mean by no witnesses. If I kill them, there are no witnesses, is that what you mean?'*

According to Amaral, Dickens again said, *'No witnesses.'*

At that point, Amaral shot Laura Bernstein in the head, killing her instantly. He turned the gun on Bryan, who was crouching over his wife and fired again.

Dickens meanwhile was driving across the road and into the rest area. Amaral jumped in and they fled the scene.

Bryan Bernstein was discovered semi-conscious next to his dead wife by a deputy sheriff about 20 minutes after the attack. He was unable to provide any information before he died at the scene.

The pair burnt the evidence of the robbery after removing cash, traveller's cheques and a single credit card, which Amaral unsuccessfully tried to use at a Yuma K-Mart the day following the murders. After spending a last night together, they split up, with Amaral returning to his mother's home who persuaded him to return to the youth centre and Dickens fleeing to Carlsbad, California.

Meanwhile, the Bernstein murder investigation went cold as there were no clues or leads for investigators to follow other than the unsuccessful card use at Yuma.

Police got their first break in the case when Amaral ran away from the centre again and ended up at Dickens's San Diego apartment. The centre reported Amaral to the police as an absconder and when they approached his mother she told them about his gay relationship with Dickens and gave them Dicken's address. When Amaral was located San Diego authorities charged Dickens with sexually abusing Amaral and other young men, as well as assault with a deadly weapon for a botched robbery.

Whilst interviewing Amaral he told police he and Dickens were involved in a double homicide in Yuma, Arizona. Why he did this is unclear.

When police interviewed Dickens about the homicide he realized the depth of the trouble he was in and attempted suicide by slashing his wrists whilst in remand. Dickens later claimed that blood loss from his suicide attempt clouded his thoughts during further interrogations.

He gave a different version of events than Amaral. According to Dickens, he and Amaral were at the east-bound rest area because he was having trouble with his truck that had broken down when Amaral decided that they could make some money by robbing people. Suddenly, without warning, the teen ran across the highway and robbed and killed the Bernsteins.

Dickens told police when he heard the gunshots he was shocked and started driving back to Yuma (in a broken-down truck?) on his own but when he saw

Amaral running after the truck, he stopped and picked him up.

*'It's all right, I didn't leave any witnesses'*, Amaral reportedly told him.

Two weeks before Dickens went to trial, Amaral agreed to a plea deal in return for his testimony against his former lover. He changed his mind and as a result, did not testify during the prosecution's case-in-chief.

After Dickens placed most of the blame for the murders on Amaral he then changed his mind again and agreed to testify in return for the state not seeking the death penalty against him.

The prosecution moved to reopen its case to present Amaral's testimony, and the judge granted the motion, giving Dickens's attorney one week to prepare for Amaral's prosecution testimony.

Amaral, being 15 years old at the time of the murders, was sentenced to 55 years in prison for his role in the murders and although Dickens was acquitted of the murder and robbery charges, the jury convicted him of felony murder and sentenced him to death. He committed suicide in prison on January 27th, 2014.

# RICHARD KENNETH DJERF

Born November 6th, 1969 - sentenced to death May 22nd, 1996, a Stay of Execution issued by U.S. District Court March 4th, 2002.

On September 14th, 1993, over the course of seven hours, Djerf killed Albert Luna Sr., 46, his wife, Patricia, 40, and two of their children, 18-year-old Rochelle, whom Djerf also raped, and 5-year-old Damien. The family's only surviving member was Albert Luna Jr., a former friend of Djerf with whom he worked at a Safeways store. He claimed that the murders were in retaliation for Albert Jr. allegedly stealing a TV, VCR, stereo unit plus several other electronic items and an AK-47 rifle from Djerf's apartment. Albert Luna Jr. confessed to stealing the items from Djerf's room during Djerf's later trial. It was also revealed that Djerf had reported the theft to the police but despite pestering them to act nothing was done which Djerf claimed was why he took it on himself to seek revenge.

The case is significant for multiple reasons. First, under a rule 11 law Djerf insisted on his right to dismiss his legal counsel and represent himself in court so that he could forgo a trial and enter a guilty plea. His case is often cited as a self-representation case where it is not in the client's best interest to represent themselves even if the person can prove competency to do so.

On the day of the murders, September 14th, 1993, Djerf showed up at the Luna home with flowers and forced himself in at gunpoint brandishing a 9mm

Beretta handgun. Patricia Luna and her 5-year-old son Damien were at home. Djerf had Mrs Luna retrieve some of the items stolen from his room and put them in his car before he secured Mrs. Luna and her son by tying their arms and legs and gagging them. When Rochelle Luna arrived several hours later, Djerf took her to her bedroom, where he raped and killed her. When Albert Luna, Sr. arrived home Djerf forced him into his bedroom at gunpoint. Djerf handcuffed Mr. Luna to a bed, smashed his head with a baseball bat, and then removed the handcuffs because he believed Mr. Luna was dead. He was not. Djerf then returned to the kitchen with Mrs. Luna and Damien. Mr. Luna regained consciousness, took a knife and charged at Djerf stabbing him several times. Djerf used his gun to kill Mr. Luna and then shot both Mrs. Luna and Damien in the head.

Before he left, Djerf spread gasoline around the house and over the bodies, turned on the stove and left a pizza box and a cloth on the burner, they caught fire but the house didn't burn.

The scene was found the next morning when Albert Luna Jr. came home after a night shift. Police searched Djerf's home and found the items and the handgun. Forensics tied the gun to the killings. He was arrested on September 18th, 1993.

The judge who sentenced Djerf to death in 1996 said that Djerf had 'relished' the time he spent killing the Luna family to get revenge against his friend for burglarizing his apartment.

There were four death sentence rulings. Djerf scoffed at the multiple death sentences, saying, 'They can only kill me once.'

The Arizona Supreme Court rejected his appeal, and the U.S. Supreme Court has refused to hear it. The Arizona Supreme Court issued a warrant of execution in February 2002. The U.S. District Court issued a stay one month later.

Djerf has continued his appeals to the Federal Courts. Under Ring v. Arizona the Supreme Court ruled that only a jury, not a judge, could hand down the death penalty. That put Djerf's case on permanent hold until the Supreme Court clarified its ruling in Schriro v. Summerlin. All three far-reaching cases, Ring, Summerlin, and Djerf, are Arizona capital murder cases.

In April 2017, the district court dismissed all of his claims, and Djerf appealed the dismissal. On July 24th, 2019, the Ninth Circuit Court of Appeals affirmed the district court's dismissal. He was given an execution date of April 3rd 2002 which was quashed by a Stay order from the U.S. District Court on March 4th, 2002. As of December 2023, Djerf is one of the 20 Arizona death row inmates who have exhausted all their appeals.

# EUGENE ALLEN DOERR

Born June 25th 1959 – sentenced to death
November 27th 1996

At approximately 10.00 a.m. on September 24th, 1994, two Phoenix police officers responded to a 'check welfare' dispatch following a 911 call. Upon arriving at a bungalow-style apartment in Phoenix, they found the front door open and Eugene Doerr sitting on the coffee table in the living room. He wore only shorts and was covered with blood.

When asked what had occurred, Doerr replied: *'I don't know. I woke up with this, there's a dead body back there.'* In a bedroom doorway, Officer Wirth found a naked woman lying in a pool of blood. Finding no pulse, he instructed his partner to radio the fire department. Doerr responded, *'You don't need fire because she's dead.'* He told the officers that when he had woken up he had gone to the bathroom and found the body on the floor. He denied knowing who the victim was.

The four-room apartment showed signs of a violent struggle, with blood in every room. Later at Doerr's trial, the medical examiner testified that the victim, 39-year-old Karen Bohl, died of multiple blunt force trauma. She suffered numerous injuries to the head, including a fractured nose, abrasions, cuts, bruises, and a two-inch laceration that exposed her skull. Her left hand was swollen and bruised. Her right hand was clenched in a fist holding hairs consistent with her own. Her left nipple and areola had been cut off, and above her right nipple were small lacerations. The body was covered in blood and fecal matter. Blood also formed a V-shaped pattern down her back from her saturated hair.

Bohl had been assaulted vaginally and rectally with an instrument of some kind. The doctor testified that the wall between her rectum and cervix had been destroyed. A bloody pipe, apparently part of a broken lamp stand, and a bloody broom handle were found nearby—objects that the medical examiner said could have produced the rectum injuries. Because of significant blood loss, swelling, and bruising, the doctor concluded that the injuries likely occurred prior to or during the victim's death. There were twenty-six other areas of injury to her body. Tests for semen were negative.

Defendant Doerr was also injured. His right hand was swollen, and he had minor cuts on his forearm, his wrist, and his left foot. His chest, stomach, pubic area, and hands were smeared and caked with blood. Defendant first claimed that he had no idea how the woman had got there. Later, as officers waited for a search warrant, he told them that he thought her purse and ID were in the bathroom *'because I remember seeing a purse and I don't own a purse.'* He also said the white car parked out front belonged to the victim. *'That is her car . . . I think.'* One of the officers testified that Doerr hesitated before adding the *'I think.'*

Doerr voluntarily went to the police station and during questioning he asked one of the officers if he thought a judge would give him life for the murder. He also said, *'She must have really made me mad for me to do something to her like this.'* Doerr was tested for drugs and alcohol at 3.00 p.m., five hours after the 911 call. The tests were negative.

Tina Allgeir last saw her sister, Karen Bohl, at about 4.30 p.m. the previous day, when Karen dropped off her 7-year-old daughter before going to work. Bohl had just started a new job as a manager trainee at a fast food restaurant. Her supervisor reported that she had called to say she would be late. However, she never arrived at work. When she later failed to pick up her daughter Allgeir and other family members went to Bohl's apartment. They found her work uniform there, and food was still on the stove. Police investigators were unable to determine where or when Bohl and the defendant met on the day of the murder. There was no evidence that the two had been previously acquainted.

☐ While in custody, Doerr told his cellmate, Victor Rosales, that he did not remember anything about the incident. However, a few weeks later he told Rosales that he remembered picking up Bohl, going on a *'partying binge,'* and arguing with her. Rosales testified that Doerr *'flew off the handle'* because descriptions contained in police reports were not *'the way it happened.'* ☐ For instance, the defendant told Rosales that he struck the victim with a pipe when she started screaming, and not with a lamp as a police report indicated.

☐ According to Rosales, Doerr wanted to have sex with Bohl, but she refused. Rosales further testified that Doerr said that *'he should have buried the bitch in the back yard'* with the cement he had purchased to use at work. □

□ At Doerr's trial his defence counsel suggested that a third party could have entered the apartment, murdered Bohl, and injured the defendant. □ Investigators, however, testified that the apartment windows were locked. □ Some, in fact, were painted shut. The front door was open when police arrived, but the back door was locked. No blood was found outside the apartment, except for a smear on the driver's side of Doerr's truck. Its location was consistent with his account of using the truck's mobile phone to call 911.

□ A jury convicted Doerr of premeditated first degree murder, felony murder, sexual assault, and kidnapping. Following a pre-sentence hearing, the trial judge found the heinous, cruel, or depraved aggravator and insufficient mitigation did not warrant leniency. He sentenced the defendant to death.

A warrant of Execution was issued by the Arizona Supreme Court for March 21st, 2002 followed by a Stay order issued by the U.S. District Court on May 1st, 2002. He is now in Arizona State Prison Complex in Florence, as far as I can find out.

# CHARLES DAVID ELLISON

Born July 3rd, 1965 - sentenced to death February 17th, 2004.

On the morning of February 26th, 1999, police went to the Kingman home of Joseph, 79, and Lillian Boucher, 73, after their daughter, Vivian Brown, could not contact her parents. When no one answered the door the police entered the home through the kitchen where they noticed a telephone with its line cut and cord missing and a knife block with a missing knife.

Police searched the house and discovered the body of Joseph Boucher on a bed in a bedroom. He had defensive wounds and minor cuts and scrapes on his wrists and arms indicating he had been bound. In another bedroom, police found Lillian Boucher's body on the floor. She had bruises on her face and body, consistent with an altercation, and a small amount of blood around her nose. According to the medical examiner, Mr. Boucher had been killed by asphyxiation by smothering. Mrs. Boucher had been asphyxiated by smothering or a combination of smothering and strangulation. Vivian Brown, the daughter, confirmed that missing from the house were a .22 calibre handgun, a pellet gun, Mr. Boucher's wedding ring and watch, and Mrs. Boucher's diamond wedding ring, anniversary ring, watch, earrings, and crucifix.

On February 26th, 1999, local businessman Brad Howe contacted police with information that he had obtained from a person named Richard Finch about the murders. Finch worked for Howe and his father as a 'lot boy' at their auto dealership in Lake Havasu City and also lodged at Howe's house. According to Howe, Finch was *'simple'* and, because he could not manage his own finances, Howe and his father gave Finch money only as he needed it.

Howe did not see Finch on the night of the killings, February 24th , however, they went drinking at several bars the next night. Howe offered to pay as usual and was surprised when Finch offered to buy drinks and showed him $250 to $300. Howe told police that Finch was drinking heavily and acting strangely as if something was on his mind. Howe repeatedly asked Finch what was distracting him. Finch became *'very upset'* and admitted he had been involved in *'some bad things.'* The two then left the bar and, on the way home, Finch told Howe details about the Boucher's murders and his 'friend' Charles Ellison .

Once at home, Finch retrieved a bag of stolen items from the Boucher's house and showed it to Howe. Howe, not wanting the items in his house, took the bag and hid it in the desert in the early morning hours of February 26th. ⬜ Later that morning he told the police of Finch's involvement and led them to the bag, which contained several items that Vivian Brown identified as stolen from the Bouchers' home.

The same day, police officers went to Howe's house and arrested Finch, who had packed his belongings as if planning to leave. After being advised of his rights, Finch agreed to speak with police and confessed his involvement in the murders. He also identified his companion as *'Slinger,'* a nickname used by Ellison. Two days later, Finch helped police find the missing kitchen knife in a field behind the Bouchers' house where Ellison had thrown it as they left..

On March 1st, 1999, after unsuccessfully searching for Ellison at the house of his girlfriend, Cathie Webster-Hauver, Kingman detectives Steven Auld and Lyman Watson learned that he had been arrested in Lake Havasu. □ They went there and after informing Ellison of his rights, the detectives interviewed him at the Lake Havasu police station just before 9:00 a.m. Ellison told the detectives he had met Finch two or three weeks earlier at Darby's, a Lake Havasu bar. The two men met again at Darby's on February 24th, 1999, where Ellison agreed to do *'a job'* with Finch in Kingman. Ellison said that he intended only to commit a burglary, not to kill anyone. Ellison also denied killing either victim.

Ellison claimed that on the night of the murders he and Finch drove Ellison's van to Kingman, where they stopped at the Sundowner's Bar. According to the bartender, Jeannette Avila, Ellison entered the bar first, ordered and paid for two beers, talked to her at length, and led the way when the two men left the bar. Finch, in contrast, never spoke to Avila he simply sat without removing his sunglasses. Avila later identified Ellison in a photographic line-up, but was unable to identify Finch.

Ellison said they next drove to a nearby movie theatre and parked the van in its carpark. Finch led the way to the Bouchers' house nearby and entered first. Once inside, Ellison and Finch ordered Mrs. Boucher from the living room and into Mr. Boucher's bedroom. Ellison admitted binding the victims with the phone cords and masking tape, but claimed to have done so only at Finch's direction. □ Ellison said Finch then pointed a gun at him and ordered him to kill Mr. Boucher. Ellison then held a pillow over Mr. Boucher's face for a period of time, possibly only a few seconds, while Finch strangled Mrs. Boucher. □ Ellison said he removed the pillow when Mr. Boucher stopped struggling, but claimed he thought Mr. Boucher was still alive because his chest was moving up and down. Ellison said he told Finch that he, Finch, would have to finish off Mr. Boucher. Ellison also said that after Finch strangled Mrs. Boucher, Finch moved her body to another bedroom.

Ellison claimed throughout that it was Finch's idea to '*hit*' the house and that he did not know why Finch had picked the Bouchers' home. Ellison admitted he was familiar with the area because his parents lived nearby. □Additionally, at trial, Vivian Brown identified Ellison as having worked on her parents' home in October 1997 and at a nearby house the next year. According to Howe, Finch did not possess a gun or a vehicle and had never gone to Kingman before February 24th, 1999.

The police acknowledged at the trial that no physical evidence proved who actually killed either victim. None of the approximately 170 fingerprints found in the house matched Ellison or Finch□ Police found a latex glove in the Bouchers' yard. Ellison later admitted he had supplied the latex gloves that he and Finch wore during the burglary and murders. None of the Bouchers' property was found on Ellison, in his van, or at his girlfriend's home. Ellison admitted removing jewellery from Mrs. Boucher's body, but said he did so only at Finch's direction. He also admitted using twenty dollars stolen from the Bouchers to buy gas for his van.

The detectives attempted to record their initial interview with Ellison but due to a machine fault failed to do so. Detective Watson re-interviewed Ellison at 10:06 a.m. In this nine-minute recorded interview, Detective Watson tried to summarize the main points of the first interview. This tape was played for the jury proceeding the verdicts.

On March 4th, 1999, Ellison and Finch were indicted for the murders and first degree burglary. The State sought the death penalty for each defendant. Judge Robert R. Moon seperated their trials. In September 2000, a jury convicted Finch on the murder and burglary charges. In March 2001, Judge Moon sentenced Finch to natural life imprisonment, finding, among other things, mitigating factors due to Finch's having acted under duress from Ellison and later cooperating with the police in their investigation.

Ellison was tried in January 2002. With Judge Moon presiding, the jury convicted Ellison on the murder and burglary charges, specifically finding him guilty of both premeditated and felony murder of the Bouchers and that he had either killed, intended to kill, or acted with reckless indifference.

When Ellison was sentenced his jury determined that death was the appropriate sentence for each murder, after finding six aggravators: 1) previous serious felony conviction; 2) pecuniary gain; 3) especially cruel; 4) murder committed while on parole; 5) multiple homicides; and 6) victims more than seventy years old.

He is on Death Row in Arizona State Prison Complex in Florence, as far as I can find out.

# ROBERT DWIGHT FENTON

Born June 7th, 1934 – executed by asphyxiation-gas in Arizon March 11th, 1960.

Robert Fenton journeyed from his home in Springfield, Illinois to Tucson on January 22nd, 1958 looking for work. His friend John Mahoney, an acquaintance of Fenton's step-father, was already there working in Keller's Drug Store and had offered to give him help in gaining employment.

Mahoney introduced Fenton to Mrs Opal Coward, the owner of Keller's Drug Store who offered him the guest room in her bungalow and part time work doing odd jobs around the place until he secured permanent employment. Fenton moved in on 31st January 1958.

On February 12th, 1958 Fenton secured a full time job at Ryan-Evans drug Store, mainly on the back of a good reference from Mrs Coward. On the 14th Mrs Coward asked Fenton to move out of her guest room as she was having relatives coming to stay and he moved into the local YMCA after borrowing $20 from Mrs Coward to be repaid when he got his first pay check. He already owed her quite a large amount he had borrowed whilst unemployed and they agreed he would pay it back by doing odd jobs around the house on his days off at $1 an hour.

On Sunday 23rd February 1958 Fenton arrived at Mrs Coward's large bungalow to do some work in the garden that afternoon. Before Mrs Coward left for the store he asked for $200. She gave him $40 to add to his debt with her and left for the store.

Whilst Mrs Coward was at work Fenton ransacked the bungalow for anything of value packing it into two suitcases. He had a plan to knock her out from behind so she would not recognise him when she returned, tie her up and then steal her car and leave the State.

He wrote a note to establish an alibi. The note was addressed to Mrs Coward saying he had left early because it was raining and was going back to the YMCA and would see her on his next day off. He would leave it on the kitchen table. He then sat and waited for Mrs Coward in her bedroom for her to return home from the store. When she did return Mrs Coward read the note and Fenton hit her with the barrel of the gun three times and on the fourth hit the gun fired and she fell down. Fenton then shot her six more times until she remained still on the floor. He then went through her wallet and pocket book taking any money. He then went outside to steal her car but the keys were not in it so he returned to the house to find them. However the back door that he used had shut and locked itself so he had to smash the bedroom window to get in. He found the keys and drove away in Mrs Coward's 1950 Chevrolet.

Fenton went to the YMCA and packed his belongings with the intention of going to California. He drove to a drive-in cinema and stayed there until midnight thinking any police hunt for him would have stopped for the night by then. He was wrong. He drove towards Nogales, Arizona and 25 miles out from there was spotted by a police highway patrol who red lighted him to stop. Instead Fenton fired three times at the patrol car before pulling over and leaving the Chevrolet. He pointed the pistol at the officers as they left their car and fired three times. He was shot in the leg and taken into custody.

A pre-trial mental assessment was made of Fenton. The expert psychologists found that Fenton fitted into the category of psychopathic personality. The experts defined the condition of a person having a psychopathic personality as one usually of average intelligence, with a likeable pleasant and rather ingratiating personality. One of the experts testified: *'They are people who are able to recognize right from wrong; who seem to know right from wrong, yet they seem to repeat anti-social acts and they seem not to profit or learn by experience, and they seem at times to be best classified not as immoral but amoral.'* The experts also reported to the court that as a result of their examination of the defendant it was their opinion that he was dangerous to society and that a person of his mental condition did not often profit by incarceration; that at the present time the only treatment is a protective environment such as institutional care.

Fenton's past was also made available in written form to the court. It disclosed that he was a member of the Air Force for two years but saw no overseas service. He received a dishonourable discharge for AWOL because he 'hit a lieutenant and a non-com, escaped and went AWOL again.' He served a sentence of ten months before being discharged. He then returned to his home in Ohio and went from one menial job to another, usually being sacked because of disagreements with his superiors. During this time he became involved with an underage 17-year-old girl, and was sentenced by the juvenile court to nine months imprisonment. Fenton admitted his previous juvenile record, dating back to the age of ten, indicating frequent hostile, aggressive anti-social behaviour. After the sentence by the juvenile court it was discovered that the 17-year-old girl was pregnant, and the defendant was released after serving five months and later married the girl involved. This marriage was not a happy one, particularly after the birth of the child. During this period of time Fenton had various jobs, some of which he lost because of shortage in receipts. He was arrested for the theft of a car belonging to a friend and was sentenced to two months in jail and placed on probation for three years. Finally in October, 1957, he left his family and job, and in December of that year was arrested as a fugitive, released on bail, and after spending Christmas with his family left with a friend for Tucson, Arizona and ended up at Mrs Coward's bungalow.

Fenton pleaded not guilty to the murder charge later changing his plea to guilty in the hope of a manslaughter charge being accepted which didn't carry the death penalty. The judge refused to accept that charge and sentenced Fenton to death for first degree murder. The Supreme Court of Arizona affirmed that sentence on June 17th, 1959 and denied any further hearings.

Fenton was executed by asphyxiation-gas on March 11th, 1960, aged 25 at Florence Jail, Pinal County, Arizona and buried in the Evergreen Memorial

Park, Tucson. The history of the J.C Higgins .22 calibre pistol he used to murder Mrs Opal Coward with is unknown.

# ROBERT WILLIAM FISHER

Born April 13th, 1961 – wanted for murder of his wife and two children. Remains at large.

Robert William Fisher is an American fugitive wanted for allegedly killing his family and blowing up the house in which they lived in Scottsdale, Arizona, on April 10th, 2001.

Fisher served in the United States Navy and later worked as a firefighter and in the medical field. He married Mary Cooper in 1987, and they had two children, Bobby and Brittney. The Fishers had a difficult family life. Robert Fisher was described as displaying cruel and controlling conduct towards his family, and on many occasions was reported to have exhibited disturbing and violent behaviour. He was unfaithful to his wife at least once. His own parents had divorced when he was 15, and this was believed to have played a role in the difficulties that he later experienced.

On April 10, 2001, the family's home exploded without warning. Inside, Fisher's wife and two children were found dead. The children's throats had been slit and Mary had been shot in the back of her head. Robert Fisher, along with Mary's car, was nowhere to be found. Police named him as their only suspect in the killings. On April 20th, Mary's car was discovered abandoned in a forest near Young, Arizona. On June 29th, 2002, he was named by the FBI as the $75th fugitive to be placed on its Ten Most Wanted list. On November 3rd, 2021, he was removed from the Most Wanted Fugitives List but remains a wanted fugitive.

Robert William Fisher was born on April 13th, 1961, in Brooklyn, New York City. His father was William Fisher, a banker, and his mother was Jan Howell. They had three children, Robert and two daughters. The parents divorced in 1976, when Robert was 15 and he and his sisters went to live with their father in Arizona. All three attended Sahuaro High School in Tucson, Arizona. According to friends and relatives, the divorce was pretty nasty and had a long-lasting effect on him. He thought his life would have been far better if he had been with his mother, not his father.

Fisher enlisted in the United States Navy and attempted to become part of the SEALs but was not successful. He was an avid outdoorsman, never more happy than when he was hunting or fishing. His work as a firefighter in California ended after a back injury. He then moved his family to Arizona and embarked on a career in the medical field. He worked as a surgical catheter technician, and respiratory therapist. Fisher was a surgical technician at a Mayo Clinic in Scottsdale at the time of the murders.

Fisher married Mary Cooper in 1987. It was not a happy marriage. He and his wife fought about sex and money, with Mary taking a job that she told friends was a 'security fund' as she couldn't see the marriage lasting. Fisher would not allow the walls inside their house to be painted anything other than white, and only a small number of pictures were allowed on the wall.

Friends noticed him exhibiting disturbing behaviour on hunting trips and other outdoor activities. In one case, after killing an elk, he began smearing its blood on his face. On another occasion, he sneaked up behind a family that was picnicking and emptied his gun into the air behind them. Several years before his wife and children were murdered Fisher shot a stray pit bull dog. He claimed that he shot it because it attacked his Labrador retriever, but police maintained that he orchestrated the encounter because he wanted to shoot the dog. Fisher had been an active participant in the Scottsdale Baptist Church's men's ministry, but, in contrast to his wife, he had begun to withdraw from church activities a few months prior to the murders. In 1998, the Fishers went to the senior church pastor for marital counselling, Fisher told co-workers about a one night stand with a prostitute he met in a massage parlour. He fretted that Mary would find out that it was the cause of a urinary tract infection that left him ill for several days in December 2000.

Fisher told a hunting companion that he was thinking of renewing his commitment to his faith and marriage because he 'could not live without his family', possibly hinting that he would consider suicide rather than divorce. According to psychologists, an intense fear of loss is not unusual among individuals who were traumatized by a divorce in adolescence. Mary told several friends that she was going to divorce Fisher in the weeks before her murder. Neighbours heard a loud argument coming from inside the Fisher home at 10 pm on April 9th, 2001, approximately ten hours before it exploded into flames. Police theorized that the murders took place between 9:30 pm and 10.00pm

A neighbour reported hearing Fisher's car leaving around 10.15pm. At 10:43 pm, Fisher was spotted on an

ATM camera, where he withdrew $280. Mary's Toyota 4Runner was in the background. It is possible that Fisher later returned to the house to commit the murders, but police believe that they had already taken place by then because he was using Mary's car, in which he is alleged to have fled.

At 8:42 am on April 10th 2001 the house exploded. Firefighters were immediately alerted to the explosion, which was strong enough to collapse the front of the house and rattle the frames of neighbouring houses for 800 metres in all directions. A series of smaller secondary explosions, believed to be caused by either rifle ammunition or paint cans, forced firefighters to keep their distance.

Investigators found that the gas line from the back of the house's furnace had been pulled. The accumulating gas was later ignited by a candle that Fisher had allegedly lit, waiting for the gas to accumulate and descend to the flame hours after being lit. This delayed fuse would have given him an approximate ten-hour head start in his successful attempt to evade law enforcement. The decision to have the house explode is believed to have been an attempt by Fisher to conceal evidence of his murders and possibly to cause police to believe that he had died. The burned bodies were found lying in bed in the burned-out remains. They were identified as Mary, age 38, Brittney, age 12, and Bobby, age 10.

Fisher, who disappeared at the time of the murders, was named as a suspect, and to date, the only person of interest in the case on April 14th, 2001, when Arizona Department of Public Safety officers were instructed in a state wide bulletin to arrest him. On April 20th, the last physical evidence of his whereabouts surfaced when police found Mary's Toyota 4Runner in Tonto National Forest near Young, Arizona, one hundred miles north of Scottsdale. The family dog Blue was found outside the car. It had taken shelter beneath the car and was in a hungry and thin state. An Oakland Rangers hat identical to the one that Fisher was seen wearing in the ATM footage was inside the vehicle. A pile of human excrement was found near the passenger door. Although police searched the area immediately around where the vehicle was discovered, they only searched one out of dozens of nearby caves. Some of these caves form a complex underground network, extending for miles beneath the surface. Several professional cavers have suggested that Fisher used them as a hiding place before escaping, killing himself, or dying from low oxygen levels. Professional cavers have visited these caves many times in the years since the murders, but no sign of Fisher has ever emerged.

The Toyota was discovered less than a mile from the Fort Apache Indian Reservation, an area which police never searched. They followed a set of footprints from the vehicle that led onto the reservation, but uncovered no sign of Fisher. A couple reported seeing a man resembling Fisher walking along the nearby Young Road several days before the discovery of the car. According to them, when the woman saw him, she said to her husband, 'That looks like Robert Fisher.' However, they waited until after the vehicle was found to report the tip. Lori Greenbeck, an acquaintance of the

116

Fisher family, said that her husband had gone camping with Fisher in the area where the Toyota was found shortly before April 10th. Her husband believed that Fisher was scouting the area. According to her, he was very familiar with the region.

On July 19th, a state arrest warrant was issued in Phoenix, charging Fisher with three counts of first-degree murder and one count of arson. Subsequently, he was declared a fugitive and a federal arrest warrant was issued by the United States District Court for the State of Arizona, charging him with unlawful flight to avoid prosecution.

On June 29th, 2002, Fisher was named by the Federal Bureau of Investigation as the 475th fugitive to be placed on its Ten Most Wanted list. He was also on America's Most Wanted's "Dirty Dozen", the list of its most notorious fugitives, and was profiled on The Hunt with John Walsh. The FBI still offers a reward of up to $100,000 for information leading to Fisher's capture. By April 2003, the FBI had received 'hundreds and hundreds of leads.' However, all reported sightings of Fisher have been either inconclusive or false.

In the years immediately following Fisher's disappearance, some people living in his old neighbourhood reported seeing a man resembling him driving slowly in the area. In February 2004, an individual with a striking physical resemblance to Fisher was arrested in Vancouver, Canada, by the Royal Canadian Mounted Police. He had a missing tooth where Fisher had a gold tooth as well as a surgical scar on his back, as Fisher had. However, his fingerprints did not match. He was held by Canadian police for approximately one week, until a relative correctly identified him. Responding to speculation that his fingerprints had been altered, Scottsdale Detective John Kirkham said that there was no scarring on them to suggest this. The man's identity was not released. The FBI alerted local law enforcement in 2012 that Fisher may have been living in the area near where Mary's car was discovered. In October 2014, police raided a house in Commerce City, Colorado after receiving a tip that he was hiding there. Despite arresting two occupants, they did not find any sign of Fisher.

In April 2016, FBI officials and Scottsdale police displayed new digitally age-enhanced photos of Fisher during a news conference on the fifteenth anniversary of the murders.

On November 3rd, 2021, Fisher was removed from the FBI Top 10 Most Wanted List. The FBI said 'Because the extensive publicity Fisher's case received during its nearly 20 years on the list has not resulted in his successful location and/or capture, the case no longer fulfils that requirement,'. Despite his removal from the Top Ten List, Fisher remains a wanted fugitive.

# ROBERT STEWART FLORES Jr.

Born1961 – committed suicide October 24th, 2002 after murdering three others.

Robert Flores, 41, a Gulf War Veteran was divorced with two young children aged 15 and 10. He was having money problems keeping up the child payments to his ex-wife. He was upset at failing his grades in nursing at the Arizona College of Nursing and Medicine, so upset that he methodically shot and killed three of his professors on October 24th, 2002 and then turned the gun on himself in a pre-meditated shooting.

At 8.30 am as most students were talking their midterm exams, third year student Flores entered the second floor office of Robin Rogers,50, an assistant professor of nursing and shot her many times.

Flores then took the stairs to the fourth floor, walked into a classroom of 40 students taking their exam and calmly shot and killed his second victim, Cheryl McGaffic, 44, another assistant professor of nursing whilst shouting at her 'Cheryl McGaffic, I am going to give you a lesson in spirituality.'

Barbara Monroe, 45, another assistant professor on the course with McGaffic was standing at the podium when this happened and crawled beneath a desk. Flores walked over to her and asked, 'Are you ready to meet your maker?' and then killed her with three shots.

Flores then looked around the room where the students were cowering beneath desks and calmly told them to 'Get the Hell out,' which they did.

Once the room was empty Flores killed himself with one of the five guns he was carrying.

Police called to the scene thought he was probably going to kill more professors as he had five guns, a Norinco .45semi-automatic pistol, a Glock .40 semi-automatic pistol, a Smith and Wesson .357revolver, a Colt.357 semi-automatic revolver, a Czech 9mm semi-automatic pistol and over 200 rounds of ammunition. No sensible reason could be advanced for his actions that day other than the three professors he killed were all teachers of the classes he failed his exams in and their death was some kind of revenge in his mind.

The day after the shooting the local newspaper the Arizona Daily Star received a letter written by Flores going some way to explaining his actions, I won't paste all 22 pages here but just some of the more relevant parts.

He opened by saying 'Greetings from the dead. You have received this letter after a rather horrendous event. I guess what it is about is a reckoning, a settling of accounts. The university is filled with too many people who are filled with hubris. They feel untouchable. I am tired, tired and weary. Rather than spend the next month or two selling what little I have I am going to end it now.' He ends with, 'As the curtain falls I will exit the stage for a well deserved rest.'

And that he did, unfortunately taking three other innocent people with him.

# MICHAEL STEVEN GALLEGOS

Born November 10th, 1971 – sentenced to death May 24th 1991. Stay of execution October, 2001. Appeals ongoing.

Kindall Wishon was 8 years old when Michael Gallegos, 21, raped and murdered her. He was her step-uncle.

The victim's mother Mrs. Wishon, met Michael Gallegos's brother Jerry Gallegos in Flagstaff in 1984. They moved to Phoenix in 1986 and eventually lived together in West Phoenix with Michael. In November 1989, Kindall's half-brother, George Smallwood, moved to Flagstaff. Smallwood visited his mother Mrs. Wishon and half-sister Kindall in Phoenix during holidays, and Michael Gallegos sometimes accompanied him. Michael Gallegos and George Smallwood were on spring break in March 1990 and spent the week in Kindall's home in Phoenix. They worked on their respective vehicles most of the week. In the afternoons, they were responsible for supervising Kindall when she came home from school because both Mrs. Wishon and Jerry Gallegos worked during the day.

Jerry Gallegos worked as an automotive repair foreman at a truck and trailer repair shop in Phoenix. On Thursday, March 15th, 1990, at about 4:30 p.m., Michael Gallegos and George Smallwood went to Jerry Gallegos's repair shop to work on their own vehicles. After the other employees left for the day, Jerry Gallegos supervised both Michael Gallegos's and George Smallwood's repair work. They drank some beer and worked on their vehicles until about 9:30 p.m. and then drove the vehicles home. Jerry Gallegos purchased a case of beer on the way. They arrived home about 10:00 p.m. and continued working on the vehicles until about 10:30 p.m. During this time Jerry Gallegos shared a couple of beers from his case with them. When Michael Gallegos and George Smallwood came into the house at about 10:30 p.m. Kindall was taking a bath; she went to bed shortly thereafter. Mrs. Wishon stopped by her room to kiss her goodnight on her way to bed. Jerry Gallegos took a shower and then played a video game with Michael Gallegos and George Smallwood before he retired at about 11:30 p.m. On his way to bed, Gallegos checked the case of beer and found that the case was all 'basically there.'

After Jerry Gallegos had retired, Michael Gallegos and George Smallwood continued playing video games and drank more beer. Michael suggested and George agreed that they go into Kindall's room to fondle her. Once they were inside the room, Michael Gallegos lifted Kindall's nightgown and rubbed baby oil on the small of her back. When she woke up, George put his hand over her mouth, and Michael put his hand over George's hand and over Kindall's nose. Kindall gasped for air and made sounds 'like a little pig' and eventually went limp. Believing that she was dead, they decided to 'finish her off.' They pulled her body off the bed and placed her on the floor. George attempted to insert his penis into Kindall's vagina. Michael then had anal intercourse with her for 15 to 20 minutes. During this time, George stuck his penis inside Kindall's. After Michael had completed the sex act, the two carried

Kindall's body out of the house and down the street where they dropped her naked body under a tree. They then returned to the house and went to bed.

Early the next morning, Mrs. Wishon and Jerry Gallegos got up to go to work. The couple did not attempt to awaken Kindall or go into her room, because she did not have school that day. Mrs. Wishon did, however, go into Michael and George's room to give them money to buy milk. George took the money and went to the store to purchase the milk. When he returned Michael went outside to work on his vehicle. After talking with Michael, George called Mrs. Wishon at her work and told her that Kindall was missing. Mrs. Wishon left work and arrived back at the house at about 10:00 a.m. George also contacted both Jerry Gallegos and the police. When Jerry Gallegos and the police arrived at the house they began an extensive search of the neighbourhood. Michael and George participated in the search, but they deliberately avoided the area where they had dropped Kindall's body. About 1:00 p.m. the police found the victim's naked body under the tree where Michael claims that he and George left her the night before. Michael's confessions and testimony in his own defence are the only evidence implicating George Smallwood.

The detective in charge of controlling the crime scene testified that the body was located 252 feet from Kindall's house. The naked body was lying supine with her legs spread apart. The body was dirty and covered with grass. The officer noted obvious trauma to the vaginal area and some type of oil located on one leg and in the vaginal area. He further stated that he observed that the victim had sustained contusions to the left side of the face, the centre    forehead, the right eye, and the right side of the nose.

George Bolduc, M.D., the medical examiner who performed the autopsy, determined that Kindall died of asphyxiation due to suffocation. He later testified at trial that her rectum was 'markedly dilated' and that the anal trauma occurred while the victim was alive. He noted that Kindall had various bruises and abrasions all over her face and body, some of which were red, indicating that they occurred while she was still alive. She also suffered a blunt force injury to her head, which caused a hemorrhage of the scalp. Mrs. Wishon testified that, before the night of the murder, the victim had no noticeable bruises or marks.

The police searched the house and seized numerous articles of evidence, including her underwear, nightshirt, and bed sheet. In the kitchen area, the police found an empty beer bottle and 2 empty cardboard beer cartons in a plastic trash container. They also found 2 empty beer cans across the room on the dishwasher and noted the presence of several hard liquor bottles on the kitchen shelves. In the carport, the police found another empty beer can and noticed a large cardboard box that was filled 3 to 4 feet high with empty aluminium beer and soda cans. After photographing the victim's room, the police dusted the room for fingerprints.

Because the house showed no signs of forced entry, the investigation focused on Michael Gallegos and George Smallwood. The police took them to the police station for questioning. Officer Armando Saldate, Jr. and Detective Michael Chambers escorted them into separate interview rooms. Officer Saldate advised Michael of his rights and then questioned him while Detective Chambers simultaneously questioned George. After initially denying any involvement in the victim's death, Michael confessed to Officer Saldate. He later confessed a second time in the presence of both Officer Saldate and Detective Chambers. The trial court determined that these confessions were voluntary.

When George was confronted with Michael's confessions, he denied any involvement in Kindall's death. He stated that if Michael had implicated him, it was only because he did not want to take the blame alone. The two were subsequently both indicted for the murder and sexual molestation of Kindall Wishon.

The state submitted blood samples taken from Michael and George, along with the evidence obtained at the crime scene, to Cellmark Diagnostic Laboratories, Inc. for deoxyribonucleic acid (DNA) testing. Cellmark later notified the state that George Smallwood could not be included as a contributor to the evidence. The state then dismissed the case against George Smallwood based on insufficient evidence.

During Michael's trial, the parties made the following stipulations regarding the tests of the physical evidence: (1) a fingerprint removed from the victim's bedroom matched Michael's right middle finger; (2) semen was detected on the victim's panties, nightshirt, and bed sheet; (3) DNA testing showed that the stain on the victim's panties contained a banding pattern that matched the banding pattern obtained from defendant's blood; and (4) the probability that an individual other than Michael Gallegos was the source of the stain on the victim's panties was 1 in 10 million for Caucasians and 1 in 67 million for Hispanics.

Michael Gallegos, a Hispanic, took the stand in his own defence and testified that he participated in the victim's death. He nevertheless maintained that he was drunk and that her death was accidental. He also testified that he believed that Kindall was dead at the time of the sexual penetration. On cross-examination, however, he was unable to explain the various bruises and abrasions on Kindall's body. Michael Gallegos was prepared to call George Smallwood as a witness, but on advice of George Smallwood's counsel, George Smallwood invoked his Fifth Amendment right not to testify.

The jury unanimously found Michael Gallegos guilty of first degree murder and sexual conduct with a minor. The jury was divided, however, on whether the murder was premeditated or felony murder.

In the special verdict, the trial judge found two aggravating circumstances (1) Michael Gallegos committed the murder in an especially heinous, cruel, or depraved manner; and (2) Michael Gallegos was an adult at the time of the offense and the victim was under 15 years of age. In mitigation, the judge found the defendant's age of 18 to be a statutory mitigating factor. He also found 2 non-statutory mitigating factors: (1) the defendant's remorse and (2) the recommendations of leniency from Officer Saldate and Detective Chambers. After considering and weighing each of the mitigating circumstances, the trial judge found that they were not sufficiently substantial to outweigh the aggravating factors and the call for leniency. Accordingly, the trial judge sentenced Michael Gallegos on May 24th, 1991, to death for murder and to a presumptive consecutive 20-year term for sexual conduct with a minor.

A Warrant of Execution was issued by the Arizona Supreme Court on October 4th 2001for the execution of Michael Steven Gallegos on November 14th, 2001. This was followed by a Stay of Execution issued on October 15th, 2001 as Gallegos has not yet exhausted his appeals.

Gallegos still sits on Death Row as his appeals move through the system.

# RUBEN GAZA

Born March 26th, 1980 – sentenced to death September 20th, 2004.

In September 1999, Ellen Franco moved into a two-bedroom house in Waddell, Maricopa County, Arizona occupied by Jennifer Farley and Farley's boyfriend, Lance Rush. Ellen had recently separated from her husband, Larry Franco.

At approximately 10.30 p.m. on December 1st, 1999, Farley heard a knock at the door. She opened it and saw a Hispanic male who was five feet nine or ten inches tall, about 180 to 200 pounds, and had bad acne. He had a large prominent tattoo on his left arm. He pointed at Ellen, who was standing behind Farley, and said, 'I am here to see her.' Ellen identified the man as Ben, whom Farley understood to be Ellen's relative.

Ellen then went outside shutting the door behind her and Farley went to her bedroom and told Lance Rush about the visitor. They then heard two gunshots. Rush and Farley scrambled to grab one of the guns they kept in their bedroom. Farley took a pistol from her bedside table drawer. Rush, who had not been able to get one of the other firearms, motioned for Farley to stay in the room and went out into the hallway. Farley heard a gunshot almost immediately and quickly hid in the bedroom closet. From inside the closet, she heard several more shots.

After waiting briefly, Farley came out of the bedroom and saw Ellen lying face down in the living room in a pool of blood. After determining that Ellen was still alive and breathing, Farley looked for Rush. She found him in the guest bedroom opposite their bedroom. He was conscious but bleeding. □ Farley dialled 911, and police and paramedics arrived within minutes. Rush was lucid and told them, 'Someone kicked the door in and started shooting.'

Ellen never regained consciousness and died at St. Joseph's Hospital shortly after the shooting. Lance Rush died at John C. Lincoln Hospital approximately an hour after the shooting.

Around two hours later at 12:45 a.m. on December 2nd, Ruben Garza bought bandages, gauze, and hydrogen peroxide from a drugstore in West Phoenix. Later that morning, he was treated at Phoenix Baptist Hospital for a gunshot wound to his left arm. The hospital contacted Phoenix police who talked to him at the Hospital. Garza told the officer that he was walking down the street when an unknown assailant drove by and shot him.

Maricopa County Sheriff's Office detectives questioned Garza the next morning after being identified by Farley. Garza first stuck by the claim that he had been shot in a drive-by, but changed his story when told that he had been identified by Farley as the visitor to the Waddell house. He then stated that he had gone there to persuade Ellen to reconcile with Larry. Ellen came out and talked to him. When their conversation turned into an argument, Garza pulled out his gun and shot her. Garza said he then 'blacked out' and was 'in a daze.' □ and did not remember seeing a man at the house, but that the woman who had originally answered the door charged at him with a knife and he shot at her in self protection. At some point someone shot at him from inside the house and he felt a "sting" in his arm and returned fire.

Garza was arrested and on December 2nd made two phone calls from jail to Laurel Thompson. In the first conversation, Garza said he was 'going to be in jail for a couple years' and that he had 'done to someone else' what the two of them had discussed doing to a boyfriend who had assaulted Thompson.

In the second conversation, Thompson told Garza that he was on every newscast and asked Garza how he had got caught; he told her, 'I got shot' □ Garza questioned Thompson about the news coverage and their friends' reaction to it. Garza asked her how many victims were being reported, and she said that he had killed two people. Garza told Thompson that he did not remember whom he shot, and they both chuckled. When asked whether it was self-defence, Garza said, 'On one count it was, on one count it wasn't. The guy shot me, then I shot him.'

Garza's car was searched on December 4th. Two white cloth gloves were found on the front seat floorboards. One glove was stained with blood identified through DNA testing as Garza's. Under the front seat was a bloodstained green cloth glove. DNA testing also identified the blood as Garza's. Garza's blood was also found on the passenger side of the car and in two locations in the hallway of the Waddell house.

A box of 9 mm ammunition was found under the driver's seat; Garza's fingerprints were on the box. These bullets were the same type as those found at the murder scene. A 9 mm pistol was found in Garza's belongings at his apartment when police searched it, testing showed that the pistol had fired the bullets found at the murder scene. No bullets fired by any other gun were discovered at the scene, which suggests that Garza's wound came from his own gun.

Jennifer Farley identified Garza at his later trial as the intruder. Eric Rodriguez, a longtime friend of Garza's, testified that before the murders he rejected Garza's offer to join him in a venture that would require that they 'get a little dirty' in order to make some money. Charles Guest, a more recent acquaintance, testified that two or three weeks before the murders Garza asked if he was interested in helping Garza sort out some 'family problems.'

Sent to trial in 2004, Garza denied committing the murders and said Larry Franco had been there and committed them. He claimed Franco was a police informant which is why they had not arrested him. There was no evidence to support this claim and the jury rejected it and found Garza guilty on two counts of first degree murder and one count of first degree burglary. The jury declined to impose a death penalty for the murder of Ellen but authorised the death penalty for the murder of Rush. The Superior Court affirmed the death penalty for Rush and sentenced Garza to life without parole for the murder of Ellen.

In 2017, age 43, another appeal was launched after a ruling in a different trial arguing that the original jury should have been informed of his release ineligibility as the prosecutors had used the possibility of him being a future danger to oppose it. The appeals continue.

# DARRICK LEONARD GERLAUGH

Born June 17th, 1960 – executed by lethal injection in Arizona on February 3rd, 1999.

Scott Schwartz, 22, was a young disabled man who walked with the aid of a leg brace and crutches because of a motorbike injury. Shortly before midnight on January 24th, 1980, he picked up hitchhikers Darrick Gerlaugh, Joseph Encinas, and James Matthew Leisure in his Lincoln Continental car. What Mr. Schwartz did not know when he offered the group a ride was that they had previously agreed amongst themselves to rob whomever picked them up.

As they drove on in Mr. Schwartz's car, Gerlaugh, who was already on probation for robbery, suddenly pointed a gun at Schwartz and forced him to drive to a deserted area near Mesa, Arizona.

There, the three men forced the victim out of his car. Gerlaugh pointed the gun at Schwartz and demanded money. Schwartz grabbed the gun from Gerlaugh pointed the gun at Leisure who was approaching him with menace and pulled the trigger. The gun did not fire. 'You fucked up' Gerlaugh laughed, 'There's no bullets in the gun.' The three men knocked Schwartz to the ground, where they beat and kicked him continuously for ten to fifteen minutes. Gerlaugh then announced that they would have to kill Schwartz to prevent him from identifying them and ordered Encinas and Leisure to hold Schwartz on the road so he could run the victim over with the car. Schwartz succeeded in dodging the car several times until Gerlaugh finally ran over him with the Lincoln Continental and felt the impact of hitting Schwartz's body with the car. Gerlaugh then ran over the Schwartz two more times and struck his head with the car bumper at least one time. At one point Gerlaugh even positioned the car's left rear wheel on top of Schwartz and floored the accelerator. Although badly hurt Schwartz was still alive and writhing in pain on the roadside. He began to plead with his assailants to tell him the reason for their attack. Gerlaugh took a screwdriver from the rear of the car and stabbed the victim in the head, neck and shoulders at least twenty times. Leisure also stabbed the victim ten to twenty times.

A pathologist testified that these various assaults caused severe injuries, any of which would have been fatal. The Schwartz suffered numerous fractures, puncture wounds and internal injuries from his head to his mid-section. His entire body was covered with bruises and abrasions. The three men then dragged Schwartz's body off the road to an adjoining field and covered it with alfalfa. Gerlaugh kept all of the money taken from their victim, $36.

The three men returned to the road and drove away in Schwartz's car. When the car ran out of gas they resumed hitchhiking and were picked up by Harry Roche in his pickup truck at about 2:00 a.m. Gerlaugh levelled the gun at Roche and forced him to take an apparently random series of turns. Finally, Gerlaugh ordered Roche to pull off to the side of the road for a comfort break. Roche at first refused and complained that the roadside was too muddy at that particular point to stop. When Gerlaugh pointed the gun at his head Roche stopped the truck and the three jumped out. Roche quickly put the truck in gear and sped away.

Roche informed the police but no names could be put to the three killers until Encinas told a friend what had happened and that person told the police who arrested all three and uncovered Schwartz's body. The Lincoln Continental had been vandalised and stripped.

Leisure and Encinas testified against Gerlaugh and received life sentences without parole. Gerlaugh was convicted of first degree murder and sentenced to death. He was stabbed in the back by other prisoners whilst in jail in 1987.

A stay of execution was dismissed as was a clemency claim. Darrick Leonard Gerlaugh was executed by lethal injection in Arizona on February 3rd 1999, age 38, 18 years after the murder. What makes this case unusual is that Gerlaugh was the first Native Indian to be executed in Arizona since the restoration of the death penalty in 1976 and was allowed Indian rights. He spent two hours three days prior to being executed preparing for his death by singing ancient Indian songs and praying inside an existing sweat lodge in the prison grounds and on the day of the execution took part in a pipe ceremony, the equivalent of Holy Communion.

# JESS JAMES GILLIES

Born October 18th, 1960 – executed by lethal injection in Arizona on January 13th, 1999.

Suzanne Rossetti, 26, was reported missing by her parents on January 29th, 1981, when she failed to pick them up, as promised, and drive them to the airport for their holiday trip. Her body was discovered several days later buried under a small pile of rocks in a ravine on Fish Creek Hill in Susperstition Mountains. She had been beaten and died from loss of blood.

Jess James Gillies, 21, lived and worked at Weldon's Riding Stables in Phoenix at the time of the murder. On January 28th, 1981, Gillies, 21, and Mike Logan were in the U-Totem Convenience Store at 52nd Street and Van Buren when Suzanne Rossetti drove up to do some shopping. When she returned to her car, she discovered she had locked herself out and the two young men helped her retrieve the keys and open it. In gratitude for their help Rossetti bought the men a six-pack of beer and offered them a lift back to the riding stable. En route, one of the men grabbed Rossetti and, after stopping the car, they pulled her to the ground where they both raped her. Gillies and Logan then drove their victim to Papago Park and then to her apartment, apparently raping her at both locations. The men rifled her purse and ransacked her apartment for valuables. When later arrested, Gillies was found in possession of several of Rossetti's belongings, including her credit cards. Rossetti was finally driven to the Superstitions where she was pushed over a cliff, tumbling 40 feet down the rocky hillside. Gillies and Logan checked on their victim and found her still alive. Rossetti begged for mercy, told the men she was going to die anyway and to let her die in peace. According to Gillies, Logan responded: 'That's right, bitch, you are.' According to Logan, Gillies began calling the victim a whore and a bitch. The victim was then beaten on the head with rocks until she lost consciousness. Gillies and Logan then covered her with rocks. A detective later testified that two men were needed to lift one of the rocks from her body, and drove back to Phoenix in her car. According to the medical examiner, Suzanne Rossetti died in approximately ten to fifteen minutes, presumably after she was buried.

When the body was discovered hair and blood drops were found nearby. Damage caused by small animals had been sustained by the body. The right cheek had been crushed and the eye was missing from the right socket. The medical examiner described various lacerations, abrasions, avulsions, and fractures to the skull and body of the victim. The victim tested positive for seminal fluid.

Between January 28th and February 3rd, Gillies and Logan accessed the Valley National Bank 24-hour automated teller twenty-eight times using Rossetti's card. Because only $250 can be withdrawn in any given 24-hour period, 13 of the attempts to obtain cash were unsuccessful. Each attempt was photographed by the ATM system.

Gillies continued to drive Rossetti's car for two days and couldn't resist telling his friends what had happened. One of them contacted the police and both he and Logan were arrested. Logan co-operated with the police and took them to the place where Rossetti's body was buried and agreed to testify against Gillies in return for a life sentence without parole for 25 years. He remains in prison today.

Gillies was tried on August 20th, 1981 and was convicted of first degree murder on August 27th, 1981 and sentenced to death. He was executed by lethal injection on January 13th, 1999.

Suzanne Rossetti is buried at Riverside Cemetery, Saugus, Essex county, Massachusetts.

# RICHARD J. GLASSEL

Born September 20th, 1938 – sentenced to death January 13th, 2003. Died age 74 from natural causes in prison in 2012.

Richard Glassel lived in a home he owned at Ventana Lakes, an active adult community for people age 55+ in Peorian and Sun City, Arizona. He had many disputes with the Lakes Home Owners Association over community charges, people parking in front of his property, hedges bounding his property being trimmed and in the end his house was foreclosed and he left and moved to California. There his hatred of the Ventana Lakes Homeowners Association festered and grew inside him.

On April 19th, 2000 the Association held its regular scheduled meeting at the Yacht Club. Seated at the head table was Board Member Duane Lynn and new Board Member Esther LaPlante attending her first Board Meeting. Duane Lynn's wife Nila was sitting in the front row of the audience of members.

The day before the meeting Glassel had driven to Arizona from California and on the day of the meeting drove into the community, parked his car and walked into the Board Meeting carrying an AR-15 assault rifle fully loaded with 30 rounds of ammunition plus two fully loaded 9mm pistols in holsters strapped to his chest and a ten round .22 calibre pistol in his hand. He had 384 rounds of ammunition on his person plus a further 359 more rounds in his truck.

Glassel entered the meeting, stood by the door and shouted that he was back and going to kill everyone in the room. He then fired all 10 shots from the .22 pistol.

One bullet hit Nila Lynn, 69, in the back of her head and killed her. Esther LaPlante was struck in the arm and head and also died, she was 59. The Association Vice Chairman was shot in the stomach and resident owner Kenneth Yankowski shot in the thigh. Glassel dropped the now empty pistol and was tackled as he tried to raise the AR-15 assault rifle. He managed to fire one round which struck owner resident Gilbert McCurdy in the foot fracturing the bone. Glassel was grounded by the rest of the group and held down until the police arrived. When a member asked him why he had done it he told them 'I did it to get even, you fucking sons-of-bitches. You fucked me over long enough.'

On April 26th, 2000 a Maricopa County Grand Jury indicted Glassel with two counts of first degree murder and thirty counts of attempted first degree murder. The trial began on November 18th, 2002. The day before Glassel's defence attorney had asked for it to be delayed and for himself to be replaced as Glassel was obstructive and wanted to defend himself. The judge refused both demands and after a 5 day trial the jury found Glassel guilty on all counts. On January 10th, 2003 Glassel was sentenced to death on two counts of first degree murder.

Glassel died in 2012 from 'apparent natural causes' after 9 years on Death Row aged 74. His court appeals against his sentence were ongoing at the time of his death.

# FABIO EVELIO GOMEZ

Born ? – sentenced to death June 5th, 2003.

Joan Morane lived in the Chandler Park Tower Apartments in Chandler, Arizona. On December 2nd, 1999, a friend stopped by Joan's apartment after work. The door of the apartment was unlocked and various items inside were in disarray.

Gomez lived across the landing from Joan. Shortly after 5:00 p.m., a resident of the apartment complex heard a woman screaming 'No!' from Gomez's bathroom and called 911. Chandler police officers responded to the call and when the officers arrived, Joan's friend informed them that Joan was missing. After looking through Joan's apartment, the officers left. Joan's friend remained and attempted to talk to neighbours about the 911 call. Gomez initially did not respond to knocks on his door, but later emerged, denying that he had seen Joan or heard any screaming. Shortly after he left his apartment to pick up his live-in girlfriend.

The neighbour who had made the 911 call left the complex shortly after the officers had arrived. The officers therefore apparently did not know Gomez's apartment had been the scene of the alleged screaming and did not go to his apartment.

Joan still had not returned, so her friend telephoned Joan's ex-husband, who arrived at the complex at about 6:00 p.m. The ex-husband found two red buttons outside of Gomez's apartment door, and Chandler police were again called to the scene. An officer returned, collected the buttons, and left the complex at approximately 8:00 p.m.

Gomez and his girlfriend returned to their apartment at about the same time as the officers were leaving. The girlfriend saw blood in their apartment and complained to Gomez. Gomez told her that earlier that day he had gone outside to smoke, leaving the door open, and that a cat had come in and scratched their baby. Gomez said that he bludgeoned the cat to death in the bathroom and threw it into a dumpster at the complex. The girlfriend went down to look in the dumpster but saw no cat; on returning to the apartment she discovered more blood.

Chandler police officers were themselves not happy with the situation and came back to the complex later that evening to briefly questioned Gomez outside of his apartment. Gomez again claimed to know nothing about Joan's disappearance or sounds of screaming coming from his apartment. The police returned to the complex several times during the early morning of December 3rd. On one of these occasions, an officer saw Gomez on the staircase carrying a deflated yellow raft to his girlfriend's vehicle. Gomez again denied any knowledge of Joan's disappearance.

The officer returned about an hour later and looked into the girlfriend's car with his flashlight and noted what appeared to be two small bloodstains on the yellow raft, he called for backup, went upstairs, and asked Gomez whether he and another officer could enter the apartment. Gomez agreed.

Once inside, one officer saw what appeared to be blood spots on the living room carpet. He asked Gomez where the blood had come from; Gomez replied that his girlfriend had cut her foot. The officers noticed more blood on the bathroom walls. In the bedroom, an officer found the girlfriend asleep, woke her, and asked if she had cut her foot. She replied she had not; the officer looked at her feet and found no injuries. He then asked her about the blood in the living room, and she related Gomez's explanation about the cat.

Gomez was asked what he had done with the cat and he said that he had put it in a garbage bag and thrown it into a dumpster at a nearby restaurant. After radioing for a search of the restaurant dumpster, officers noticed more spots of what appeared to be blood in the bathroom and by the front door. They  found wet throw rugs hung up to dry in the bathroom.

A search of the restaurant dumpster proved futile. However, an officer subsequently saw what appeared to be dried blood on the front of a dumpster at the apartment complex. Inside that dumpster, an officer found a blanket, a newspaper, and a woman's blouse, all with dried blood on them. A more thorough search revealed Joan's body, clad only in a red nightshirt with missing buttons similar to the ones found outside Gomez's apartment. In nearby dumpsters, the police found a pair of stained shorts, duct tape with blood on it and hairs attached to it, and bloodstained socks and washcloths.

Joan's body was bruised extensively. She had bruises on her arms and wrists consistent with someone gripping her tightly. The bruises to her right hand and wrist were consistent with defensive wounds. Joan had numerous lacerations and contusions on her face and

144

head. Her nose was broken and an abrasion at the back of her hairline was consistent with duct tape having been applied and then removed. Joan's skull was 'extensively' fractured; the shattered bone fragments had torn into her brain.

Subsequent searches of Gomez's apartment revealed bloodstains on the walls and floor and a large bloodstain near the patio door that had been covered up with several towels and a pillow. A bloodstained comforter was found inside the washing machine. Police also found socks and towels in the apartment similar to the bloodstained items in the dumpsters. They also found a receipt dated December 1st, 1999, showing the purchase of duct tape; the only duct tape found in the apartment was a small strip stuck to the carpet.

Vaginal swabs taken from Joan's body revealed the presence of semen. Subsequent DNA testing identified the semen as Gomez's and the bloodstains in the apartment as Joan's. No cat blood was ever found in the apartment.

At his trial in 2001 Gomez denied any knowledge of or involvement in Joan's disappearance and murder. He admitted to having sex with Joan but claimed it was consensual. He again claimed that the blood in his apartment was from a cat.

The jury returned verdicts finding Gomez guilty of first degree murder, kidnapping, and sexual assault. Sentencing proceedings were commenced before the trial judge, but before sentence could be pronounced, the United States Supreme Court decided in the Ring v. Arizona case that Arizona's capital sentencing scheme unconstitutional. The legislature then amended the capital sentencing statute and assigned to juries the responsibility of finding aggravating circumstances and determining whether a sentence of life imprisonment or death should be imposed.

The Gomez sentencing proceedings therefore began anew under the amended statutes before a new judge and a newly empanelled jury. Gomez represented himself during these proceedings with the assistance of advisory counsel. At the conclusion of the aggravation phase, the jury unanimously found that the murder was committed in a cruel and depraved manner but was not unanimous as to whether the murder was heinous. After hearing mitigation evidence in the penalty phase, the jury found death to be the appropriate sentence. The superior court subsequently sentenced Gomez to death for the first degree murder and to aggravated sentences for the kidnapping and sexual assault, the non-capital sentences to run concurrently with each other and consecutively to the death sentence. Various appeals with new attorneys were raised and all dismissed. In 2022 Gomez asked leave of court to be able to contact the various prospective jurors in any future appeals under the 14th Amendment of due process right to a fair trial to question them on racial criteria, he being black. The leave of court was denied. His appeals are still working through the system as he sits on death row.

# ERNEST VALENCIA GONZALES

Born February 8th, 1964 – sentenced to death April 27th, 1992.

Shortly before 7:00 p.m. on February 20th, 1990, Roger Daughtry returned home from work and noticed that his porch light was on. He went inside and saw that someone had disassembled his stereo units and moved his large speakers. Suddenly, a man appeared from behind the speakers, looked at Daughtry, and ran out of the house. Daughtry later identified that man as Ernest Gonzales.

Minutes later, Jeri Sheer, Daughtry's neighbour, took out her trash with her dog which ran toward a man holding what looked like a tyre iron. Sheer looked at the man, grabbed her dog, and went back into her house. When she looked out the window, she noticed the man heading in the direction of Darrel and Deborah Wagner's townhouse. Sheer later identified the man as Gonzales.

About 7:10 p.m., Darrel Wagner, his wife Deborah, together with Deborah's seven-year-old son arrived home from dinner out. As they walked into the small courtyard of their townhouse, they noticed that their front door was ajar. Darrel went to investigate while Deborah and her son waited at the gate. As Darrel pushed open the front door, both he and Deborah saw Gonzales standing on the stairway inside holding their VCR under his arm. Deborah immediately told her son to run to the neighbour's house and call 911. When she turned back toward her home, she saw Gonzales shove her husband out of the front door. Darrel lost his balance and fell backward. Gonzales then stabbed him seven times.

Deborah pleaded with Gonzales to leave. When he did not she jumped on Gonzales's back and wrapped her arms around him to keep him from stabbing Darrel again. Gonzales then swung at Deborah and stabbed her twice. He also apparently wounded himself as he was flailing at Deborah. When Deborah fell off his back, Gonzales snatched her purse and ran off. A few minutes later, Darrel helped his wife up and both went inside to call 911. Darrel collapsed on the floor during the call and died later that night from a stab wound to the heart. Deborah spent five days in intensive care. She had a damaged spleen, colon and diaphragm plus a punctured lung.

Gonzales went from the Wagner residence to his girlfriend's house. She helped clean his wound. Her daughters, Catherine and Martha Trinidad, were there and testified later at Gonzales's trial about comments Gonzales made on the night of the murder, his clothing, and the 'bag' he had with him containing a woman's driver's license and pictures of a boy with red hair, the colour of Deborah's son's hair.

Gonzales was quickly identified, arrested on February 23rd, 1991 and charged on a six-count indictment: felony murder of Darrel Wagner, first-degree burglary, aggravated assault of Deborah Wagner, armed robbery of Deborah Wagner, theft, and burglary of Roger Daughtry's residence. The first trial ended in a hung jury. Gonzales claims that this was because of Deborah's less-than-positive in-court identification. The second jury found Gonzales guilty on all six counts. At that trial, on May 23rd, 1991, Deborah identified Gonzales without hesitation. At sentencing on October 27th, 1992, the trial court found two aggravating factors, no mitigating factors, and sentenced Gonzales to death on the murder charge and various prison terms for the other crimes. The appeals followed until the Arizona Supreme Court issued a Warrant for execution on December 8th, 1999. On November 16th, 1999 they issued a Stay of Execution as the appeals went on. In 2006 based on evidence of Gonzales deteriorating mental condition and psychotic disorder another Stay was issued by the 9th Circuit. The prosecution suggests the mental condition is faked. The case goes on.

# MARK GOUDEAU
# ( THE BASELINE KILLER )

Born September 6th, 1964 – sentenced to 1,634 years in prison December 14th, 2007.

Mark Goudeau is an American serial killer, kidnapper, thief and rapist who became known as the Baseline Killer. He terrorized victims in the Phoenix Metro Area between August 2005 and June 2006. Goudeau was active at the same time as two other Phoenix serial killers, jointly known as the'Serial Shooter.'

Trouble began for Goudeau in 1982 when he was 18. He and one of his brothers were accused of raping a young woman. They were not charged as the victim did not want to be identified in court. In 1987 he was charged with trespass and drunk driving. In 1989 he was charged with kidnapping and sexual assault. Before that came to trial he robbed a cashier at Fry's supermarket of $850. He was sentenced to 15 years for the assault and 21 years for the robbery. He was paroled after 13 years in 2004. One year later he started his year long spree.

In addition to committing nine murders, his extensive crime spree included 84 other felony crimes that totalled 93 felonies over the ten-month period. He faced two separate trials—one for 19 charges related to an attack on two sisters whom he raped and sexually assaulted, and another related to 74 other charges including murder, robbery, rape, kidnapping, sexual abuse and/or assault of minors and adults. All but one of his victims were female. Goudeau was convicted on a total of 76 of 93 crimes, and was sentenced to death 9 times (one for each murder conviction) and given a sum total of 1,634 years in Arizona state prison.

Goudeau was first referred to as the Baseline Rapist when Phoenix Police announced that a light-skinned black male was sexually assaulting females as young as 12 years old at gunpoint near Baseline Road. Goudeau would later be named as the Baseline Killer in the spring of 2006 after investigators linked him to a series of murders and armed robberies. The crimes later spread north, primarily in the North Central area of Phoenix, Arizona.

Goudeau is believed to have committed nine counts of first degree murder, the victims being eight women and one man, in addition to 15 sexual assaults on women and young girls, 11 counts of kidnapping, and a number of armed robberies. Although not initially linked, the crimes were distinguished by having no apparent motive. The murders were particularly vicious and brutal, with the killer more often than not shooting the victims in the head. The attacker was often described wearing various disguises such as a Halloween mask as well as attempting to impersonate a homeless man or drug addict.

Police say that forensic analysis of the shell casings found at each of the crime scenes all came from the same gun. Phoenix police spent thousands of hours patrolling and following up on hundreds of tips during the summer of 2006. As residents of Phoenix became increasingly alarmed by the random nature of the violent crimes, community meetings were called by the police to distribute a sketch based on the description given by the surviving victims. Frustration and fear blanketed the city as posters and billboards displayed the sketch of the Baseline Killer and offered a $100,000 reward for information leading to an arrest. It took the police over a year to finally come up with a viable suspect.

At the time Mark Goudeau was on community supervision (parole) with the Arizona Department of Corrections and supervised out of the Northeast Parole Office. In August 2006 suspicious parole officers in the Northeast Parole Office provided information to the Phoenix Police Department task force suggesting that Goudeau matched the sketch of the Baseline Killer and should be investigated further. Parole officers searched Goudeau's residence and found a ski mask and a realistic toy handgun. Police used this information to obtain a search warrant for a detailed search of the residence and found additional items that linked him to crimes committed by the Baseline Killer.

On September 4th, 2006, Mark Goudeau was arrested in connection to the sexual assault of two Phoenix sisters, an attack which was tied to the Baseline Killer investigation. The sisters, one of whom was visibly pregnant, were assaulted in a Phoenix city park on September 20th, 2005. Goudeau was linked to the attack by DNA evidence collected shortly following the time of the assault. On September 7th, 2007, Goudeau was tried and convicted of all 19 charges relating to the attack on the sisters. He was sentenced on December 14th, 2007, to 438 years in prison for the sexual assault charges. On November 30th, 2011, a Phoenix jury sentenced him to death on the murder charges relating to the Baseline Killings. Goudeau is held on death row in ASPC Florence, awaiting execution.

## Timeline

August 6th, 2005, two sexual assaults.

9:45 pm, 7202 S. 48th Street, Phoenix. Police say Goudeau forced three teenagers behind a church near Baseline Road, and molested two of the girls.

August 14th, 2005, combined sexual assault and robbery

4:10 am, 2425 E. Thomas Rd, Phoenix.

September 8th, 2005, homicide

1:00 am, 3730 S. Mill Ave, Tempe, Georgia Thompson, 19.

September 15th, 2005, sexual assault

9:40 am, 4512 N. 40th St, Phoenix.

September 20th, 2005, sexual assault

10:30 pm, 3100 W. Vineyard Rd, Phoenix. While walking home from a Phoenix city park at night, two sisters (one of whom was clearly pregnant), were approached by Goudeau who was armed with a gun. He sexually assaulted one of the sisters while pushing the gun into the other sister's pregnant belly. He was arrested one year later when DNA evidence found on the women matched his profile. This was the breakthrough that led to the arrest in the Baseline Killer investigation.

September 28th, 2005, robbery

1425 W. Baseline Rd, Tempe.

September 28th, 2005, combined sexual assault and robbery

9:30 pm, 7202 S. Central Ave, Phoenix.

November 3rd, 2005, robbery and sexual assault

Separate robbery at 8:01 pm, 4019 N. 32nd St, Phoenix, then sexual assault at 8:10 pm, 3131 E. Indian School (across the street from the robbery), Phoenix. A robbery occurred on North 32nd Street. A man with dreadlocks and a fisherman's hat walked into a shop and robbed it at gunpoint for $720. Less than 10 minutes later, he abducted a woman placing items in a parking lot donation receptacle, across the street. He sexually assaulted her in her car and demanded she drive him to the corner because he just committed a robbery. The victim said he wore a Halloween costume and black plastic glasses.

November 7th, 2005, three separate robberies

8:08 pm, 2950 N. 32nd St, Phoenix. A string of robberies occurred starting with four people at gunpoint inside Las Brasas, a Mexican restaurant. He then went next door to a Little Caesar's Pizza restaurant and robbed three people inside. Immediately before entering the pizza restaurant, he robbed four people outside on the street. He reportedly stole $463 and fired a round into the air as he fled.

December 12th, 2005, homicide

At 6:55 pm there was a murder on 6005 S. 40th Street, Phoenix. Tina Washington, 39, was on her way home from a pre-school where she worked. A witness spotted a man with a drawn gun standing over her body behind a fast food restaurant. She had been shot in the head.

December 13th, 2005, robbery

4:00 pm, a woman was robbed at 700 E. South Mountain Avenue, Phoenix.

February 20th, 2006, two murders

7:38 am, the bodies of 38-year-old Romelia Vargas and 34-year-old Mirna Palma-Roman were found shot to death inside their snack truck at 91st Avenue and Lower Buckeye Road. Initially, police did not connect this crime to the Baseline Killer and believed that the murders were drug-related. The murders were officially linked by police in July 2006.

March 15th, 2006, two murders

At 9:00 pm, a double murder was discovered on 4102 N. 24th Street, Phoenix. Two employees of Yoshi's restaurant at 24th Street and Indian School Road were on their way home in the same vehicle. Liliana Sanchez-Cabrera, age 20, was found dead in the parking lot of another fast-food restaurant while the body of Chao Chou was discovered about a mile away. Both victims were shot in the head.

March 29th, 2006, murder

12:00 am, 2502 N. 24th St, Phoenix. A body was discovered on North 24th Street. A local businessman noticed streaks of blood on the gravel of a parking lot. The police were called, but a search of the area turned up nothing of real value. A week later, the businessman discovered the badly decomposed body of Kristin Nicole Gibbons as he was investigating a horrible smell in the area. She had been shot in the head.

May 1st, 2006, sexual assault

At 9:00 pm, 2950 N. 32nd St, Phoenix. A man in a latex Halloween mask abducted a woman in a car and sexually assaulted her at gunpoint. She was taken from outside the same restaurants where the November 7th, 2005 crimes occurred.

May 5th, 2006

Phoenix police went public with a list of 18 crimes that they believed were the work of the Baseline Killer. This number has since risen to 23, as of August 2nd, 2006.

June 29th, 2006, murder

At 9:30 pm, a murder occurred on 2924 E. Thomas Rd, Phoenix. Carmen Miranda, 37, was abducted from a self-serve carwash, located half a block from the May 1st and November 7th crimes, while she was on her cellular phone. She was found dead from a gunshot to the head behind a barbershop about 100 yards (91 m) away. The attack was captured on closed-circuit television. This is the last crime attributed to the Baseline Killer.

Phoenix police released hundreds of pages of documents that detailed their investigation into the Baseline Killer. The paperwork reveals that police had at least 10 names of possible suspects that they had looked into, and that they had already ruled out some of those people. The 20,000 pages of police reports were primarily of other suspects and contained very little mention of Mark Goudeau. The documents revealed information on nine cases ranging from a double homicide to sexual assaults, robberies and kidnappings. The new information included police reports and narratives that described where and who police were looking at in the investigation. They also discussed investigative leads; however, much of the information is redacted.

According to the un-redacted pages, the Baseline Killer posed as a homeless person in one incident, pushing a shopping cart toward a woman in a parking lot near 32nd Street and Thomas Road. He forced himself into her car and told her to perform oral sex upon him or he would kill her. The records state that she fought him off. In that incident, the man believed to be the Baseline Killer was wearing gloves, a mask and clothing that covered his entire body. The records show police worked to obtain partial hand prints, DNA and ballistics reports to build their case; but those results are redacted on the paperwork.

Police recommended that prosecutors charge Goudeau with 74 crimes, including nine counts of first-degree murder, five counts of sexual assault, three counts of attempted sexual assault, 10 counts of kidnapping, 12 counts of armed robbery, four counts of attempted armed robbery, three counts of sexual abuse, nine counts of sexual conduct with a minor, 13 counts of aggravated assault, and three counts of indecent exposure. On October 31st, 2011, Mark Goudeau was found guilty of a total of 67 felony counts, including all murders attributed to the Baseline Killer. On November 30th, 2011, Goudeau was sentenced to death 9 times for the murders and 1,196 years for the other 58 crimes he was convicted for while already serving a 438-year sentence after being convicted for 19 separate crimes related to the rape and assault of two sisters during this same crime spree. The final sentence totals 1,634 years.

In October 2015, Goudeau appealed his nine death sentences, with an appellate attorney arguing to the Arizona Supreme Court that Goudeau should have been tried separately for each of the murders and some other counts. In June 2016, The Arizona Supreme Court upheld nine death sentences and more than 60 other felony convictions against Mark Goudeau.

Goudeau is held on death row in ASPC Florence awaiting execution.

# JIMMY LEE GRAY

Born September 25th, 1948 – executed by asphyxiation gas September 2nd 1983.

Jimmy Lee Gray was born in 1949 in Whittier, California. At the age of 18, Jimmy murdered his girlfriend Elda Louise Prince. 16 year old Elda was a sophomore at Parker High School in Parker, Arizona where Jimmy was also a student and a school friend of Elda's brother, 18 year old Ervin. The Prince family had made Jimmy welcome in their house and even helped out by buying him clothes. They also took him to ball games and on fishing trips. On the day of the murder, January 5th, 1968, Elda was to leave school early for a doctor's appointment and her mother, Opal, was going to the doctor's office to pick her up at 4.30 pm. The receptionist told her that Elda had not shown up so Opal went home presuming that her daughter had caught the school bus as usual. When this arrived without her, Opal called the police and reported her daughter missing. Jimmy went with the Prince's to the sheriff's office and later that evening helped in the search for Elda. The sheriff was suspicious of Jimmy, having noticed his muddy shoes and under questioning the following day he led deputies to a culvert near the Colorado River, and showed them where he had dumped her body. The shoe's pattern exactly matched the prints at the crime scene. Examination showed that the Elda had been strangled and had her throat cut, before being thrown into the culvert. It appeared that Jimmy had met Elda after school and that whilst walking home they had quarrelled and he had killed her. Elda was buried in the Cottonwood Cemetery on 11th January. Jimmy was convicted of 2nd degree murder and received a sentence of 20 years to life. Sadly he was released on parole after just 7 years despite the protest of the trial judge who regarded him as a dangerous individual. How right he would be proved to be.

Just one year later on June 25th 1976, Gray kidnapped 3 year old Deressa Scales from her family's apartment in Pascagoula . He drove the terrified little girl to a remote part of the Mississippi Gulf Coast and raped and sodomised her. He then kept her head held down in a muddy ditch until he thought she was dead and walked away. She wasn't dead, and when she gurgled in the muddy water he returned and stamped on the back of her neck breaking it before throwing the body from a bridge into a creek below.

Gray lived in the same apartment complex as the Scales' and was questioned by police after neighbours mentioned that they had seen Deressa with a man with a red Volkswagen car, whom they identified as living in the apartments. When Jimmy showed up in the car police noted that the lower legs of his jeans were wet, which he explained by his having been swimming in the complex's pool. Under questioning he admitted to them that he had taken Deressa for a ride in the country and that on a back road had touched the little girl. He claimed that she had wandered off and fallen into a shallow ditch. He rescued her from the ditch and put her, still breathing into the trunk of his car. He then began the homeward journey, stopping on a bridge over Black Creek where he removed Deressa from the trunk and threw her into the water below. He led police to the crime scene at 3.30 am the following morning. The full story came out under further questioning and him being confronted with forensic medical evidence.

Jimmy Gray came to trial in Pascagoula on December 13th, 1976, before Judge Merle, charged with 1st degree murder and sodomy. Once again shoe prints would help convict the killer and chemical analysis would show the presence of semen in the little girl's body, although at that time DNA was not sufficiently advanced to enable it to be linked to Gray. It took jurors just an hour to convict Gray and he was then sentenced to death in the gas chamber. His mandatory appeal to the Mississippi Supreme Court reversed the original verdict and gave him a new trial in 1978, where he was allowed to address the jury on his own behalf. However they were not impressed and reached the same verdict. Both juries recommended the death penalty at the conclusion of the sentencing phase, as the victim's age and sodomization were aggravating factors. In 1979, the same court upheld the verdict and the sentence from the second trial. Further appeals followed, including one based upon the cruelty of execution by lethal gas in which the 5th Circuit Court sitting in New Orleans granted a stay of execution in July 1983 hours before he was due to be executed.

Gray's appeals ended after 7 years on death row on September 1st, 1983 when the US Supreme Court dismissed his final appeals in a 6 to 3 decision clearing the way for his execution the following day, Friday, September 2nd, 1983 at the Mississippi State Penitentiary.

His execution at the Mississippi State Penitentiary was not straightforward.

It took two minutes for the guards to strap him into the seat. He kept his head bowed and his eyes closed, whispering occasionally. At 12:10 am., the door to the chamber sealed, and Sheriff John Ledbetter signalled T. Berry, a school custodian who has been Mississippi's executioner since the chamber was built in 1955 to proceed. He threw the lever that dropped a small container of white cyanide crystals into an acid solution under Gray's seat. A white wisp of gas writhed up between Gray's legs and he visibly sucked in his breath, breathing deeply. Within a minute his head fell forward and he appeared to be unconscious.

But then his head jerked back, he began to choke and strain at the straps holding him to the seat by his arms, legs and chest. His fists clenched. His face contorted, and prolonged, agonized groans and shuddering gasps could be heard in the witness room.

Three times his head dropped and he appeared dead, but each time it snapped up, striking with an audible clang a steel pole running from floor to ceiling behind his seat. After eight minutes of this, assistant Warden Joe Cook entered the steaming, mosquito-filled witness room and said 'Gentlemen of the press, let's go.' The chamber was still filled with gas and mosquitos and Gray's head was strained back against the pole, his head turned to the side, his eyes open and rolled back in his head, his mouth open, and his head was moving slightly. Gray was finally pronounced dead at 12.47 am. by doctors monitoring his heart beat via a remote stethoscope.

The parents of Deressa Scales later sued the State of Arizona for releasing Gray after 7 years from his previous 20 year sentence.

In part due to Gray's botched execution Mississippi passed legislation making lethal injection the only method of execution for inmates sentenced after July 1st, 1984. The gas chamber was decommissioned in 1998.

# RANDY GREENAWALT

Born February 24th, 1949 – executed by lethal injection in Arizona January 23rd, 1997.

In early January 1974, Greenawalt went on a trip to Miami, Florida, where he had planned to exchange his car with a couple from Denver, Colorado. On January 12th, the body of 42-year-old Henry A. Weber, a Global Van Lines truck driver who had been shot in the head, was found at a highway rest area in Mississippi County, Arkansas. Initially, nobody could be connected to the crime until four days later, when police officers in Tempe, Arizona detained brothers Randy and James Greenawalt, 25 and 23, respectively, for the January 15th murder of 33-year-old Stanley Edward Sandage at a rest area near Flagstaff. Like Weber, Sandage was a truck driver working for Whitfield Tank Lines who was found shot dead in his truck in an apparent robbery as $42 had been stolen from his wallet.

The Greenawalts were arrested for trying to purchase stereo equipment using Sandage's MasterCharge card, and upon inspecting their vehicle, police found a .32-caliber pistol that was positively identified as the murder weapon, and a .243-caliber rifle that might have been the second murder weapon. A third man, 33-year-old George Sanders, an acquaintance of the brothers, was also arrested for federal firearms violations and credit card fraud in relation to the case. Due to the similarity of the two cases, a sheriff from Arkansas was dispatched to question Randy about the earlier Henry Webber killing, but decided to wait until the case in Arizona went first.

In a bid to avoid the death penalty, the elder Greenawalt pleaded guilty to the murder and was sentenced to life imprisonment in exchange for testifying against his brother who had pleaded innocent on all charges. During the trial, it was made apparent that in the Sandage murder, Randy had pre-emptively painted an "X" on the window of the truck before proceeding to open fire and kill his victim. Thanks to his testimony, James was also convicted and sentenced to life imprisonment, which he was to spend at the Florence State Prison. In the meantime, Randy was extradited to face charges in Arkansas, but despite his willing confession to both this and another murder committed in Colorado, the case fell through and he was returned to serve his sentence in Arizona.

During his time in prison Greenawalt was considered a model inmate and granted a cushy job as an office clerk. Another inmate placed in the trustee unit with him was 43-year-old Gary Gene Tison, who was serving a life term for stabbing a prison guard and had a history of escape attempts from the prison. On July 30th, 1978, Tison's three sons (Donald, Ricky, and Raymond), who regularly visited their father in prison, entered the prison, ostensibly for another one of their visits. While Ricky was talking to his father, his brothers pulled out a sawn-off shotgun concealed in a cardboard box they had been carrying and ordered the guards to go into the booth. Greenawalt, who had been working in the booth and was in on the plan, then cut the alarm and phone lines, and was provided with a pistol. After locking the remaining guards, visitors, and prisoners into a supply closet, all five men escaped in the Tisons' 1969 Ford Galaxie with their planned final destination being a small ranch across the border in Saric, Mexico, where Gary Tison allegedly had connections with a drug smuggling network.

On the way towards Yuma, the gang changed their car with a black Lincoln Continental and drove on dirt roads to avoid roadblocks. The next day, the gang was near Quartzsite when their car blew a tyre and they were left stranded by the roadside. The Tisons and Greenawalt then established a campsite in the area, where they were noticed by 24-year-old Marine Sgt. John Lyons, who was driving along the highway with his 23-year-old wife Donnelda, their 22-month-old son Christopher, and 15-year-old niece Teresa-Jo Tyson. Lyons stopped and offered to help them out, but he and his family members were then forced at gunpoint into the Continental and driven out in the desert. There, both Gary and Greenawalt proceeded to shoot the Lyons to death, while niece Tyson was left to bleed out, dying while attempting to crawl away from the car. The Lyons' corpses were discovered on August 6th, while Tyson's was found five days after.

In the meantime, the gang had stolen the family's orange Mazda and headed to Wenden, where they spray-painted it a silver colour. After this, they headed towards Flagstaff, where they established a campsite on the outskirts of town. While the other three rested, Greenawalt and Donald went to visit a female pen pal of Greenawalt's who bought them a truck and ammunition. Shortly after that, Gary arranged for a plane to fly them out of the United States from Clovis, New Mexico, but the authorities were onto them and set up an ambush at the airport. Upon arriving at the airport however, the gang realized the police were waiting and headed towards south western Colorado instead. Along the way, they came across Texas newlyweds James and Marlene Judge, 26 and 23, who were on their way to Denver to watch a football game. The gang killed them near Pagosa Springs on August 9th, stole their van, and then buried their bodies, which were not found until months after their disappearance.

After stealing the Judges' van, the gang headed to Casa Grande, Arizona, where they stayed with a relative of Gary Tison. After resting for a day, they continued their trip towards Mexico, unaware that by then, the police had set up roadblocks along every intersection of the roads. Along the way, the gang attempted to break into a gas station near Gila Bend, but were unsuccessful in doing so. On August 11th at night they approached their first roadblock in rural Pinal County. They pulled up and then opened fire on the approaching officer, barely missing him, before they drove off right through the blockade.

About six miles ahead, they faced another roadblock, but this time, the deputies opened fire on the van. Donald Tison, who was driving, was fatally hit in the head, causing the vehicle to swerve off the road. After it halted, the remaining four fled on foot in the darkness towards the desert, with the deputies chasing after them. A helicopter was dispatched to illuminate the area, revealing that Greenawalt and the two living Tison brothers had been hiding in a ditch. While all three were armed, they surrendered peacefully to the authorities. Gary Tison remained on the run for 11 days, until his body was discovered by chemical worker Ray Thomas under a mesquite tree near his workplace in Chuichu. He had died of thirst and exposure in the desert heat, about a mile and a half from where the van had crashed.

Following their capture, Greenawalt and the Tison brothers were first arraigned on charges of prison escape and assault, for which they were speedily convicted in December 1978. Soon after, Greenawalt was charged with four counts of capital murder, three counts of kidnapping, two counts of armed robbery and one count of auto theft, while Ricky and Raymond, who claimed that they took no part in the killings, pleaded guilty to one count of murder as part of a plea bargain to testify against Greenawalt. However, once in court they refused to do so, the judge declared a mistrial and reversed the verdict, allowing the brothers to be charged anew. On February 16th, 1979, Greenawalt was convicted on all charges, showing no emotion when the verdicts were read out. On March 26th, he was officially sentenced to death for the four murders, as well as being given concurrent life terms for his other convictions. Justice Douglas Keddie later stated that he had no reason to be lenient with the convict, as he found no mitigating circumstances in the case and determined the killings to be cruel and unnecessary. The murder charges in Colorado were dropped following the Arizona convictions, and that case was officially closed.

After spending 18 years on Arizona's death row with unsuccessful attempts to have his sentence commuted, Greenawalt was executed via lethal injection at the Florence State prison on January 23rd, 1997. His last meal consisted of two cheeseburgers, French fries, coffee, and milk from the prison cafe, and his final statement was, *'I have prayed for you many times and the Lord is using you well. Don't worry about me. I'll be fine.'*

Ricky and Raymond Tison, who had also been sentenced to death for their roles in the murders, later had their sentences commuted to life imprisonment after the Arizona Supreme Court determined that they were not active participants in the shootings and under twenty years old at the time.

# BERTRAM GREENBERG

Born March 31st 1932 – killed in a hail of bullets after running a police road block.

Coming into Houck, Arizona, from the west there are the remains of several billboards along the road, most have fallen or are slowly falling to pieces. It was by one of these billboards that one of the more awful episodes in Houck's history started on the cold night of February 7th 1971, on the road that superseded Route 66 and ending on the old road itself in New Mexico.

That evening police patrol dispatchers received two messages almost at the same time. Both were from Highway Patrolmen in desperate circumstances, but these were two separate incidents a couple of miles apart. Just west of Houck on Interstate 40, Patrolman James Lee Keaton stopped a car for a number plate discrepancy. For the 27-year-old officer, who lived in Sanders, it should have been nothing more than a routine traffic stop on his local patch. Keeton had served six years in the Army Reserve and had completed a degree in police science in 1968.

Behind the wheel of the '68 Pontiac with the gold and vinyl top that he pulled over was 38-year-old Bertram Greenberg. That he was on parole after serving a prison sentence for extortion and had crossed the state line from his home in California might have been enough to warrant a stop, but Greenberg was the subject of an all points bulletin issued just hours earlier which was unknown at that time to Patrolman Keeton – the APB declared Greenberg as a    suspect in the rape and murder of 13-year-old Mary Louise Hill in Griffith Park, Los Angeles, on the afternoon of 4th February. A hiker had seen Greenberg dragging the body of the young girl into undergrowth and had noted the license plate of his car which was swiftly traced back to relatives of Greenberg.

Greenberg had a history of violence and mental illness that stretched back several years. At 23 he had been charged with robbery and battery after a bloodstained car in his garage was linked to an assault on a local woman. As soon as he was released from jail he was arraigned on charges of raping a UCLA co-ed and a West Los Angeles housewife. He served just a year before being released and was rearrested on charges that he posed as a policeman to lure a woman into his car and rape her. He was once more sent to prison and paroled in 1963. Four years later he was returned to state prison after being convicted of extortion, having blackmailed a woman whom he took nude photos of. That sentence included time at the California Medical Facility at Vacaville, a special institution for mentally disturbed inmates.

After killing Mary Louise Hill, Greenberg had returned to his home in West Covina where he was visited by his parole officer, Robert Conway. During that visit, Greenberg was telephoned by relatives notifying him that the car he was using was being sought by the police who had visited the relatives who were the registered owners. Conway was suspicious enough to ring the police himself and ask why they were looking for the Pontiac. When they told him of the girl's murder he immediately advised them to put out a bulletin for Greenberg. But, by then, Greenberg was on the run.

At 4.14pm the following day, Officer Keeton pulled the Pontiac over on Interstate 40 just west of Houck. A passing motorist saw the officer and another man struggling in the front seat of the police patrol car but, by the time he was able to turn around and return to the scene, the man had driving off in the Pontiac leaving Officer Keeton, who had managed to radio in a distress call dead at the scene, shot with his own service revolver. A few minutes later the Pontiac was stopped by Patrolman Don Allen Beckstead, this time east of Houck. Beckstead was also familiar with the local area as he lived in Houck with his wife and two young sons. Again, this should have been a simple traffic stop for speeding as Beckstead was not aware of the shooting of Keeton. As Beckstead approached the car, Greenberg pulled out the revolver he had taken from Officer Keeton and fired. Shot in the stomach, Beckstead was able to radio for help as Greenberg sped away. Beckstead fought hard for his life in hospital but kidney failure meant he had to be urgently transported to Albuquerque to the nearest artificial kidney machine and sad to say he didn't make it.

Crossing into New Mexico on Route 66, Greenberg pulled to the side of the road and flagged down a yellow Volkswagen Beetle, telling the occupants that he had a problem with his generator and that he needed a lift to Gallup. Once in the car, he pulled out the gun and ordered them to drive up a dirt road towards an abandoned mine. Realising the peril they were in, James Brown and his wife, Karen Dianne, a law student and school teacher on holiday from Missouri, lunged at the hitchhiker but were unable to disarm him. Greenberg forced Brown to strip to his underpants before sexually molesting his wife. Then he shot Brown in the back of the head before shooting Dianne in the head, too. James Brown died but Dianne was able to escape and would later recover in hospital.

Stealing the yellow VW, Greenberg headed for Grants where he was finally stopped by a local police road block and a barrage of handgun, carbine and shotgun fire at the junction of Highway 117 and Interstate 40. The VW was virtually cut in half by the hail of bullets and skidded off the road. Greenberg tried to make a run for it but was cut down by some nine or ten bullets finding their target in his body and killing him on the spot. It transpired he had tried to stab himself with a pocket knife before the shooting, stabbing himself in the chest and cutting his wrist, almost severing his left hand.

A rather poignant addition to this story is the fact that both the murdered patrolmen's widows Betty Beckstead and Connie Keeton would later take up positions as police dispatchers.

# BEAU JOHN GREENE

Born April 2nd, 1966 – sentenced to death August 26th, 1996.

Roy Johnson, 59, a music professor at the University of Arizona, was last seen around 9:30 p.m. on February 28th, 1995 as he was leaving the Green Valley Presbyterian Church where he had just given an organ recital. Although his wife expected him home before 10:00 pm., the usually punctual Johnson did not make it back that night. Four days later, authorities found his body lying face down in a wash.

At his later trial Greene admitted that he killed Johnson. He testified that he had been using methamphetamine continuously for several days preceding the murder and that he had neither slept nor eaten much during that time. He said that he was suffering from withdrawal from drugs when he killed Johnson.

On the day of the murder, Greene's friends, Tom Bevan and Loriann Verner, both drug users themselves, told Greene he could no longer stay in their trailer located west of the Tucson Mountains as a drug dealer they used had threatened to shoot Greene over an outstanding debt and Bevan and Verner thought Greene's presence in their trailer would ruin their relationship with that dealer. Greene left, stole a truck and drove to Tucson where the truck broke down.

Sometime that night, during Roy Johnson's drive home from the concert, Greene and Johnson's paths crossed. Greene's story, disbelieved by judge and jury was that Johnson approached Greene in a park. Greene claims that Johnson wanted to perform oral sex on him, and offered to pay him for it. Greene accepted, and the two drove to a secluded parking lot in Johnson's car. Greene says he then changed his mind and told Johnson. In response, Johnson smiled and touched Greene's leg. Greene claims he 'freaked out' at Johnson's touch, and struck him several times on the head with his fist knocking Johnson unconscious. He then moved Johnson's motionless body to the back of the car, drove to a wash, and dumped the body, walked back to the car and drove away. He then claims he realized that he needed money so he returned to the wash, walked down to the body, and stole Johnson's wallet.

Several pieces of evidence undermine Greene's version of the killing. First, medical testimony indicates that a heavy flat object -- not a human fist -- damaged Johnson's skull. Fist bones striking a person's head will ordinarily shatter long before the thick bones of the skull, yet neither of Greene's hands showed injuries or bruising. Secondly, only one set of tyre tracks and footprints entered and left the wash, suggesting that Greene did not return for the wallet. After dumping Johnson's body in the wash, Greene drove Johnson's car directly to the Bevan/Verner trailer and told Bevan about the killing. Greene asked Bevan for some clean shoes. He also took a small rug to cover the blood soaked car seats.

Greene left the trailer and headed for K-mart, the first of several stops he made on a spending spree using Johnson's cash and credit cards. To explain any discrepancies between his signature and those on the credit cards, Greene had wrapped his hand with K-Y jelly and gauze and feigned an injury to it. Among other things, he bought clothes, food, camping gear, an air rifle and scope, and a VCR (which he later traded with a street dealer for methamphetamine). He eventually abandoned Johnson's car in the desert. On March 2nd, the police were contacted by an informant and they arrested Greene at a friend's house on March 3rd. He led them to Johnson's body on March 4th.

Greene was sent to trial on charges of first degree murder, robbery, kidnapping and 6 counts of forgery on March 5th, 1996. He was found guilty and sentenced to death on August 16th 1996. His automatic appeal was dismissed on October 10th, 1998 and the sentence affirmed. A warrant of Execution was issued by the Arizona Supreme Court on December 5th, 2003 after other appeals were dismissed and a Stay of Execution was issued by the same court on January 14th, 2004, which was the actual date of his proposed execution. Further appeals took place with the Supreme Court of the State of Arizona affirming the death sentence on April 14th, 2023. Greene now 57 sits on death row.

One little niggle, although the judge dismissed Greene's story of being approached for sex by Johnson mainly on evidence from Johnson's wife that he was not homosexual, one has to ask, why did Mrs Johnson take a book from the local library about 'Living with a Homosexual Husband' some time before the murder?

# RICHARD HARLEY GREENWAY

Born October 14th, 1968 – sentenced to death June 15th, 1989.

On March 27th, 1988 Greenway and his friend Christopher Lincoln robbed the Tucson home of Lili Champagne, 62, and her daughter Mindy Peters, 17. Greenway shot and killed both females with a .22 rifle by shooting them in the head. The two then made off in Mrs Champagne's Porsche car later abandoning it and setting it on fire.

Police found the bodies of Lili Champagne and her daughter in their home when they went to ask about the Porsche fire having established Mrs Champagne was the owner. Evidence suggested that the two had been killed in the course of a robbery and following a news bulletin asking for information regarding the victims, Greenway's sister notified homicide detectives that Greenway knew something about the incident.

Detectives picked up Greenway and his co-defendant, Chris Lincoln, for questioning during which Lincoln, a juvenile, confessed to participating in the robbery and killings and implicated Greenway as the killer. Greenway and Lincoln were then both arrested and charged with several counts, including first degree murder.

Before his trial, Greenway was placed in a cell with Anthony Schmanski. Schmanski, according to his trial testimony, asked Greenway why he was in jail, and Greenway told him, 'I just blew two people away' because 'they had seen my face.' Further investigation revealed Greenway had attempted to sell the victims' car stereo to Brian Mize, a co-worker. According to Brian Mize's trial testimony, Greenway told Mize that he went to the victims' house and, after taking 'some stuff,' shot the victims. Greenway also told Mize that, after he shot the older lady, 'her body rolled over and blood gushed out of her head.' There was also evidence that Greenway knew the victims. He had been to a party with Mindy Peters in late 1987. Greenway met Lili shortly thereafter when Greenway went to their house to return Mindy's wallet which he said he had found but had probably stolen.

Both Greenway and Lincoln received guilty verdicts on the first degree murder charges and other supplementary charges and on June 15th, 1989 Greenway was given the death sentence plus 57 years for the other charges whilst Lincoln, being a juvenile, received life in prison sentences for both murders to be served concurrently. In 1991 the Arizona Supreme Court upheld the convictions and sentences on appeal. Both are in prison with further appeals ongoing.

# SHAWN RYAN GRELL

Born February 17th, 1975 – sentenced to death July 9th, 2001 overturned in 2013 and given a sentence of natural life in prison.

(Personally I think death is too good for this asshole.)

Thirty-five-year-old Shawn Ryan Grell was one of those kids who grew up hard and mean. He killed his family's cat, set fire to their dog, and even burned down the house they lived in. In 1988, when he was 13, police arrested Grell after he fondled a young girl's breasts.

Grell was sent to a juvenile facility after the incident, where he continued assaulting staff and other inmates and earned a reputation for being an unstable kid whose violent behaviour needed to be controlled. He was tested and was diagnosed as borderline retarded with an IQ somewhere between 70 and 80.

Grell spent the rest of his youth in and out of that juvenile facility, committing offenses like disorderly conduct, shoplifting and assault.

Things did not improve for Grell as he got older. By 1992 he had been convicted of assault and sent to prison. In 1995 he was back in jail again for robbing a convenience store. Grell was granted parole, but his Parole Officer sent him back inside when he was caught possessing drug paraphernalia in 1998.

During the three years or so that Grell was out on parole, he had managed to find himself a steady girlfriend, Amber Salem, and when he ask her to marry him in 1998, she accepted. He also became a father.

Kristen Salem was born in 1997, and by all accounts was a happy, well adjusted little toddler. All three had moved in to Amber's parent's home by the time Grell violated his parole and was sent back to prison.

After Grell was released in 1999, he tried to get work but his criminal record made it difficult for him. Because of his felony convictions, companies would either not hire him, or, if he lied and didn't tell them about his record, fire him in a couple of months after his background check was completed and his past had come to light.

His inability to remain employed caused a great deal of conflict in the home between Grell and Amber Salem's parents.

Grell was at home December 2nd, 1999, when Amber's mother found out he'd lost his job once again. Amber Salem then called to meet Grell for lunch. Grell cashed his last pay check, put in some job applications at Desert Sky Mall and met Amber outside the food court. She told him how upset her parents were, and that they were threatening to throw Grell out of the family home.

When Amber returned to work, Grell bought some 32-ounce bottles of beer and drank them in her car. He went to a bar in Phoenix, to meet Amber for her break about 2:45 p.m. After that, Grell later told police, he decided to pick up two-year-old Kristen and drive out to visit his sister.

He picked up little Kristen Salem at the day care she attended, then took her to McDonald's for a hamburger. They ate in the McDonald's parking lot, then cruised around for a while, looking at the Christmas displays.

Kristen got fed up and started whining that she wanted her mother.

Grell told police, 'I just got tired of it and slapped her in the mouth. After she stopped crying a few minutes later, she said, 'Sorry, Daddy,' and then she started being good, and then she just went nuts again because she wanted to see her mom again.'

Then things took a horrific turn.

Grell took Kristen to the Target store and purchased a red plastic 3-gallon gasoline jug for $4. He filled it at a gas station and then he drove around the desert for about 45 minutes until he found a ditch on the side of the road that appeared to be just what he was looking for.

His recorded statement continues, 'Kristen was asleep, so I got out of the car, then I picked her up out of the car. I said, 'Kristen, Mommy's here. Let's lay down,' so I laid her in the dirt next to the car. I took the gasoline and poured it on her."

Even Kristen's screams and pleas of 'No, Daddy, no!' weren't enough to stop him.

'I took a match and threw it on her.'

Detective Donald Walsh of the Maricopa County Sheriff's Office testified in court that forensic analysis at the crime scene showed that Kristen was laying on the ground when the blaze began on the front of her body. She got up and ran about 12 feet, walking in circles at one point as the flames spread upwards to her face. He said that the heat was so intense, a barrette on the left side of her head melted, the plastic running down her face. She finally collapsed face-first in a ditch and died.

Grell drove back and forth until he couldn't see the flames anymore. Then he went back, got out and walked over to Kristen.

'I just looked at her,' he says.

Six hours after he burned his daughter to death, Shawn Grell was pulled over in downtown Phoenix on suspicion of drunk driving. He was arrested and, during a 30 minute interview with police officers, laughed, joked, and even suggested a lingerie bar he thought the cops might enjoy. Not once did he mention his two-year-old daughter.

Two days later as a hunt for missing Kristen intensified Shawn Ryan Grell turned himself in and confessed to the murder of his daughter.

At his trial he pleaded guilty to first degree murder and threw himself on the mercy of the court giving up the right to trial by jury.

Judge Barbara Jarrett had sat on the bench for 12 years. During her long and illustrious career, she presided over many cases where capital punishment was an option, but never found cause to use it. Not once.

On July 9th, 2001, in one of her last acts before she retired from the bench, The Honourable Judge Barbara Jarrett sentenced Shawn Ryan Grell to Death.

Sadly, Judge Jarrett's sentence was not the end of this story.

On June 6th, 2006, the Arizona Supreme Court unanimously decided that Shawn Grell did not give up his right to a jury sentencing when he waived his right to a jury trial in 2000. His death sentence was vacated, and it was ordered that a new sentencing hearing be held.

At the centre of the issue is whether the trial court erred by failing to find that Grell is mentally retarded and appropriately weighing that factor in mitigation of his sentence, and whether the execution of a mentally retarded person violates the Eighth Amendment's prohibition against cruel and unusual punishment.

Grell's public defenders called for evidence of his mental state and found that he had brain damage and recommended life with parole. In 2013, the Arizona Supreme Court settled the issue when they concluded that Grell was indeed mentally disabled and overturned his death sentence reducing it to one of natural life in prison ruling that it would be constitutionally prohibited cruel and unusual punishment to execute someone with mental retardation. He remains in Florence prison today.

# DOUGLAS EDWARD GRETZLER

Born May 21st 1951 – executed by lethal injection June 3rd 1998

Strap in for a long ride, this case has many twists and turns and a host of participants, good and bad.

Douglas Edward Gretzler was an American Serial killer who, together with accomplice Willie Steelman, committed seventeen murders in the States of Arizona and California in late 1973. All the victims were shot, strangled, or stabbed to death, and the majority of the murders were committed in the commission of robberies or for the purpose of eyewitness elimination.

Gretzler was born on May 21, 1951, in the Bronx, New York, he was the second of four children born to Norton Tillotson Gretzler, a Roumanian national, and his wife, Janet (née Bassett). His father served as President of the Tuckahoe School District, and his mother was a homemaker. In the early 1950s, the Gretzlers moved to the working class suburb of Tuckahoe, where they were regarded as upstanding residents.

Although Gretzler repeatedly attempted to please his father as a young child, by the time he was eleven, he had stopped trying; instead seeking avenues to spite him and frequently pursuing leisure activities outside the home or playing his drums at night in the family basement. By 1966, Gretzler had begun smoking marijuana. His father soon discovered his recreational usage of the drug and attributed it to his lackadaisical attitude toward his studies

On August 16th, 1966, the oldest of the Gretzler children, Mark, committed suicide by shooting himself in the head in his bedroom at the age of 17. His suicide came just days after his father discovered he had stolen upcoming examination papers and handed copies of the answers to other students as a prank which had resulted in the school banning him from all senior year activities. His suicide note offered no explanation for choosing to end his life, but simply thanked an aunt for lending him the gun he used to do it with.

Two years after his brother's suicide, Gretzler began extending his drug habit by taking narcotics such as mescaline and LSD, as a result of which his relationship with his father further deteriorated.

While Gretzler was not popular at school, his friends and acquaintances later spoke well of him. After graduating in 1969, Gretzler chose not to continue his education; instead deciding to become an auto mechanic. He worked for several months in a local car service centre.

The following year, Gretzler left New York and relocated to Florida, where he met a young woman named Judith Eyl, they began dating, and shortly thereafter announced their engagement.

Shortly after their February 1970 marriage in Miami-Dade County, Florida, the Gretzlers returned to the Bronx, where they bought an apartment. However, although Gretzler held a variety of jobs, he invariably left his employment of his own volition after a matter of days or weeks frequently leading to arguments with his wife who worked full-time in a local bank. In 1972 Judith gave birth to their daughter Jessica. Initially, Gretzler relished his role as a father, although he soon began to tire of the responsibility, however, he was never harsh or directly neglectful to the child, instead opting to leave her in the care of his wife as he spent increased amounts of time away from home. The two began to experience increased financial difficulties and Gretzler began committing petty crimes for money, although he was never arrested for these.

Via a wealthy relative, Gretzler inherited a generous trust fund of several thousand dollars on his 21st birthday; he spent the majority of this inheritance on a 1967 MGB sports car and improvements to the vehicle and little, if any, on his wife and child.

On December 26th 1972 Gretzler abruptly abandoned both his job and his family altogether. He waited until his wife left the apartment with their baby before packing some belongings into a duffel bag and heading West in his MGB with ambitions to ultimately relocate to Colorado. He arrived in Casper, Wyoming, on December 27th and lived in this city for six months undertaking a series of low-paying jobs. After 6 months on June 28th, 1973 he was arrested for a minor traffic offence and vagrancy. Approximately eight weeks later, Gretzler left Wyoming and drove to Denver. His life changed when he met Willie Steelman.

Willie Luther 'Bill' Steelman was born on March 21st, 1945, in San Joaquin County, California, the youngest of three children born to Lester Steelman and his wife, Ethel.

The Steelman family had migrated to California from Oklahoma in 1935 where Lester initially obtained work as a foreman at a San Joaquin farm. The family had little money, but were close-knit. As both parents worked to provide for their children, the responsibility for raising Steelman was largely delegated to his 14-year-old sister, Frances.

. When Steelman was 13, his father died. Shortly after that Steelman dropped out of school and began committing petty crime. Despite his mother's efforts, he refused to recommit to his studies or find employment. She re-married.

In March 1962, Steelman's mother and his stepfather persuaded him to enlist in the United States navy; this enlistment lasted only a few months before his service was terminated. The following fall, Steelman relocated to Denver to live with his sister Frances who soon evicted him from her home due to his unruly and threatening behaviour toward her and her children. He returned to California to live with his mother and step father.

In January 1965, Steelman was convicted of three counts of forgery and involving a minor in a crime and was placed in the custody of the California Youth Authority, who in turn sent him to the Pine Grove Work Camp, where he remained for seven months.

Following his release, Steelman obtained employment as a field hand. He met a 15-year-old girl, whom he later married, with the ceremony conducted in Reno, Nevada. He soon quit his job, and the couple moved into his mother's home. In December 1965, a warrant was issued for Steelman's arrest for cashing stolen cheques. He was arrested in early January the following year and remanded in custody at Stockton County Jail, where he attempted suicide. Days later, his young wife had had enough and annulled their marriage.

In February 1966, Steelman was transferred to the Stockton State Hospital. He was classified as mentally ill, and transferred to the Atascaderor State Hospital, where his 'remarkable progress' saw him returned to Stockton State Hospital after several months. He was later sentenced to 14 months' imprisonment for his second forgery conviction, to be served at the California Men's Colony where he proved to be a model prisoner.

Steelman was granted parole after serving just two months' imprisonment at the CMC; he was released on September 16th, 1968, and returned to Lodi, obtaining employment as a shipping clerk. Three months later, he was arrested for supplying LSD to two 16-year-old girls. For this, he was sentenced to 43 days imprisonment and fined $625. While in prison he became acquainted with a young woman named Kathy Stone. He moved into Stone's house shortly after his release in the spring of 1969. Via Stone, Steelman became acquainted to a young woman named Denise Machell. The two wed in June 1969, relocating to Sacramento and, later, MountainView.

Throughout 1970 and 1971, Steelman was frequently arrested for a variety of minor offenses, although on each occasion, the charges were either dropped, or he was given a small fine. By 1972, his drug dependency had increased. He became an orderly at the

Vista Ray Convalescent Hospital in Lodi, earning $320 a month, but lost this job for forging prescriptions. His wife left him on New Year's Day 1973.

In August 1973, Steelman travelled to Colorado to visit his sister. Although Frances initially welcomed her brother, he soon outstayed his welcome, but refused to leave her house, remaining in an unfurnished area of the house and refusing to pay rent or find employment. Although Frances resented her brother's freeloading off her, and his refusal to return to California, Steelman's oldest niece, Terry Morgan, enjoyed her uncle's company. Via Terry, Steelman became acquainted with a 17-year-old named Marsha Renslow. She was one of many youngsters who became impressed with Steelman's outlandish and somewhat embellished stories of bravado and crime. The following month, Gretzler met Steelman at his sister's home. The two initially became acquainted via Renslow.

Although Gretzler had initially arrived in Denver to seek enough work to maintain his vehicle and feed his drug habit, he and Steelman soon became close friends, although Gretzler always considered himself the follower of the two. The pair frequently discussed their mutual desire to obtain quick cash via crime, with Steelman also teaching Gretzler how to snatch purses and cheque books. Shortly thereafter, the two duped a teenage boy into providing them with a shotgun, and they began devising ways of committing more serious crimes without being caught. They continued these discussions after Frances abandoned her home on September 30th just hours after Steelman had stolen her purse. She moved with her children into a nearby apartment, informing Steelman the house was about to be repossessed in the coming days.

Within days of Frances and her children leaving the house, Steelman announced to Gretzler and Renslow his decision to relocate from Denver to 'someplace warmer, maybe Phoenix'. Gretzler agreed to accompany him. On hearing this, Renslow asked if she could accompany the two, hoping to become reacquainted with a 21-year-old acquaintance named Katherine Mestites, with whom she was infatuated. The two agreed to take her, and the trio drove from Denver to Phoenix on October 9th. En route, they stopped for one night in a motel; the following evening, Gretzler accidentally discharged a firearm through a window of the motel, resulting in them being thrown out and all three spending the night of October 10th in Gretzler's car at a nearby roadside pull-in.

By October 13th, the trio had driven to the town of Globe, where Steelman robbed a nude sunbathing couple of $5 at gunpoint. Hours later, close to Tempe, the trio picked up a hitchhiker, whom they drove to a secluded orange grove, stripped, pistol-whipped, and robbed. The ring stolen from this hitchhiker netted the trio $60 at a Phoenix pawnshop when they arrived in the city later that evening.

They spent the night of October 13th at the Stone Motel, resolving to drive the following morning to the address of the man whom Mestites had relocated to Phoenix with named Kenneth Unrein, 21, whom Renslow knew through maintaining correspondence with Mestites, lived on 18th Street.

On the morning of October 14th, the trio arrived at Unrein's address, only to learn Mestites and Unrein had recently separated. At Renslow's request, Unrein provided the trio with the Apache Junction trailer park address of Katherine Mestites, adding she now lived with a 19-year-old named Robert Robbins.

Intentionally or otherwise, Unrein provided the incorrect address. Two days later and again out of cash and furious at being lied to Steelman decided to return to Unrein's address. On this occasion, Unrein was in the presence of 19-year-old Michael Adshade. At gunpoint, the two men were forced to drive to Mestites' apartment, where they all consumed alcohol and drugs before Unrein and Adshade discreetly exited the residence and returned to their home. In their absence, Mestites divulged to her guests the details of a physical assault she had endured at Unrein's hands two months previous. Robbins then drove Gretzler and Steelman back to their motel. Mestites and Renslow remained in each other's company at Apache Junction for several days, although Renslow never mustered the courage to inform Mestites of her love for her. On October 22nd having neither seen nor heard from either Steelman or Gretzler for six days Mestites purchased a plane ticket for Renslow to return to Denver.

On October 17th, 1973, Gretzler and Steelman returned to Unrein's address and both he and Adshade were forced at gunpoint into Unrein's Volkswagen van. Upon Steelman's instructions, the four drove to California. Niether Unrein or Adshade were bound, although Gretzler and Steelman alternated between driving and sitting in the passenger seat pointing a gun at them. By the following morning, they had reached Oakdale, where Steelman purchased food and drink for all of them.

After driving aimlessly for several hours, Steelman ordered Gretzler to park the van close to Littlejohn Creek in Knight's Ferry, where both captives were ordered out of the van and told to walk down to a creek bed. They were then bound with microphone cord and rope before Steelman informed them that he and Gretzler were going to abandon them, adding both should wait one hour before attempting to free themselves. Steelman and Gretzler left but minutes later, the two returned to the creek. Steelman then partially strangled Unrein before stabbing him to death, and then helped Gretzler to strangle and stab Adshade. The victims were then stripped naked before their bodies were concealed beneath bushes.

The following morning, Gretzler and Steelman visited an acquaintance of Steelman's in the town of Clements. On October 20th, Unrein's van broke down close to California State Route 1. Minutes later, they stopped a young couple in a car near Petaluma. and ordered them to drive the two to Santa Clara, the driver was ordered to stop close to the town of Marshall. The male hostage, James Fulkerson, was then bound and a gun placed against his head. In response, Fulkerson referred to his companion by name, stating: 'I know I don't have much say in this, but please don't hurt Eileen, okay? Please don't hurt her.' This statement unnerved Steelman, who untied the young man and dragged him to his feet, informing him he had had ,'every intention of blowing your fucking head off'. One hour later, with the male hostage in the trunk of his car, Steelman attempted to rape Hallock, but was unable to sustain an erection. The couple were robbed, then released in Mountain View the following morning after Gretzler and Steelman stole a brown Ford sedan from a parking lot.

Concerned that Robbins and Mestites could link them to the disappearances of Unrein and Adshade, and aware the two teenagers they had released would soon inform police of their ordeal, Gretzler and Steelman decided to return to Phoenix. En route to Arizona, on October 21st, they picked up 18-year-old hitchhiker Steven Allan Loughran close to Monterey Bay. Loughran agreed to accompany the two to Arizona, also purchasing gasoline for them on route.

Upon their arrival at Mestites' address, Steelman was informed Renslow had returned to Denver; he introduced Loughran as a friend from California. The five spent the evening and early hours drinking, smoking, and taking drugs.

On the afternoon of October 23rd, Robbins drove Mestites to work at the Playful Kitten massage parlour. In their absence, Steelman initiated a fight with Loughran, although Loughran, approximately 6 feet 1 inch (1.85 m) tall and weighing 180 pounds, easily won this confrontation. In response, Steelman retrieved his shotgun and a sleeping bag, ordering the teenager out of the apartment with Gretzler following, carrying the sleeping bag. The trio drove to a deserted gully close to the Superstition Mountains, where Steelman ordered Loughran out of the car, to hand over his wallet and then crawl inside the sleeping bag. Steelman then shot the teenager in the head; the two then returned to the trailer.

In the afternoon of October 24th, Steelman convinced Gretzler the two should murder Robbins. This decision was partly due to fear the teenager suspected their involvement in the disappearances of Unrein and Adshade. The two devised a plan to murder the teenager while Mestites was at work later that day. According to Gretzler he strangled Robbins that evening from behind with an electrical cord. The two then shot him once in the head to ensure his death, and hid his corpse beneath a mattress in his bedroom. Hours later, Steelman drove Mestites back to the trailer from her place of work, explaining Robbins was 'out of town for a few days.'

The following morning, the trio drove to a local store in Robbins' Chevrolet convertible as Mestites remarked of her relief that 'Ken and Bob' were 'out of her life', and her need to 'do some coke' that afternoon prior to conducting a spiritual reading to direct her future. Although Steelman attempted to persuade Mestites to go to work at the massage parlour that evening in order that he and Gretzler could dispose of Robbins's body, she refused. Shortly after dusk, Steelman shot Mestites once in the head from behind as she knelt and conducted a séance at a small altar she had constructed. Robbins and Mestites bodies were discovered on October 28th.

Within 24 hours of their murders, friends and neighbours of Mestites and Robbins had alerted authorities to their disappearance. Through interviewing local residents following the October 28th discovery of their bodies, investigators learned that two men named 'Bill and Doug' had recently stayed at the trailer with the victims, having left the residence in the early hours of October 26th, and that a young girl named 'Marsha, from Denver' had also stayed at the trailer until approximately one week before. One eyewitness informed police that 'Bill' had claimed to hail from California, whereas 'Doug' had a notable New York accent. Both had stated their intention to travel to San Fransisco. By October 31st police had determined Marsha was Marsha Renslow. She initially refused to co-operate, but when shown Polaroid crime scene photographs of the bloated bodies of Robbins and Mestites she changed her mind and agreed to co-operate, naming 'Bill' as Willie Steelman, and although not positive as to 'Doug's' surname, she thought it was possibly "Gritzler". The information provided by Renslow included details of robberies and car jackings the pair had committed and the paying for motel rooms with stolen cheques between October 9th and 16th; this information was soon followed by the discovery of a motel receipt dated October 16th listing Gretzler's name and his address in the Bronx. This information proved sufficient to issue warrants for the suspects' arrest on suspicion of robbery and fraud on November 1st.

Hours after police interviewed Renslow for the second time on November 1st, Arizona investigators received a fax from their California counterparts informing them they had traced an abandoned green Volkswagen van linked to the October 20th kidnapping and robbery of a teenage couple to a missing Arizonian named Kenneth Unrein, adding the teenagers had named their abductors as 'Bill' and 'Doug'.

Within hours of Mestites' murder, Steelman persuaded Gretzler to accompany him to Tucson. The two left Apache Junction in Robbins' Chevrolet in the early hours of October 26th but abandoned the car hours later. The two then travelled to Tucson via bus, purchasing the tickets with money stolen from Mestites. They arrived in the city on October 27th, residing in a cheap boarding house on 4th Avenue. The two remained at this boarding house until November 1st, having by this date become acquainted with a young woman named Joanne McPeek, the younger sister of their boarding house landlady, Susan Harlan.

Late in the evening of November 1st, Gretzler and Steelman decided to steal a car and flee the city. Shortly after they began hitchhiking close to the University of Arizona the two approached a Dodge Charger driven by 19-year-old Gilbert Rodriguez Sierra, as he slowed the vehicle close to a stoplight, with Steelman thanking him for stopping before pointing a gun and stating, 'We need a ride. We need a car, your car!' Sierra was then ordered into the back seat at gunpoint as Gretzler began to drive. As had been the case with the two teenagers they had held hostage at gunpoint, then released, on October 20th, Steelman claimed to be a notorious hitman on the run, having 'just wasted a cop'. It is unknown if Sierra believed these boasts as according to Gretzler, he simply stared blankly at Steelman, muttering a brief sentence in Spanish as opposed to English for the first time.

Steelman then forced Sierra into the trunk of his car before the two returned to the Tucson apartment of Joanne McPeek and her partner, Michael Marsh, which they had left hours earlier; McPeek and Marsh were persuaded to accompany the two to purchase hard drugs, with Steelman adding, 'We've got a dude in the trunk, a narco.' When McPeek stated she didn't believe him, Steelman rummaged through the glove box for identification, before shouting to the rear, 'Hey! Is your name Gilbert?' to which Sierra replied, 'Yeah!' Steelman then asked Marsh for directions to the desert, adding 'I'm gonna kill this sonofabitch!'

Shortly after, at a deserted canyon close to Gates Pass, Steelman dragged Sierra from the trunk at gunpoint, forced him to hand over his T-shirt, then ordered him to his knees and accused him of being a "pig" and a "narco". Steelman then twice attempted to shoot Sierra, although on each occasion, the pistol misfired as he had covered the firearm with Sierra's Tee-shirt which blocked the hammer. As Sierra desperately tried to run, Steelman removed the T-shirt and shot him once in the back causing him to collapse to his knees and fall down a small ravine. Steelman then ran down the ravine and shot Sierra in the face and forehead at close range as Gretzler laughed. The four then returned to Tucson and purchased amphetamines off a local drug dealer before spending the remainder of the night at a Mabel Street drug den with a teenager named Donald Scott, whom they first encountered at this address.

After wiping all fingerprints from Sierra's car the following day, Gretzler and Steelman abandoned the vehicle in a parking lot. Sierra's body was discovered approximately twelve hours after his murder. He was formally identified on November 5th.

On the morning of November 3rd, a young student named Vincent Armstrong observed the two hitchhiking close to the site of Sierra's abduction. He stopped to offer the two a lift, although shortly thereafter, Steelman pressed a gun against his torso, ordering him to continue driving. When Armstrong began shaking in panick, Steelman punched him before ordering him to 'pull over, then' close to an intersection. Armstrong then climbed into the passenger seat of his Pontiac Furebird as Gretzler took over driving. Moments after Gretzler took control of the vehicle, Armstrong threw himself head first from the passenger seat to the pavement sustaining severe bruising and abrasions and shattering his glasses. Gretzler performed a U-turn and drove the vehicle at him. Armstrong then scrambled over a low wall and ran into the grounds of a nearby church as Gretzler sped from the scene.

Armstrong reported his ordeal to the Tucson Police Department who recovered his broken glasses at the location of his escape. He was driven to a nearby hospital and given appropriate medical attention before assisting police in creating Identikit drawings of his two assailants.

After Armstrong had jumped from the vehicle, Gretzler and Steelman drove in an aimless manner around Tucson until they drove by a condominium in the Villa Paraiso complex close to Vine Street. Outside this address, they observed a 28-year-old former Marine Captain and student teacher named

Michael Sandberg washing his Datsun car. Steelman threatened Sandberg with his gun before the pair forced him to take them into his condominium where his 32-year-old wife, Patricia, was preparing food in the kitchen. Gretzler pressed a knife to her neck as Steelman informed the couple they were to remain hostages until after dusk, after which they would be left unharmed.

At Michael's request, Patricia was given Vallium to help ease her nerves. She then prepared a sandwich for Gretzler before Steelman decided the two should adjust their appearances. Gretzler then dyed his blond hair brown before Steelman shaved off his moustache and attempted to disguise a black eye he had recently received with Patricia's cosmetics. Both then changed into clean clothing from Michael's closet before Gretzler bound Patricia's arms behind her back with twine and ordered her sit on the floor of the bathroom. Michael was then forced to lay face-down on the couple's bed before his ankles and neck were bound in a manner which ensured he could not move his ankles without choking himself.

Minutes later, Patricia was dragged from the bathroom to the couch where she was further bound before Gretzler walked into the bedroom and shot Michael in the head; he then shot Patricia once in the head through a cushion Steelman had placed over her skull to muffle the sound of the discharge. Steelman then fired four further rounds into her head. Noting Patricia was still just alive Steelman repeatedly beat her about the head with a golf club until her twitching ceased. After destroying any potential incriminating evidence at the crime scene, the two packed some of Michael's clothes into a suitcase before stealing the Sandbergs' credit cards, a camera and other items of material value from the house. They then fled the scene in the Sandbergs' Datsun, leaving Armstrong's Firebird parked beneath a canopy close to the condominium.

Immediately after leaving the Sandberg residence, the two returned to the Mabel Street drug den they had left that morning. Only Donald Scott, who they had met earlier, was still at this address; he agreed to their offer to accompany them to California. The trio drove to a nearby motel in Stanfield, Arizona, where they spent the night of November 3-4. The following evening, they stopped overnight in another motel, again signing the register as Michael Sandberg and again paying for their room with a forged cheque taken from the Sandbergs' residence.

By the afternoon of November 5th, the three had reached Pine Valley, California, where Gretzler and Steelman agreed to Scott's request to part company with them, allowing him to exit the vehicle close to Interstate 8. They then continued driving in the direction of Victor, California with Steelman talking increasingly frequently of robbing the owners of the downtown United Market, assuring Gretzler that the owners, Walter and Joanne Parkin (with whom he had previously had a heated confrontation), were wealthy. He also explained the family lived in a rural ranch house surrounded by vineyards and estimated a robbery of the Parkins' Orchard Road house and their supermarket would net the pair anything up to $20,000.

By the afternoon of November 6th, 1973, the pair had returned to Steelman's hometown of Lodi, where they slept at the home of an acquaintance until shortly after 5:00 p.m. Steelman persuaded a friend named Duff Nunley to telephone his 17-year-old nephew, Gary Steelman Jr. and convince Gary his uncle's life was in danger and persuade him to hand Steelman his father's Derringer pistol without his father's knowledge. The ruse worked.The two thanked Steelman's acquaintance and nephew for the firearm and then informed them they were leaving the state. Gretzler and Steelman then drove to the United Market at closing time, expecting to find Walter Parkin alone at the premises, only to discover the building already closed; they then drove two miles toward Orchard Road.

At the time of their arrival, the Parkins were not home; the couple's two children, 9-year-old Robert and his 11-year-old sister, Lisa, were being babysat by 18-year-old Debra Earl and her 15-year-old brother, Richard. The two entered the property by Steelman briefly deceiving Debra to lower her guard by believing they owed the Parkins money before pushing past her and immediately threatening the teenagers at gunpoint, with Steelman shouting: 'Now listen! We're only here for Walter, so both of you stay cool and nobody is gonna get hurt! That understood?' As Richard stood in shock, Debra comforted the Parkin children as she wept explaining Walter and Joanne were bowling and wouldn't return for "a couple of hours." All four were then forced to sit on the sofa to wait.

They were not aware that prior to the two entering the house, Debra had phoned her father,

Richard Sr., in distress at two strangers in the yard; he sped to the Parkin residence, where he too was held at gunpoint as Debra again burst into tears, shouting 'Oh Daddy!' Upon learning Richard Sr. had told his wife, Wanda, to contact police if he was 'not back home in fifteen minutes', Steelman ordered Gretzler to watch the child and teenage hostages at gunpoint as he and Richard Sr. went to fetch Wanda from their home at gunpoint, adding he should 'shoot the hostages' if he, Richard Sr. and Wanda were not back at the Parkin residence in twenty minutes. 10 minutes later, Steelman returned to the Parkin residence with Richard Sr. and Wanda Earl.

At approximately 9:25 p.m. Debra's fiancée, 20-year-old Mark Lang, arrived at the Parkin residence by pre-arrangement to drive Debra and her brother home. He was also taken hostage at gunpoint, and allowed to comfort his weeping girlfriend.

Walter and Joanne Parkin returned to their home at approximately 10:45 pm. All adult hostages were then forced to hand over all the money and jewellery in their possession before, at Joanne's pleading, she was allowed to put her two children to bed in the master bedroom—pleading with the two to go to sleep in order that they become oblivious to the ongoing ordeal. Steelman then ordered the adult and teenage hostages, except Walter, into the bathroom, where Gretzler bound the hostages with nylon cord he had retrieved from the Sandbergs' vehicle. The male hostages were bound first, before Wanda, then Debra, and finally Joanne. All were ordered to sit in a semi-circle inside a large walk-in closet in the master bedroom with Gretzler observing the hostages as Steelman forced Walter to drive to the United Market to retrieve money from a floor safe he knew the Parkins kept there. This robbery netted approximately $4,000 (the equivalent of about $26,840 as of 2024). The two then returned to the Parkin residence, where Walter was also bound and placed in the walk-in closet. All adult hostages were then bound together by their ankles and then gagged.

According to Gretzler, once the two had wiped their fingerprints from surfaces they had touched, he exclaimed to Steelman, 'Listen, why don't we split? We got what we came here for. Let's just get outta here!' Steelman refused, saying 'I said all along, no witnesses. I know you remember me sayin' it'.

Gretzler then shot and killed the two Parkin children in the master bedroom. Each was shot once between the eyes as they slept. The two then opened the walk-in closet, where the remaining seven hostages had heard the gunshots and begun desperately screaming and writhing. Richard Earl Sr. was then shot and wounded in the temple; Gretzler then shot Walter Parkin, Richard Earl Jr., Wanda Earl, Debra Earl, and Joanne Parkin. After reloading his gun, Gretzler then shot Mark Lang to death before Steelman fatally shot Richard Sr. before repeatedly firing into the bodies of all deceased and dying hostages inside the closet.

Gretzler then consumed a slice of chocolate birthday cake and a bottle of wine found in the family kitchen as Steelman drank from a bottle of whisky as he searched for further money and valuables within the residence. The two then left the Parkin household at approximately 1:20 am. One hour later, they checked into a Holiday Inn under the alias of W. J. Siems.

At 3:00 am., a young house guest and employee of the Parkins, 18-year-old Carol Jenkins, returned to the Parkin residence. Although she noted two lights remained on which should have been turned off, she decided not to investigate, for fear of waking the family. Jenkins immediately fell asleep in her bed.

Four hours later, two friends of Mark Lang, having been alerted to his disappearance by his mother, discovered his Chevrolet Impala parked outside the Parkin residence. When the two friends knocked on the door of the property at approximately 7:03 am., Jenkins groggily agreed to ask the Parkins if they knew of Lang's whereabouts—believing the couple to still be asleep in the master bedroom. Jenkins entered this bedroom as Lang's friends remained in the hallway.

One of the first responders to the scene would later state the first sight he observed as he arrived at Orchard Road was two distraught males in their late teens or early twenties themselves chasing and attempting to catch and comfort a young woman running in and out of the house, frantically flailing and screaming 'Oh my God!' The officers entered the residence to discover the bodies of the two Parkin children in the master bedroom.

Upon learning the children's babysitter, her boyfriend, and younger brother were unaccounted for, investigators drove to the Earl residence at 7:40 am., only to discover the house unoccupied, and a loaded .410 shotgun upon Richard Earl Jr.'s bed. When they returned to Orchard Road, a sergeant named Steven

Mello searched a hallway leading to the family bathroom, where he discovered the remaining seven casualties inside the walk-in closet.

While investigating the murders of the Parkin and Earl families and Mark Lang, police found several witnesses who gave a description of the two criminals, including the owners of the motel in which the two had spent the night of November 5th, and who had paid for the room with a dud cheque in the name of one Michael B. Sandberg. The license plate of the cream Datsun vehicle had been an Arizona plate, number RWS 563. From this, the California State Department contacted their colleagues in Arizona, who determined that the car was registered to one Michael Bruce Sandberg, who resided in the Villa Paraiso apartment complex in Tucson.

Just hours after the discovery of the nine victims at Orchard Road, a Tucson investigator named David Arrelanes secured updated arrest warrants for Gretzler and Steelman in relation to the Mestites and Robbins murders, with bail for the fugitives set at $220,000 each. Arrelanes returned to his office to receive a teletype notifying his department of the nine homicides in San Joaquin County. He immediately contacted his California counterparts, whom he updated on his department's manhunt for Gretzler and Steelman in relation to two recent murders in Phoenix, and who he stated his department had 'every reason to believe' may have returned to Steelman's home turf in Lodi. Arrelanes provided his counterparts with a recent booking photo of Steelman and copies of the existing arrest warrants. At a press conference held late in the evening of November 7th, San Joaquin County Sheriff Michael Canlis informed the media the chief suspect in the Victor murders was one Willie Steelman, adding his department had reason to believe he was also responsible for two recent killings in Phoenix. All media personnel were provided with copies of the photograph provided by Arrelanes.

On November 8th, California investigators were also contacted by an individual who had been in their company for a brief period of time the previous afternoon confirming Gretzler and Steelman had been in Lodi immediately prior to the murders at Orchard Road. The same day, Donald Scott also contacted authorities to state that Gretzler and Steelman could be involved in the killings, having discussed the imminent robbery of a Victor supermarket belonging to a Wally Parkin as he had travelled with the two just days previously. Arrest warrants were also issued for the two men in California, and their names. accompanied by a recent mug shot of Steelman, were published in the Sacramanto Union Paper on the morning November 8th, and the Sacramento Bee that afternoon.

After leaving the Holiday Inn in the late morning of November 7th, Gretzler and Steelman drove north for several hours, with agreed plans to ultimately reach Nevada before Steelman decided they should 'lay low' for a few days before attempting to cross state lines. The two parked the Sandbergs' Datsun in a multi-storey car park before purchasing new clothes and checking into the nearby Clunie Hotel in Sacramento, paying in advance for three days. Steelman signed the register as Will Simen, whereas Gretzler signed using his real name.

On the morning of November 8th, Steelman purchased a copy of the Sacramento Bee from the hotel lobby, only to observe his mug shot on the front page and to read that he and Gretzler were the prime suspects in eleven homicides. This revelation unnerved Steelman, who decided their best plan was to flee California immediately. Realizing returning to the Sandbergs' Datsun was too risky, Steelman decided the two should try and convince a young female acquaintance named Melinda Ann Kashula, whom he had encountered the previous afternoon at a massage parlour, to accompany the two to Florida.

As the two exited the hotel, a clerk named William Reger recognized Steelman. Reger waited until the two had exited the lobby before discreetly informing the police of their whereabouts. Within minutes, numerous armed police had surrounded the hotel.

At Kashula's apartment, the young woman feigned interest in Steelman's offer before declining to drive the two to Florida. She then indicated she may know of alternate accommodation for the two in Davis. Minutes later, Steelman encouraged Gretzler to return to the Clunie Hotel via taxi to retrieve their belongings, adding his own picture had been published on the front page of the Sacramento Bee, but that the media were unaware of his own physical appearance. He had changed using Patricia Sandbergs make-up and hair dye.

It didn't work. Gretzler was observed entering the hotel and entering an elevator bound for his room on the third floor. Police sealed the second floor of the premises and positioned sharpshooters to cover every escape serving the third floor.

As he attempted to enter his room, Gretzler overheard an officer talking in hushed tones on the telephone behind the door. He fled to the fourth floor in a vain attempt to escape from the building concealing the Derringer in a small portal above a doorway before descending to the second floor, raising his arms and waiting for his inevitable arrest.

The time of Gretzler's arrest was 10:04 am. As Gretzler was searched for weapons, he informed police, *'Man, I'm glad this is over. I've seen enough killing, and man, I don't wanna see any more.'* He then provided police with the address where Steelman could be located, adding Steelman was in the company of a young woman, that he was armed, and had sworn never to be taken alive if arrest was impending.

At 10:50 am., the first of over 70 armed police officers arrived outside Kashula's apartment. Their presence was quickly noticed by Kashula, who became hysterical as a police chief shouted through a bullhorn: *'Willie Steelman, this is going to be your last chance to give yourself up peacefully.'* Although Steelman heard this message, he initially refused to surrender; first claiming to Kashula he was the victim of mistaken identity as he threatened to commit suicide before Kashula dissuaded him from doing so, then agreeing to surrender but only if the media were present outside the apartment to record his arrest and after the police chief persuaded a disc jockey to announce live on a local rock radio station that he and Kashula would not be harmed if they exited the apartment separately, with their hands aloft. The chief negotiator agreed to these requests.

Two minutes after the terms of Steelman's surrender were broadcast across the airwaves of KZAP, police fired a single tear gas canister into the apartment as Kashula argued with Steelman to honour his promise to surrender. In response, Steelman shouted his intentions to surrender, but only after Kashula had been allowed to safely exit her apartment. The two exited the apartment separately after Kashula tossed Steelman's firearm onto the lawn. Steelman was then manacled and placed in a police car as he shouted, 'Guess I'm going back to Stockton!'

Much of the money stolen from the United Market was discovered in the suspects' possession at the time of their arrest; this money was traced to a batch of notes issued to Walter Parkin shortly before the Orchard Road murders. In addition, Gretzler was found to have placed the Sandbergs' door key on his key ring.

A police search of the hotel room the two had rented recovered several firearm cartridges, a Smith & Wesson .38 calibre revolver later determined via ballistic testing to have been used in numerous homicides linked to the pair, the Sandbergs' chequebook and stolen identity cards in addition to other physical and circumstantial evidence linking the two to numerous recent crimes in both Arizona and California. Several shell casings discarded by Steelman alongside a highway following the Orchard Road murders were later recovered and forensically proven to have been discharged by the firearm in his possession at the time of his arrest.

Upon locating the Sandbergs' vehicle on the evening of November 8th investigators discovered a bloodstained pair of boots and jeans and a brown grocery sack filled with numerous wallets, purses, credit cards, driving licenses and items of jewellery belonging to those murdered at the Parkin residence.

Gretzler and Steelman were extensively questioned by Sacramento County investigators in relation to the Orchard Road murders before they were transferred to the custody of San Joaquin authorities on the evening of November 8th. The two were separately escorted to French Camp, San Joaquin under armed guard to formally face charges pertaining to the nine murders committed in Victor. Both were held in solitary confinement at Deuel Vocational Institution, and prohibited from contact with each other.

Steelman refused to divulge much information about the murders prior to being assigned an attorney, at which point he refused to talk with any investigators, Gretzler consented to interview requests from both Arizona and California investigators. He was initially cooperative but evasive falsely claiming all the abductions and robberies the pair had committed in both Arizona and California over the previous three weeks had been at Steelman's behest and that Steelman had committed all the murders, but gradually he admitted his culpability in several of the murders.

On November 9th, both defendants were arraigned on nine counts of first degree murder, each in relation to the Orchard Road murders (a further charge of kidnapping with intent of robbery was later added on November 14th). Both were assigned public defenders. By November 10th, both had confessed to 17 murders, with Steelman revealing the location where they had concealed the bodies of Unrein and Adshade in addition to Loughran, whose disappearance had not been linked to the two before. Loughran's body was discovered on November 10th; Unrein and Adshade were recovered the following day.

Gretzler provided investigators with a full confession on November 10th. He began with the events at Orchard Road before outlining the previous eight murders.

Hours later, Steelman also provided investigators with a full confession. His account of the murders contained only minor discrepancies with Gretzler's.

California investigators decided the two would first be tried for the Orchard Road murders, and thereafter extradited to Arizona to be tried for further murders committed in that state.

Gretzler and Steelman were tried jointly for the Orchard Road murders in June 1974. Gretzler formally pleaded guilty to nine counts on June 4th. Steelman, on advice from his attorney, pleaded no contest to all charges in exchange for the prosecution agreeing not to pursue the charge of kidnapping against him. Sentencing was postponed until the following month.

On July 8th 1974, both were sentenced to life imprisonment, Gretzler for nine counts of murder, and Steelman for nine counts of murder and five counts of robbery.

Two weeks after their convictions for the Orchard Road murders, the thenGovernor of California, Ronald Reagan authorized the extradition of Gretzler and

Steelman to Arizona for the murders of Michael and Patricia Sandberg and Gilbert Sierra. The prisoners were escorted to Tucson on September 17th, and a gag order subsequently issued, prohibiting any pre-trial publicity.

Both defence attorneys filed numerous pre-trial motions delaying the commencement of their clients' respective Arizona trials by several months.

Although Arizona had initially planned on trying both defendants together, the judge ruled on February 10th that the defendants be tried separately. On March 3rd, prosecutor David Dingeldine offered a stipulation that if he obtained a first degree murder conviction for the Sandberg murders, he would not try either defendant for the Sierra murder. This offer was accepted by both defence counsels.

Steelman was brought to trial at the Apache County Courthouse in St. Johns, Arizona, on July 10th, 1975. The prosecution called numerous witnesses to testify as to Steelman's participation in the Sandberg murders over the following days. The first physical evidence was introduced on July 11th, when an investigator named Larry Hust formally identified a bloodstained cushion and blanket as items he had removed from the sofa upon which Patricia Sandberg's body was found, adding the cushion had evidently been used to silence the discharge from the firearm used to kill her. Hust's testimony was followed by that of the owner of the motel the defendant and Gretzler had stayed in on the night of November 3-4, a Mrs Francisco. This witness stated Steelman had paid for a room with a $5 check in Michael Sandberg's name, had signed the motel register as Michael Sandberg and had displayed a Veteran's Card issued to a Captain Sandberg as a form of identification. Francisco also formally identified Steelman as the individual who had stayed at her motel on the night in question.

On July 14th, an FBI fingerprint analyst testified numerous fingerprints recovered from the apartment matched Steelman's. His testimony was followed by that of a firearms expert, who testified that numerous bullets recovered from the heads of both decedents had been fired by the revolver discovered in Steelman's possession at the time of his arrest. The prosecution rested their case the following day.

The defence produced their first witnesses on July 17th. The first witness to testify was Steelman's former wife, Denise Machell, who outlined Steelman's sudden bouts of anger throughout their marriage and his inability to recall incidents triggered by his extreme rage. Following a brief recess, Steelman then took the stand in his own defence to describe in greater detail extreme, recurring headaches his former wife had stated he had suffered following a fall outside a department store in 1972. In an apparent effort to convince the jury into believing he was insane, Steelman then launched into a tirade of outlandish claims portraying himself as a "fighter of the oppressed people" driven to violence by seeing 'brothers die in the streets trying to change things' and that he had begun dropping acid to alleviate his pain caused by injustices perpetrated by the government. Steelman then claimed that he had killed Michael Sandberg due to his Marine background and being part of the 'ruling class'.

The defence then called two experts to testify as to their belief Steelman was legally insane and unable to control his actions.

Three doctors testified on behalf of the prosecution as to Steelman's sanity on July 21st. The state then rested its case.

On July 23rd, both prosecution and defence attorneys delivered their closing arguments to the jury and the jurors retired to consider their verdict at 2:30 p.m. At 5:15 p.m., the jurors announced their verdict: Steelman was guilty of two counts of murder, one of kidnapping (in relation to Vincent Armstrong), two counts of robbery, and one count of burglary.

He was sentenced to death on August 27th, plus 80 to 95 years for the kidnapping of Armstrong and the burglary and robbery of the Sandbergs.

Gretzler's trial was held in the Federal Building in Prescot, Arizona before Judge William Druke in October of the same year, As Gretzler had already formally confessed to the Sandbergs' murder, the strategy chosen by his defence was to secure second degree murder convictions—thereby saving his client's life. Upon the advice of his attorney (who wanted to avoid his client being subjected to cross-examination), Gretzler did not testify in his own defence. The forensic and witness evidence from the prosecution was overwhelming.

The jury then retired to consider their verdict; they deliberated for just over two hours before announcing they had reached their verdict: Gretzler was found guilty of two counts of first degree murder, in addition to two counts of robbery and one of kidnapping.

Due to several legal mooves filed by his defence counsel prior to formal pre-sentencing hearings, Gretzler was sentenced to death for both murders on November 15, 1976; he was also sentenced to a concurrent sentence of 25 to 50 years for the charges of robbery, kidnapping, and burglary.

Following their Arizona trials for the murders of Michael and Patricia Sandberg, both men were transferred to death row at Florence State Prison to await execution. Over the next two decades, both filed numerous appeals to overturn their sentence, with Gretzler insisting that his drug addiction and mental health were mitigating circumstances for his crimes. Steelman's attorneys appealed against his conviction on issues such as legal technicalities. All of their appeals were dismissed.

By the early 1980s, Steelman had developed serious health issues in prison, including cirrhosis of the liver, which he was diagnosed with in 1983. By early 1986, Steelman was informed he had less than three years to live. Reportedly, upon being informed of his terminal illness, Steelman stated his impending death was the sole way he would ultimately 'beat the state.' His health deteriorated rapidly throughout the summer, and he was discovered collapsed in his cell on the morning of August 7th, 1986, and rushed to the Maricopa County Hospital, where he died that afternoon. He was later buried at the Temple Beth Israel cemetery in Phoenix.

Following his conviction, Gretzler shunned all contact from his family and the public alike for many years. Although initially viewed as a disciplinary problem, he gradually became a model inmate. Gretzler initially expressed neither remorse for his actions or concern for his own predicament in the years immediately following his arrest, but by the early 1980s, he claimed to have repented for his past deeds. He severed all contact with Steelman, re-instigated contact with his family—apologizing to them for the shame and stigma he had brought upon them—and wrote letters to his victims' relatives in which he expressed remorse for his actions and asked for forgiveness.

By 1998, Gretzler had informed both his family and his attorney of his wish to cease any further efforts to postpone his impending execution. He spent his final days writing dozens of letters to his family, friends, attorney, legal personnel, and relatives of his victims. Neither he or his attorney were present at a June 2nd, 1998, obligatory reprieve hearing to plead against the scheduled June 3rd execution date ordered by Justice ThomasZlaket.

Gretzler was executed via lethal injection at Florence State Prison at 3:11 p.m. on June 3rd, 1998. His execution was the first to be conducted during daylight hours in the history of Arizona. Gretzler's execution was witnessed by 35 people, including four relatives of his victims, one of his younger sisters, two close friends of his, several individuals involved in his apprehension and prosecution, and nine journalists. His last meal, served to him at 7 am, consisted of a platter of six fried eggs, four slices of bacon, two slices of toast, a cup of coffee and two cans of Coca-Cola.

Gretzler's request to wear his glasses at his execution in order that he could see his loved ones as he delivered his last words was granted. Immediately prior to his execution, Gretzler asked those present for forgiveness, and as his final words, said the following:

*'From the bottom of my soul, I'm so deeply sorry and have been for years for murdering Patricia and Michael Sandberg. Though I am being executed for that crime, I apologize to all 17 victims and their families.'*

Gretzler then turned towards his sister, telling her in Romanian that he loved her and his two granddaughters before stating in English: *"Thank you for life's lessons learned."*

At the time of his execution, Gretzler was 47 and the longest-serving death row inmate in Arizona's history. His body was later released to his family.

# DAVID GULBRANDSON

Born December 30th, 1944 – sentenced to death February 19th, 1993.

David Gulbrandson and Irene Katuran, were partners in a photography business and also romantically involved. Their personal relationship ended in January 1991, when Ms. Katuran renewed a romantic relationship with another man, but the business partnership continued. On February 14th, 1991, a drunk Gulbrandson argued with Ms. Katuran about the business in the presence of two friends, Sally and Charles Maio. Gulbrandson then physically attacked Ms. Katuran and began choking her and when Mr. Maio pulled him off Ms. Katuran, he attacked her again. As the Maios drove Gulbrandson home, he told them, "I'm going to kill her and I'm going to kill the business. I'm going to kill everything."

Ms. Katuran obtained a restraining order against Gulbrandson and when he was served with the order on February 27th, 1991, he referred to Ms. Katuran as a "bitch." During the weekend of March 8th, 1991, Ms. Katuran travelled to New Mexico on business. She returned on the evening of Sunday, March 10th, with cash and checks from the trip. The next morning, Monday, March 11th, her daughter went to Ms. Katuran's bedroom to wake her and found the bedroom door locked; there was no response when she knocked. She then noticed a dark stain on the wall leading to the bedroom. Suspecting that something was wrong, the daughter telephoned her grandmother, who then called the police. The police found Ms. Katuran dead in the bathroom adjacent to her bedroom.

Irene was killed brutally. The police found her face down dressed in only a pair of panties with her legs bent up behind her at the knee and her ankles tied together by an electrical cord attached to a curling iron. Her right wrist was bound with an electrical cord attached to a hair dryer. Her bedroom was covered in what appeared to be blood. From the bedroom to the bathroom were what appeared to be drag marks in blood across the carpet. Clumps of her hair were in the bedroom, some of the hair had been cut, some burned, and some pulled out by the roots. Four knives and a pair of scissors were in the kitchen sink and appeared to have blood on them; hair appeared to be on at least one of the knives. There was also what appeared to be blood on a paper towel holder in the kitchen. A burnt paper towel was in Irene's bedroom. A Coke can with what appeared to be a bloody fingerprint on it was on the kitchen counter; this fingerprint was identified as Gulbrandson's.

At Gulbrandson's trial, the state's criminalist testified that the knives, scissors, paper towel holder, and Coke can all had human blood on them, although the police did not determine the blood type. Gulbrandson's fingerprints were found on the paper towel holder and on an arcadia door at Irene's home which was open in the family room the morning after the crime. A blood soaked night shirt with holes in it was in Irene's bedroom; the blood on the nightshirt was consistent with Irene's blood type. A banker's bag was also in her bedroom with what appeared to be blood on it. The autopsy revealed that Irene suffered at least 34 stab wounds and slicing wounds, puncture wounds, and many blunt force injuries. The most serious stab wound punctured her liver, which alone was a fatal injury. Her nose was broken, as were 2 ribs on the back of the chest and 5 ribs in front on the same side of her trunk. Half of a wooden salad fork was embedded in her leg; the other half was found in the bedroom. On her left buttock was an abrasion that appeared to be from the heel of a shoe. The thyroid cartilage in front of her neck was fractured, which could have been caused by squeezing or by impact with a blunt object. She died from the multiple stab wounds and the blunt neck injury. The neck injury may have resulted in asphyxiation. The pathologist believed that most, if not all, of the injuries were inflicted before death.

Ms. Katuran's car was also missing. The police immediately suspected Gulbrandson and officers searched his apartment on March 11th. They discovered blood-splattered papers, a blood-stained jacket, and other black clothing with blood stains. They also located cheques from New Mexico, payable to the photography business, and other business papers. In the pocket of the black jacket they found a credit card belonging to Ms. Katuran. On the evening of March 11th, Gulbrandson called his mother and told her that "he thought he had done a terrible thing. He thought he had killed Irene." He also indicated that he was going to kill himself. Gulbrandson's mother called the police and informed them of the conversation. After the murder, Gulbrandson drove Ms. Katuran's car to Laughlin, Nevada, where he was seen gambling at a hotel casino into the early morning hours of Tuesday, March 12th. He told the casino employees that his name was David Wood. He lost between $1,100 and $1,200 and the hotel management provided him with a complimentary room. He then travelled to Montana, where, using the name David Randall, he attempted to sell Ms. Katuran's car to a bar owner who declined the deal because Gulbrandson could not produce a title to the car. On April 1st, 1991, a Montana police officer discovered the vehicle, which was damaged and had been abandoned on the side of a road. The vehicle bore Canadian license plates; the Arizona plate was found under the driver's seat. The police apprehended Gulbrandson in an apartment in Great Falls, Montana, on April 3rd, 1991. On December 15th, 1992, a jury convicted him of theft and first-degree premeditated murder. On February 19th, 1993 the trial court sentenced Gulbrandson to death on the murder conviction. On direct appeal, the Arizona Supreme Court affirmed the conviction and sentence. Gulbrandson's last appeal was rejected in 2013 when a three judge panel of the 9th U.S. Circuit Court of Appeals rejected his claims that his initial trial attorney was ineffective and that the judge at that trial should not have allowed inflammatory victim-impact statements from Katuran's family at his sentencing. Gulbrandson's current attorney advised that he would appeal that ruling. Gulbrandson sits on death row in Florence jail.

# PAUL V HADLEY

Born 1887 – executed by hanging in Arizona on April 13th, 1923.

This case is quite important for the work done on firearm identification by an amateur photographer matching the bullets to the gun barrel.

Paul V. Hadley and Ida Hadley resided in Beaumont, Jefferson county, Texas. Paul V. Hadley was indicted for assault with intent to kill in Jefferson county, Texas and fled. As a fugitive from justice he was arrested March 20th, 1916, in Kansas City, Missouri where he was going under the name of J. O. Kendrick. Sheriff Giles of Jefferson County, Texas, was notified of his arrest, and in the meantime Hadley was incarcerated in what was known as the matron's department at the police station. Whilst held there his wife, Ida Hadley, visited him several times and had several conversations with him before Sheriff Giles arrived in Kansas City on the 23d day of March with a requisition from the Governor of Texas for Paul V. Hadley. Ida Hadley met Sheriff Giles at the police station and requested that he allow her to return to Texas with her husband. Sheriff Giles told her she could come if she wanted to, but she would have to pay her own railroad fare, which she did. Sheriff Giles, with both Paul and Ida Hadley, left Kansas City on a train called the "Katy Limited" at 5:30 p m. on the 23rd of March, 1916. The train arrived in Muskogee just after midnight the next morning. Before leaving Kansas

City, Ida Hadley asked Sheriff Giles to remove the handcuffs from her husband who had agreed to return to Texas by signing a written waiver of formal requisition. The Sheriff granted her request. When the train left Parsons, Ida Hadley was sitting in the rear seat on the right side of the carriage, and shortly after the Sheriff, with Paul V. Hadley in custody, came out of the smoking car into the carriage where Hadley sat down by his wife, and the Sheriff sat down in the seat across the aisle; couple engaged in a whispered conversation, and Ida Hadley went to the ladies' toilet in the front end of the carriage several times, and each time returned to her seat by her husband. At that time the handcuffs had been removed from Hadley, and he was riding just as any other passenger would in the company of his wife. Sheriff Giles at that time was sitting across the aisle in the third seat from the rear, the back of which had been reversed, and he was facing the couple. When the train left Muskogee, Ida Hadley said to Sheriff Giles, 'You might just as well go to sleep; Paul and I are going to sleep in a minute'; and within ten minutes after leaving Muskogee, Ida Hadley got up from her seat and walked to the ladies' toilet in the forward end of the car. She returned, carrying a satchel or package and on reaching the Sheriff, she drew a pistol from the package and shot Sheriff Giles in the back of the head. The bullet passed through his head and fell on the floor; the train at that time was passing through the town of Oktaha, Muskogee County. Instantly Paul Hadley jumped across the aisle and grabbed Sheriff Giles' pistol and said to his wife, 'Hold the gun on all of them; if they move blow their heads off'. Ida Hadley told the other passengers in the carriage, 'Don't a man or woman of you get up' After taking the sheriff's pistol Paul Hadley proceeded to go through the pockets of the Sheriff, taking papers out and sticking them into his own pockets. About this time the train ticket collector came into the carriage and Paul Hadley, pointed his pistol at him, said, 'Stop this train, God damn you, or I will blow your brains out'; the collector pulled the bell cord, but the train did not stop. The train stopped next at Checotah, and the two defendants stepped off and from there walked about five miles south stopping at the home of a Mr. Ennis, where they asked permission to stop there until morning when they also arranged to have Mr. Ennis' son drive them to Briartown. After going about ten miles he left them at a Mr. Stevens' place on Hi Early Mountain. Sheriff McCune, of McIntosh county travelling fast with a posse of deputies, caught up with them there and arrested them at about mid-day. Ida Hadley asked Sheriff McCune if Sheriff Giles was dead, and he told her he was, she then asked, 'What are you going to do with us?' and the sheriff said, 'We are going to take you to Eufaula, the county seat of the county where you killed Sheriff Giles.' It appears that Sheriff Giles never spoke after he was shot, and died two or three minutes after he was taken from the train at Checotah. Paul Hadley did not testify as a witness. Ida Hadley testified as a witness on her own behalf and also in behalf of her husband.

Paul Hadley was convicted of assisting a murder and sentenced to life in prison. Ida was judged to be insane and pleaded guilty to a conspiracy charge which meant she would be housed in a prison rather than an institution.

Hadley appealed his conviction but it was affirmed.

His story doesn't end there. In 1919, he persuaded the state of Oklahoma to furlough him for a sixty-day period. Accounts vary as to the reason why but it may have been so he could visit his dying mother

It seems that, as long as he promised that he would come back the prison authorities had no trouble granting a sixty-day leave to a cop-killer with a history of escaping from custody!!

You'll be shocked to hear that Paul Hadley didn't turn up after sixty days for re-incarceration. By the time the police went looking for him, the trail was two month's cold. Hadley was gone.

By November 1921, he was going by the name William S. Estaever and hitch-hiking his way west. In Denver, Colorado he got picked up by an elderly married couple named Peter and Anna Johnson, who were driving to California. Just southwest of Tucson, Arizona, Hadley pulled a gun on Peter Johnson and forced him to pull the car over.

He ordered the couple out of the car and shot them both, killing Anna instantly and seriously wounding her husband.

Leaving Peter for dead on the roadside, Hadley took their car and drove off. The vehicle ran out of gas some miles further on and as he was hitching to Yuma, Arizona, he was arrested. He was still carrying the murder weapon, a .32 calibre Mauser pistol.

Hadley was tried for attempted murder and murder in Tucson, Arizona with the judge allowing the prosecuting attorney to employ a retired local lawyer and keen photographer, A.J.Eddy, who was working on ballistic identification to participate in the Hadley prosecution. Eddy used photographic material to match recovered bullets to the inside of gun barrels. The judge allowed this evidence as that from a 'semi-expert witness' to be presented to the jury and together with other forensic and witness evidence Hadley was convicted.

Hadley claimed he and the Johnsons had been attacked by a gang of bandits and he had returned their fire, but Peter Johnson recovered from his injuries and testified against Hadley at the trial.

The first jury was unable to reach a verdict. Hadley was convicted after a second trial, however, and sentenced to death. It was only then that authorities realized the criminal William Estaever was the fugitive from Oklahoma Paul Hadley.

Estaever/Hadley's conviction was appealed all the way up to the Arizona Supreme Court, with his appeals attorney arguing Eddy's testimony should never been allowed into evidence. The court upheld the conviction in a historic ruling: this was the first time a state supreme court had recognized ballistics evidence as valid and admissible.

Hadley refused a final meal on the morning of his execution and calmly walked to the scaffold after the warden read the death warrant at 5:00 am.

His last words were, "I am innocent and ready to meet my death." The trap sprung at 5:10am and Hadley pronounced dead five minutes later. Nobody claimed the body and so it was deposited in the prison cemetery.

As for Ida Hadley? Paul never tried to get in touch with her in the two years of his extended release from prison in Oklahoma. She remained his dutiful wife, however, and when she found out he had been convicted of murder in Arizona and sentenced to death, she begged the Oklahoma governor to pardon her so she could be with him in his last days.

She got her pardon on July 22nd, 1922 and went immediately to her husband's side so she could help with his appeal. A week after Paul's execution, the widow Hadley married Jack Daugherty of Wichita Falls, Texas. She enjoyed her second marriage for less than a year, however as Ida Lee Hadley Daugherty died on March 21st, 1924.

# TRACY ALLEN HAMPTON

Born November 2nd 1970 - sentenced to death January 27th, 2003.

On May 16th, 2001, Department of Public Safety officers attempted to serve a traffic offence ticket on Tracy Allen Hampton. The officers went to a house on East Roberts Road in Phoenix, where Hampton had been staying with Charles Findley and Findley's girlfriend, Tanya Ramsdell, who was five months pregnant. Hampton was not there, but Findley and Ramsdell were. To prove that he was not the man the officers were looking for, Findley showed them a photograph of Hampton, and the officers left.
   Early the next day, Misty Ross and Shaun Geeslin went to the house on East Roberts Road where Hampton let them in and  told them of the police visit the day before and his intention to confront Findley about the incident and showing the police a photo of himself. When Findley awoke, Hampton argued with him.  Later during the morning of May 17th, Hampton, Findley, Ross, Geeslin and several others smoked methamphetamine. Sometime after 10:30 a.m., Hampton and Geeslin left. The two returned near noon and entered a back room where Findley was kneeling on the floor working on a lighter. Hampton turned on a CD player to a loud volume, walked in front of Findley, and called out his name. As Findley looked up Hampton shot him in the forehead, killing him instantly. Geeslin and Ross then walked to the front door. Hampton began following Ross and Geeslin, but stopped and went to a

bedroom where Tanya Ramsdell was sleeping and opened the door. Ramsdell told Hampton to get out, and Hampton shot her in the head. Ramsdell and her unborn child died as a result. Hampton then joined Ross and Geeslin in Geeslin's truck. After asking whether he had any blood on his face, Hampton asked to be taken to get some food. A few hours later, Hampton asked Misty Ross whether she wanted to play a game of darts which she refused and he commented, 'What, I killed two people, and we can't forget it?'

Hampton was arrested on May 31st, 2001. While awaiting trial in the Maricopa County jail in August 2001, Hampton shared a cell with George Ridley. Ridley testified at trial that Hampton admitted to committing the murders and told him the story of the murders every night for two weeks. Hampton had told Ridley that he killed Findley because 'he was a rat' and he killed Tanya Ramsdell because he was affiliated with the Aryan Brotherhood and thought that Ramsdell was a 'nigger lover' who was pregnant with a Black man's child. Hampton also told Ridley that he 'thought it was funny that Ramsdell had slept through the shooting of her boyfriend', and he bragged about the fact he was able to shoot her in pretty much the same place he shot her old man. Ridley also said that before leaving the house, Hampton told him he knelt down next to Findley's body and whispered in his ear, 'I want to let you know I took care of your nigger loving old lady and her little coon baby, too. Don't worry, they didn't feel a thing.'

The State charged Hampton with two counts of first degree murder for the deaths of Findlay and

Ramsdell and one count of manslaughter for the death of the unborn child. The jury returned guilty verdicts. The superior court imposed death sentences for each of the murder convictions and a twelve and half year sentence for the manslaughter conviction to run concurrently.

Hampton has so far been able secure stays of execution so he can pursue various appeals. The last one filed in 2019 in the U.S. Court of Appeals, Ninth Circuit and is pending at this time.

# CHRISTOPHER ALLEN HARGRAVE
See under **Steve Alan Boggs**


# JAMES CORNELL HARROD

Born December 27th, 1953 – sentenced to death May 27th, 1998. Re-sentenced to death October 28th, 2005.


In 2005, a jury determined that James Cornell Harrod should be sentenced to death for the 1988 murder of Jeanne Tovrea. An automatic notice of appeal was filed under Arizona Rules of Criminal Procedure

Just before 1:00 am. on April 1st, 1988, Phoenix police officers responded to an alarm company call at a private residence. A kitchen window had been completely removed and was sitting on a chair on the patio; an arcadia door was open. The police found the owner, Jeanne Tovrea, dead in her bed. She had been shot five times in the head with a .22 calibre gun. Twice shot through a pillow and three times at close range. Several drawers from a jewellery case had been removed and sat on top of the furniture, and Jeanne's purse had been emptied onto the kitchen counter. The rest of the house appeared undisturbed.

Jeanne had married Ed Tovrea, Sr., in 1973. She had an adult daughter from a previous marriage, Debbie Luster. Ed had three children from a previous marriage, Ed Jr., Georgia, and Priscilla. When Ed Sr. died in 1983, his estate was worth approximately $8 million. His will provided that each of his children would receive $200,000, which would be distributed in monthly payments of $1,500. Jeanne received certain real estate, stock, and personal property as listed in the will. The remainder of Ed Sr.'s estate was put into a trust. The terms of the trust entitled Jeanne to the income from the trust during her lifetime, and the trustees were permitted to invade the trust for her benefit. On her death, the trust would pass to Ed Sr.'s three children. At the time of Jeanne's death, the trust had an estimated worth of nearly $4 million.

Almost a year before her death, Jeanne met with a man in San Diego who called himself Gordon Phillips, a journalist; he had been contacting her for information regarding Ed Sr.'s involvement in World War II and his POW experiences. Jeanne's daughter, Debbie Luster, and Debbie's husband were present at the meeting. Phillips led Debbie to believe he had been a soldier in Vietnam but he did not seem interested in the World War II related books Debbie and her mother had brought. Debbie became suspicious of Phillips and called security after he left.

Immediately after Jeanne's death, Debbie told the police about Gordon Phillips. Debbie and her husband also found a micro-cassette tape in Jeanne's home that had several answering machine messages on it, two from Phillips.

In April 1992 a 're-enactment' of Jeanne's murder was aired on the national television show, Unsolved Mysteries and several people put Harrrod's name to the voice on the tape.

Harrod's friends testified that he had repeatedly told them that he had been in Vietnam. Harrod later admitted lying about his service.

In September 1995, the police arrested Harrod for his involvement in the murder of Jeanne Tovrea. At this point, investigators had gathered considerable evidence against Harrod, including bank records showing large money transfers from Ed Tovrea, Jr., to Harrod, telephone records showing calls between Ed Jr. and Harrod, and statements regarding the jewellery and credit cards that were missing. In addition, after being offered immunity, Anne Costello, Harrod's ex-wife, informed police that: (1) Harrod told her that he had been hired by Ed Jr. to coordinate a hit on Jeanne for $100,000; (2) Harrod said that he had posed as Gordon Phillips to interview Jeanne; (3) when Harrod left their house on March 31st, 1988, he told Anne he was going to supervise the murder and he let her know that it was done when he returned the next morning; (4) Harrod spoke to Ed Jr. on the telephone the morning of the murder, April 1st, 1988; (5) Harrod and Anne suddenly had large, unaccounted-for sums of money; (6) Harrod received Fed-Ex boxes full of cash from Ed Jr.; and (7) Harrod kept Jeanne's jewellery and credit cards in their house for a time before burying them in the desert.

Police also found Harrod and Anne Costello divorced between the time of the murder and the time she spoke to police. Numerous latent fingerprints from Jeanne's kitchen counter, the outside of the window pane, the inside of the window pane, and a gate on her property matched Harrod's fingerprints.

In November 1997, a jury convicted Harrod of premeditated murder and felony murder of Jeanne Tovrea. A judge subsequently sentenced Harrod to death in May 1998. The United States Supreme Court vacated the judgment and remanded the case for further consideration and subsequently remanded Harrod's death sentence for resentencing in 2003. The resentencing proceeding occurred in 2005. The jury found that the State had proved beyond a reasonable doubt the existence of a 'pecuniary value' aggravating factor and determined that Harrod should be sentenced to death after finding that the mitigation evidence was not sufficiently substantial to call for leniency. The judge sentenced Harrod to death by lethal injection on October 28th, 2005. His appeals are ongoing.

Ed Yovrea Jr was not interviewed regarding the murder, the money transferred to Harrod, their phone records or their business deals. Harrod's defence attorneys made little of any supposed relationship between the two so one would assume they did not give any credence to the information from Harrod's ex wife being fact. Ed Yovrea Jr died in 2011.

# DALE SHAWN HAUSNER

Born February 4th, 1973 – committed suicide in his cell June 19th 2013.

Known as the 'Serial Shooter' Dale Hausner and Samuel Dieteman terrorized the Phoenix district at the same time as the Baseline Killer, Mark Goudeau, was on the rampage. Hausner was the main killer ending up with convictions for 80 crimes, including six counts of first degree murder, attempted murder, aggravated assault, cruelty to animals and other charges.

They committed several drive-by shootings and arsons in Phoenix, Arizona, between May 2005 and August 2006 targeting random pedestrians and animals mostly whilst under the influence of methamphetamine. They also set fire to multiple objects. Investigators believe that together they were responsible for eight murders and at least 29 other shootings.

After being found guilty of 80 of 88 felony charges in one single trial including murder, attempted murder, arson, animal cruelty and drive-by-shootings, Hausner was sentenced to death. He killed himself by taking an overdose of methamphetamine in prison in 2013. Dieteman was sentenced to life imprisonment without the possibility of parole. Hausner's brother Jeff had assisted in some of the shootings, and was himself sentenced to 25 years in prison.

In addition to several dozen non-fatal shootings of people and fatal shootings of animals, Hausner and Dieteman were found guilty of the following murders:

David Estrada (20), shot to death on June 29th, 2005, in Tolleson, Arizona.

Nathaniel Shoffner, (44) murdered on November 11th, 2005, while attempting to protect a dog from being shot.

Jose Ortiz (44) and Marco Carillo (28), murdered on December 29th, 2005.

Claudia Gutierrez-Cruz (20), shot and killed by Dieteman on May 2nd, 2006, as Hausner drove in Scottsdale, Arizona..

Robin Blasnek (22), the serial shooters' last victim, shot and killed on July 30th, 2006 in Mesa, Arizona..

Phoenix police originally believed that the serial shooter was a single individual responsible for 4 murders and 25 shootings beginning in May 2005, and that a series of 13 shootings in the same area were the work of another shooter. However, on July 11th, 2006, investigators revealed that they believed the two series of shootings were related. On August 3rd, Phoenix police released a statement linking Blasnek's murder to the serial shooters, citing forensic evidence and other similarities to the shooters' past crimes.

Dale Shawn Hausner, 33, had worked as a custodian at Phoenix International Sky Harbour Airport since 1999 as well as a boxing photojournalist for Ring Sports and Fightnews.com.

Samuel John Dieteman, 31, had a history of petty crimes such as shoplifting and drunk driving and had relocated to Arizona a few years prior from Minnesota.

Hausner and Dieteman were initially identified as suspects on July 31st, 2006. The most important tip came from Ron Horton, a friend of Dieteman, who said Dieteman had confessed to being involved with the shootings whilst out drinking with him. Horton was at first uncertain whether Dieteman's confession was serious, but went to police after the shooting death of Robin Blasnek, which he said 'affected me quite a bit' due to a belief he might have prevented her death had he contacted police earlier.

On August 3rd, 2006, police arrested both suspects outside of their apartment in Mesa. On the morning of August 4th, 2006, Phoenix police announced that two arrests had been made in connection with the serial shootings. Authorities also linked Hausner and Dieteman to two arson fires at Wal-Mart stores on June 8th in Glendale Arizona started 45 minutes apart from each other that caused between $7 and $10 million in damage.

A few weeks prior to his capture, Hausner interviewed former Heavyweight boxing champion Mike Tyson as part of his sports journalism job. Police questioned Tyson regarding his brief meeting with Hausner, and the boxer later described Hausner as '...a small guy, but a nice guy.'

Hausner was charged with 88 crimes in 5 different indictments attributed to the serial shooter investigation, including 8 murders, 18 attempted murders, 17 aggravated assaults, 26 drive-by shootings, 4 firearms charges, 10 animal cruelty charges and 2 arson of an occupied structure charges. He was convicted on 6 of 8 murders, and 80 charges overall on March 13th, 2009.

Hausner's former roommate, Samuel Dieteman, pleaded guilty to two murders, plus conspiracy to commit several others. In July 2009, Dieteman received a sentence of life without parole.

On March 27th, 2009, Hausner was sentenced to six death sentences. He had instructed his attorneys not to oppose a death sentence, saying his execution would help the victims' families heal. After the mandatory appeal affirmed the death sentence, Hausner waived further appeals and requested to be put to death 'as soon as possible.' During Hausner's half-hour statement to the jury before sentencing, he apologized to several people, including his family, and compared himself to Charles Manson.

On June 19th, 2013, Hausner was found unresponsive in his cell and died later that day. His autopsy revealed no physical trauma. The medical examiner determined that he had killed himself by overdosing.

Hausner was convicted of murdering six people, and is suspected to have killed two more people in 2005:

Tony Mendez (39), shot to death on May 17th, 2005.

Reginald Remillard (56), was shot to death on May 24th, 2005.

## KNOWN VICTIMS:
### 2005

June 29 — David Estrada, 20, who was shot to death in Tolleson.

June 29 — A horse that was found shot to death in Tolleson.

July 20 — A horse that was shot and wounded in Tolleson.

July 20 — A dog that was shot to death.

Nov. 11 — A dog that was shot and wounded.

Nov. 11 — A dog that was shot and wounded.

Nov. 11 — Nathaniel Shoffner, who was killed.

Dec. 29 — A dog that was shot to death.

Dec. 29 — A man who was wounded.

Dec. 29 — Jose Ortis, 44, who was fatally shot.

Dec. 29 — Marco Carillo, who was fatally shot.

Dec. 30 — Three dogs that were shot.

Dec. 30 — A woman, who was wounded.

## 2006

May 2 — A victim who was shot in the back while walking.

May 2 — Claudia Gutierrez-Cruz, 20, who was fatally shot while walking in Scottsdale.

May 17 — A man stabbed in an attack in a parking lot.

May 30 — A man who was wounded.

May 31 — A man who was shot in the side while walking.

May 31 — A man shot in the left side.

June 8 — A man who was shot in the right side while walking.

June 8 — Arsons at two Wal-Mart stores.

June 11 — A woman who was shot in the left hip while riding her bicycle.

June 20 — A man who was shot while sitting in a parking lot.

June 20 — A man who was shot in the torso while walking.

July 1 — A woman who was shot while walking.

July 1 — A man who was shot while standing behind a strip mall.

July 3 — A man who was shot while pushing his bicycle on the sidewalk.

July 8 — A victim who was shot in the back of the head while walking.

July 8 — A man who was shot in the torso while walking.

July 22 — A man who was shot.

July 30 — Robin Blasnek, 22, who was fatally shot while walking in Mesa.

# CHARLES MICHAEL HEDLUND

Born November 22nd 1964 – sentenced to death July 30th, 1993.

Beginning February 28th, 1991, half brothers Charles Michael Hedlund and James Erin McKinney commenced a residential burglary spree for the purpose of obtaining cash or property. In the course of their extensive planning for these crimes, McKinney boasted that he would kill anyone who happened to be home during a burglary and Hedlund stated that anyone he found would be beaten on the head.

They enlisted two friends to provide information on good burglary targets and to help with the burglaries. These two friends, Joe Lemon and Chris Morris, were not physically involved in the burglaries in which the murders occurred. It was from Lemon and Morris, however, that Hedlund and McKinney learned that Christine Mertens, 40, would make a good burglary target.

The first burglary in their spree occurred on February 28th, 1991. Christine Mertens' home was the intended target that night, but she came home and scared the would-be burglars away. A different residence was chosen to burglarize, but they obtained nothing of value. All four were involved in this crime.

The second and third burglaries occurred the next night, March 1st. This time Lemon was not involved. The three participants stole a .22 revolver, $12, some wheat pennies, a tool belt, and a Rolex watch.

The fourth burglary took place on March 9th, 1991. This time only Hedlund and McKinney were involved. Christine Mertens was picked again because Hedlund and McKinney had been told by Lemon and Morris, who knew Mertens' son, that she kept several thousand dollars in an orange juice container in her refrigerator.

Mertens was home alone when Hedlund and McKinney entered the residence and attacked her. Beaten and savagely stabbed, Mertens struggled to save her own life. In the end McKinney held her face down on the floor and shot her in the back of the head, covering his pistol with a pillow to muffle the shot. The pair then ransacked the house and stole $120 in cash.

The pair then committed their fifth burglary on March 22nd, 1991. The target was Jim McClain, a sixty-five-year-old retiree who restored cars for a hobby. McClain was targeted because Hedlund had bought a car from him some months earlier and thought McClain kept money at his house. Entry was gained through an open window late at night while McClain was sleeping. Hedlund brought along his .22 rifle, which he had sawn the barrel off to help him conceal it. The pair ransacked the front part of the house then moved to the bedroom. While he was sleeping McClain was shot in the back of the head with Hedlund's rifle. They then ransacked the bedroom, taking a pocket watch and three hand guns; they also stole McClain's car.

Forensic and other evidence left at McClain's house including palm and  fingerprints meant the pair were soon arrested as were Lemmon and Morris.

Hedlund and McKinney were each indicted on two counts of first degree murder and four other counts relating to the robberies. Both were tried in the same courtroom before dual juries. Before returning its verdict, Hedlund's jury asked whether he could 'be convicted as an accomplice to the burglary and not be convicted in the murder charge.' On November 12th, 1992, the jury found Hedlund guilty of the second-degree murder of Mertens, the first-degree murder of McClain, plus lesser charges. In a special verdict, the jury unanimously found that Hedlund was guilty of the premeditated murder of McClain, rejecting a felony murder theory. The trial court sentenced Hedlund to death for the first degree murder of McClain and to terms of imprisonment on the lesser charges. McKinney was also convicted of first degree murder and sentenced to death for the murders of Mrs Mertens and Mr McClain plus he was convicted of two counts of first degree burglary and one count of theft.

Upon direct appeal, the Arizona Supreme Court affirmed the convictions and sentences. Appeals from both killers followed with the last ones taking place in 2016 affirming their convictions. More appeals are expected

# GRAHAM SAUNDERS HENRY

Born July 24th, 1946 – died in the medical unit Florence jail, Arizona in February 2018 age 71.

On June 6th, 1986 Henry and co-defendant Vernon Foote were travelling from California when their vehicle broke down outside Las Vegas. They made their way into the residential area and kidnapped Roy Estes, an elderly and partly disabled man, from his apartment in Henderson and took his pickup truck. They drove the vehicle south on U.S. Highway 93 to a spot about 30 miles south of the Arizona-Nevada border where they stabbed Estes and slashed his throat before leaving him to die in the desert hidden under some bushes.

Henry and Foote were arrested a short time later when they were pulled over on Highway 93 because an intoxicated Henry was driving Estes' pickup truck north on the southbound lanes of the highway. They were arrested and gave false names. Once the police noted their false names they were remanded in custody whilst enquiries were made. The car was registered to Roy Estes who had disappeared. The pair were still held in the Mohave County jail in Kingman days later when Estes' body was discovered and investigators connected them to the killing.

Foote was convicted of attempted murder and other charges and given a 15-year prison sentence for his involvement in the kidnapping and killing. Henry was convicted of first-degree murder and sentenced to death in 1988.

After numerous appeals a Warrant of Execution was issued by the Arizona Supreme Court on March 21st 2002 for the execution of Graham Saunders Henry on May 8th, 2002. It was followed, as per usual, on April 16th 2002 by a Stay of Execution issued by the U.S. District Court.

It is believed that Henry died of apparent natural causes and that his body was transported to the Pinal County Medical Examiner's office for an assessment or autopsy that concurred this.

# MICKEL WILLIAM HERRERA

Born May 1st 1968 – sentenced to death December 21st, 1989. Vacated May 20th, 2002 and set aside for re-sentencing.

On the afternoon of June 30th, 1988, Mickel Herrera and his girlfriend, Mary Cardenas, went driving with his father, William Diaz Herrera, Sr. (Senior), and defendant's brothers, William Diaz Herrera, Jr. (Junior) and Ruben Herrera. The family travelled in two cars, a gold Plymouth Duster and a blue Chevrolet pickup. After purchasing beer and wine, they drove to a relatively isolated dirt road in southwest Phoenix beside an irrigation canal where they stopped to allow the Duster, which had begun to overheat, to cool down. They parked the cars parallel to each other facing into some trees and shrubbery on the side of the road and began drinking, listening to music, and talking. With the exception of Senior, each of the Herreras was under the age of 21.

An hour passed without incident before a motorist driving on the road on the other side of the canal, seeing the positioning of the two vehicles and believing that an accident had occurred, flagged down Sheriff's Deputy Vernon Marconnet and told him about the possible accident. When the deputy arrived at the Herreras' location he approached the family and asked if there was a problem. Mickel responded that the Duster had overheated. The deputy then asked everyone for identification. Ruben produced an I.D., but Mickel told the deputy that he had no I.D. because his wallet had been stolen; Junior also said that he had lost his I.D. When the deputy asked Senior for an I.D., Senior became belligerent and stated that he knew the law and that he had done nothing wrong, and that he "wasn't going to show any fucking I.D." The deputy responded that if Senior refused to show his I.D., he would have to "book" him. The deputy then walked Senior over to the patrol car and placed him in the back seat.

Deputy Marconnet next asked Ms. Cardenas, who was sitting in the pickup, for the vehicle's registration. About this time, Junior, who had jumped his burglary probation in Texas and was worried about being arrested, told Mickel that he was going to fight the deputy. When the deputy again approached Junior and requested his I.D., Junior began to argue with him. At some point, the deputy requested a police backup. Junior's argument with the deputy quickly escalated into a scuffle, and Junior grabbed the deputy and hit him a few times. By this time, Ruben had released Senior from the patrol car, and Senior joined in the fray, kneeing or kicking the deputy in the groin and cussing at him. At Junior's urging, Mickel wrestled the deputy's revolver away from him and ordered him two or three times to get down on the ground. Junior then threw the deputy's portable radio, which he had grabbed during the scuffle, at the deputy and caused a severe laceration in the deputy's forehead.

There is conflicting evidence about what happened next. Ms. Cardenas testified at trial that as she was leaning over in the pickup looking through the glove compartment for the vehicle's registration papers, she heard Mickel say "freeze." She immediately sat up and saw Mickel point the gun at Deputy Marconnet while Junior shouted, "shoot him, shoot him." Although her view was somewhat limited because of the positioning of the vehicles, Ms. Cardenas testified that she saw Mickel shoot the deputy.

The information provided by Mickel in his first interview with investigators is largely consistent with Ms. Cardenas' version of the shooting. Mickel admitted that he held the deputy's gun on him for up to two or three minutes. During this time, the deputy lay on his back and, according to Mickel, appeared to say, "Just put it down." But when Senior and Junior shouted "shoot him, shoot him," Mickel shot the deputy. At his second interview, Mickel first claimed that Junior shot the deputy, but then stated that he himself shot the deputy.

During his third interview and at trial, however, Mickel claimed that when Senior and Junior told him to shoot the deputy, he refused. Senior then took the gun from him and shot the deputy, before he handed the gun back to him, telling him to "get rid of it." When questioned about the conflicting stories, Mickel testified that during his first two interviews, "I didn't know what I was thinking; I was confused."

After the shooting, the family fled the crime scene in the two vehicles. Junior, Ruben and Senior fled in the Duster toward Casa Grande. As they drove along the interstate, a tyre blew out. Junior and Ruben then separated from Senior and spent the night wandering in the desert before going to Casa Grande, where they turned themselves in. Mickel and Ms. Cardenas fled in the pickup truck. They immediately picked up Mickel's brother, Tony Huerta, from work, and Mickel told him, "I shot a cop today." After returning to the family's apartment Mickel hid the deputy's gun in some bushes. Later that night, Mickel checked into a motel, where he was arrested.

When backup officers arrived at the murder scene, they found Deputy Marconnet's body. He had been shot once through the right eye, he had a gash on his left forehead, dirt was embedded in the buttocks, crotch, and leg areas of his trousers, and his metal name plate was bent. The medical examiner determined that the deputy died from a single gunshot to the head at close range. He also found powder burns on the deputy's hands, which indicated that his hands were in front of his face when the gun was fired.

Additional physical evidence at the scene indicated that a scuffle preceded the deputy's death. Investigators found several scuff marks on the ground, and they located the deputy's sun glasses approximately 8 feet from his body. The deputy's portable police radio was found in some brush about 12 to 13 feet from his body. Ruben's fingerprint was positively identified on the right rear door of the deputy's patrol car.

Mickel, Junior and Senior were each indicted on one count of first degree murder, one count of aggravated robbery, and one count of kidnapping. The trial court separated Senior's trial from that of Mickel and Junior who went to trial together before the trial of Senior. Senior was convicted of first degree felony murder and kidnapping, and he was sentenced to death and a lengthy prison term. Ruben also faced murder, aggravated assault, and kidnapping charges. He pleaded guilty to the kidnapping charge in exchange for his testimony at Senior's trial, and he was sentenced to 10 years' imprisonment.

At the close of the evidence at Mickel and Junior's joint trial, the jury was instructed on both felony and premeditated first degree murder. The felony murder charge was predicated upon aggravated robbery and/or kidnapping. In October 1989 the jury convicted both Mickel and Junior of first degree felony murder, aggravated robbery, and kidnapping. The trial court sentenced Mickel to death for the murder, to 21 years' imprisonment for the kidnapping, and to 10 years' imprisonment for the aggravated robbery. The trial court sentenced Junior to death for the murder, to life imprisonment for the kidnapping, and to 10 years' imprisonment for the aggravated robbery.

With regard to Mickel's death sentence, the trial court found the existence of one aggravating circumstance: the murder was committed in an especially heinous, cruel or depraved manner. The trial court also found the existence of one statutory and one non-statutory mitigating circumstance: Mickel's age, he was 18 at the time of the murder. However, the trial court further determined that the mitigating circumstances were not sufficiently substantial to call for leniency. The automatic appeal challenged the death penalty and affirmed his convictions but cut the sentence to life imprisonment without parole for 25 years.

# CLARENCE DAVID HILL

Born July 25th, 1948 – sentenced to death June 5th, 1990. Released after 16 years when new DNA evidence accepted October 12th, 2005.

Shortly after 5:30 am. on June 18th, 1989, a local resident discovered a burning body in a Mohave County dump and called the Sheriff. When the deputies responded, they found the body still burning and lying on its left side. The deputies noted the presence of vehicle tracks and shoeprints. A comparison of these markings with the tyres of the resident's vehicle and his shoes indicated that another vehicle had been in the area and that other shoes had made the prints.

Deputies found a wallet that contained the victim's driver's license but no money. Based on the address on the driver's license, deputies went to the victim's home, where they observed tyre tracks and shoeprints similar to those found near the body. Clarence Hill answered the door at the victim's home wearing only a blanket. He explained that he lived in his motor home on the victim's property. He informed the deputies that the victim drove a small blue pickup truck and described the vehicle. He then asked permission to get dressed, and the deputies followed Hill to his motor home. The deputies examined Hill's tennis shoes and noted that the sole design was similar to the shoeprints found near the victim's body. There was also blood on the blanket and his clothes.

According to Hill, he and the victim had been drinking at nearby bars on the previous day. He said that the victim left a bar briefly to go grocery shopping at Best Buy Market, after which they returned to the victim's home. The victim then left again in his pickup truck to "make the rounds." Hill claimed that he stayed at the victim's home watching television and fell asleep. He said that when he woke up, he went back to his motor home, undressed, and went to bed. He awoke again at approximately 11:00 p.m. and could hear the victim's air conditioner running. Knowing that the victim regularly turned off his air conditioner in the evening, Hill went to the victim's home to see if he had returned. Finding that he had not, Hill turned off the air conditioner and fell asleep on the couch, he woke up when the deputies knocked on the door. Deputies noted, however, that the air conditioner was running when they arrived.

Detective Sergeant Lent, a tracking specialist, met the deputies at the victim's home, examined the tyre tracks and shoeprints, and took measurements. He also examined one of Hill's tennis shoes. He then proceeded to a nearby bar, where a deputy had located the victim's truck. A gallon container half full of paint thinner and a pair of gloves were found in the back of the truck.

Detective Lent observed and then followed shoeprints with distinctive markings, including the logo of "Athletix" and a distortion on the ball of the right shoe, from the bar to the back yard of the victim's home. Hill's shoes had similar markings, including the "Athletix" logo, and there was a "glob" on the right shoe. Detective Lent then went to the scene and identified the shoeprints there as having been made by the same shoes that made the prints leading from the bar to the victim's home. Based on his examination of Hill's shoes and the prints both at the scene and from the bar to the victim's home, Detective Lent concluded that Hill's shoes made the prints. Detective Lent also identified the tyre tracks at the scene as having been made by the victim's truck.

A Mohave County fire investigator, George Koskela, examined the position and condition of the body and concluded that a flammable substance had been poured on the front lower portion of the victim as he was lying on his back and that the fire was started while he was in that position. Because the body had fresh blisters, Koskela deduced that the victim had been alive when the fire was started. He further believed that the victim ended up on his side while trying to get up to escape the fire. The state's coroner, as well as the pathologist, also concluded that the victim was alive when set on fire and that he died from smoke and gas inhalation.

The victim's roommate testified that the victim and Hill had a heated argument approximately two weeks before the murder over the victim's failure to pay Hill for work done around the victim's house. When Hill was arrested on the afternoon of June 18th, deputies found over $200 in his wallet, including four $1 dollar bills folded over a receipt from Best Buy Market, dated June 17th, showing purchases for $17.75 and change of $2.25. At trial, Hill testified that he gave the victim $20 to make the purchases and that the victim returned the folded bills as change from the store along with the sales receipt.

A jury found Hill guilty on December 29th, 1989 of first degree murder. Following an aggravation-mitigation hearing, the trial judge found three aggravating factors and one statutory mitigating factor. After considering Hill's proffered mitigating factors and finding them not substantial enough to call for leniency, the trial judge sentenced Hill to death on June 5th, 1990.

Fifteen years later on October 12th, 2005, Hill was released from Mohave County Jail. During his appeals the blood found on the victim's clothing and his bed sheet had been tested with new DNA techniques and found not to be Hill's blood. The blood spots on Hill's clothing were found not to be the victim's.

The judge stated 'that it was highly likely that no reasonable juror would have convicted Hill had that evidence been available at his original trial' and ruled to overturn the conviction.

The Arizona DA took six months to work out how they could release Hill without admitting they had convicted the wrong man and open themselves to an expensive payout. Hill was by this time 58 and terminally ill and just wanted to be back with his family not to go back for a new trial to be found not guilty and exonerated. He had always denied being the killer. The answer was to allow him to plead guilty to second degree murder and be sentenced to the amount of time he had already served and therefore be released, which he accepted.

Nobody has been charged with the murder of the victim in the case which remains open.

# JOHN ALBERT HINCHLEY

Born May 10th, 1933 – sentenced to death 1992, died in prison May 22nd 2006.

In the early-morning hours of September 29th, 1985, Hinchley argued with the woman he had lived with for 12 years about her two daughters from a prior marriage. After the woman went downstairs to sleep in a chair, Hinchley followed to continue the argument and pulled out a pistol purchased the day before and shot her four times.

Hinchley then kicked open the locked bedroom door of the woman's 17-year-old daughter. The daughter was asleep but woke up when Hinchley broke in her door. The daughter's infant son was sleeping in the same room. Hinchley shot the daughter twice in the face and left the bedroom.

The mother had survived the shooting and managed to run outside. Hinchley pursued and caught her, then beat her with the pistol until the trigger guard broke, at which point he beat her head against some rocks. He left the gun lying beside the mother on the sidewalk and returned to the daughter's bedroom. Hearing the daughter moan, Hinchley took a tonic water bottle and beat her over the head until the bottle shattered. When the daughter continued to moan, Hinchley went to the kitchen, got a knife and returned to her room where he

stabbed her numerous times leaving the knife stuck in her abdomen. The daughter died but her infant son was unharmed. The mother survived.

Hinchley drove to the local police station, turned himself in, and gave a taped confession. He was charged by indictment with first-degree murder for the daughter's death and attempted first-degree murder for assaulting the mother. Originally, Hinchley entered into a plea agreement to plead guilty in exchange for a life sentence plus 21 years and was sentenced in accordance with that agreement. He subsequently requested post-conviction relief, alleging improper denial by the trial judge of his motion to withdraw his guilty plea. The superior court granted relief and reinstated the original charges.

Prior to trial, Hinchley filed a motion for a determination of his competency to stand trial and of his mental condition at the time of the offence. The trial court found him competent to stand trial after reviewing reports from appointed experts. In addition, Hinchley sought to preclude admission of other bad act evidence, specifically, an assault on the daughter with a hammer about 14 months earlier. On October 14th, 1987 the trial court heard arguments on this motion and determined that the evidence was admissible for purposes of showing preparation, plan or intent, and that the probative value of the evidence outweighed any potential prejudice.

At trial, Hinchley presented an insanity defence, claiming alcohol-induced psychosis, and did not testify on his own behalf. On October 28th, 1987 the jury returned a verdict of guilty on both counts and Hinchley was sentenced to the death penalty for the murder of the daughter and 21 years for the attempted murder of his wife. Hinchley died in prison age 74 on May 22nd 2006 whilst his appeals were ongoing 21 years after the murder.

# MURRAY HOOPER

Born November 22nd, 1945 - executed November 16th 2022 age 76, 42 years after the murder.
See **WILLIAM BRACY**

# RICHARD DEAN HURLES

Born June 1st 1959 – sentenced to death October 13th, 1994.

After serving nearly fifteen years in prison for sexually assaulting two young boys, Richard Dean Hurles was released on parole in June 1992. Following his release, Hurles moved to Buckeye, where some of his family lived.

On the afternoon of November 12th, 1992, Hurles went to the Buckeye public library, a small, house-type building in a residential neighbourhood. The only employee in the library at the time was Kay Blanton. The last patron, other than Hurles, left the library just before 2:40 pm. Hurles then locked the front doors to the library and attacked Blanton in the back room. He stripped off her underwear and pulled her skirt above her waist in an unsuccessful attempt to rape her. Using a paring knife found in the back room of the library, Hurles mortally wounded Blanton, stabbing her thirty-seven times and inflicting blunt force trauma by kicking her to such an extent he tore her liver.

At approximately 2:45 pm., Mark Porter and his friend, John Kale, went to the library and discovered the front doors were locked. Porter looked through the window and saw Blanton lying in a pool of blood. While Porter went around to the back door of the library, Kale ran across the street to a house where Dale Capper was working on his truck. Capper had noticed Porter and Kale try to open the library door and had, at the same time, seen Hurles "crash" through the back door of the library, run towards him, then turn and head down the street. After Kale explained what he and Porter had seen, Capper got into his truck and followed Hurles. Meanwhile, Porter entered the library through the open back door and called 911. The call to 911 was received at 2:50 pm.

Capper followed Hurles down the street and caught up to him at a four-way stop. While he was stopped, Capper had an excellent opportunity to identify Hurles when the latter, for some reason, approached the truck and asked Capper "How are you doing?," to which Capper responded "I'm doing okay." Capper then observed Hurles enter an apartment complex, at which point Capper left his truck and continued following Hurles on foot.

At the apartment complex, Capper saw Hurles talking to Robert Phillips, who knew Hurles. Phillips was outside fixing a lawnmower when Hurles approached and asked to borrow the bicycle lying next to him. Phillips initially refused to let Hurles take the bike but relented after Hurles asked him ten to twenty times. At approximately 3:00 p.m., Capper watched Hurles ride away on the bicycle; he then returned to the library to tell police what he had seen.

Between 3:00 and 4:00 p.m., Hurles rode the bicycle to the home of his nephew, Thomas, in Buckeye and asked Thomas for a lift to Phoenix. Hurles had changed his clothes and cleaned himself up, and Thomas, who had been asleep and was unaware of Blanton's murder, agreed to drive Hurles to Phoenix. As the two left the house Hurles was carrying a bundle of clothes. During the drive to Phoenix, Thomas noticed that Hurles had bite marks on his wrist. When asked about them, Hurles told Thomas he had been in a fight with a Spanish man at the library, that he had stabbed the man with the man's knife, and that he had received the bite marks in the fight. As part of his insanity defence at his later trial, however, Hurles claimed he had no recollection of anything that occurred between sitting in the library and going out the back door.

As they continued toward Phoenix, Hurles had Thomas pull over so he could toss the bundle of clothes out of the car window. Thomas left Hurles at a Phoenix bus station where he purchased a bus ticket to Las Vegas. Thomas returned to Buckeye, where he heard about the library murder and  made contact with the police and told them of Hurles' destination. Later that evening, the police intercepted Hurles' bus on the way to Las Vegas; Hurles was removed from the bus, arrested, and returned to Phoenix.

With Thomas's help, the police recovered Hurles's discarded clothes. Police found blood on the clothing that matched Blanton's blood type, which occurs in just one percent of the population. Police also found blood matching Blanton's type on Hurles's shoes, which he was still wearing when taken from the bus. Four bloody shoeprints at the murder scene matched the soles of Hurles's shoes, and Hurles's palm print was found on the paring knife left at the scene.

Hurles went to trial on March 31st, 1994 and on April 15th, 1994, all twelve jurors found Hurles guilty of both premeditated and felony murder. The trial court sentenced Hurles to death on October 13th, 1994 and his statute appeal followed and affirmed the guilty verdict. The lengthy appeals system is ongoing with Hurles attorneys pushing for the sentence to be vacated in 2014. No decision at this time.

# LEVI JAMES JACKSON

Born January 14th, 1976 – sentenced to death Jan 26th 1994, reduced because of his age being under 18 at the time of the murder.

See under **Kevin Miles**

# STEVEN CRAIG JAMES

Born May 24th 1958 – sentenced to death November 23rd, 1982

On November 16th, 1981, Juan Maya approached 14 year old Marty Norton and made homosexual advances towards him. Norton rebuffed Maya but suggested they might get together in a nearby trailer owned by Steven James where he might be more receptive to Maya's advances.

When Maya followed Norton into the trailer he was set upon and badly beaten by James, Lawrence Libberton and Norton. They then drove Maya's own car towards Salome where James parents owned a piece of property with an abandoned mine shaft in it. When they arrived there at around dawn James ordered Maya to stand by the mine shaft and fired a gun at him, Maya charged at James trying to wrestle the gun from him but was beaten off by all three with rocks. James tried to fire the gun three more times but it wouldn't fire.

The unconscious body of Maya was thrown down the mine shaft and then rocks and railroad ties thrown down on top of it.

In September 1982 Steven James, Lawrence Libberton and Martin Norton were each convicted of Maya's murder in separate proceedings in Arizona state court.

Norton, who was 14 years old at the time of the murder, agreed to testify against James and Libberton and to plead guilty in juvenile court to first-degree murder, kidnapping, armed robbery, and credit card fraud. In exchange for his testimony and guilty plea, he was committed to juvenile detention until he turned 18, with no subsequent incarceration.

Libberton was convicted of first-degree murder, aggravated kidnapping, robbery, and theft, and sentenced to death.

James was convicted of first-degree murder and kidnapping, and sentenced to death.

In 2009, the 9th Circuit granted Libberton habeas relief with respect to his death sentence. The U.S. Supreme Court declined then to take up the case in 2010.

James was slated for similar relief after the 9th Circuit ruled in late 2011 that the state court improperly failed to address the merits of his claim of ineffective assistance of counsel at the penalty phase.

The U.S. Supreme Court summarily vacated the decision in 2013. The two appeals continue.

# JIMMIE WAYNE JEFFERS

Born June 7th, 1946 – executed by lethal injection in Arizona September 13th, 1995.

In May, 1976, police arrested Jimmie Wayne Jeffers and his girlfriend, Penelope Cheney, on state-law charges of possession of narcotics and receipt of stolen property. Jeffers posted bond for Cheney, but hadn't enough money to post bond for himself and remained in custody at the Pima County Jail.

While in jail, Jeffers received reports from visiting friends that Cheney had been co-operating with police by providing the police with information about his heroin transactions. Jeffers wrote a note to another jail inmate offering him money if he would kill Cheney. The detention officer who was supposed to deliver the note read it and seized it.

In October, 1976, Jeffers was released from jail on bond pending an appeal of his convictions. About a week later, he met Doris Van Der Veer and began living with her at a motel in Tucson. Jeffers made contact with Cheney and invited her to the motel in order to provide her with some heroin.

On the day of the murder, Jeffers told Van Der Veer that Cheney was coming over and that they wished to be alone. When Cheney arrived, Jeffers introduced her to Van Der Veer, who then left them. After about two and a half hours, Van Der Veer returned to the motel room and knocked on the door. Jeffers admitted her, pointed a gun at her, and ordered her to sit in a chair and be quiet.

When she entered the motel room, Van Der Veer saw Cheney lying unconscious on the bed. Cheney appeared cyanotic, her skin had a blueish tint. Jeffers injected a fluid into Cheney's hand and told Van Der Veer that he had "given her enough shit to kill a horse, and the bitch won't die." Van Der Veer then noticed foam coming from Cheney's mouth, which she recognized from her training as a nurse to be a sign of heroin overdose. Van Der Veer checked Cheney's condition and determined that she was still alive and asked Jeffers if he was going to help Cheney, to which he replied, "No, I'm going to kill her."

Jeffers then removed the belt from around Cheney's waist and began to choke her with it. He then discarded the belt and choked her with his bare hands. Van Der Veer urged him to stop, saying Cheney would probably die anyway, but Jeffers carried on and replied, "No, I've seen her this way before, and she's come out of it."

After strangling Cheney, Jeffers asked Van Der Veer to check Cheney's pulse. Van Der Veer found no pulse and reported that Cheney was dead. Jeffers then ordered Van Der Veer to inject more heroin into Cheney and to choke her while he took pictures. Van Der Veer complied. Jeffers told Van Der Veer that he did this to have proof that she was an accomplice and then beat Cheney with his hands several times, calling her a "bitch" and a "dirty snitch" and stating, as each blow landed, that "this one is for [naming several names]."

Jeffers then dragged the body off the bed and placed it in the shower stall. After three days, when the body began to smell, Jeffers and Van Der Veer wrapped it in newspaper and plastic garbage bags, placed it in a sleeping bag, and transported it to a secluded area in the Sedona desert, where they buried it in a shallow grave.

A month later, prostitute Sharon Galarza, a friend of Cheney was arrested on prostitution and drug charges and phoned Jeffers to suggest that Cheney might have set her up. Jeffers told Galarza that was impossible as he had killed her. He warned Galarza not to tell anybody as he didn't act alone.

When Galarza posted bail bond she went to Jeffers hotel room to buy heroin. He attacked her and held a knife to her throat threatening to kill her if she ever told anybody about him killing Cheney.

A few days later Jeffers was arrested and subsequently convicted of theft and receiving stolen property and sentenced to 12 years in prison. Another charge of possession and use of firearms resulted in a further 20 year concurrent sentence.

While Jeffers was in jail Garlarza was arrested on drug and prostitution charges again and made a deal with the police telling all she knew about Jeffers and his claim to have murdered Cheney for the charges against her being dropped.

In 1977 a jury convicted Jeffers of the first-degree murder of Penelope   Cheney. After a sentencing hearing, the trial court found two aggravating circumstances and no mitigating factors. In accordance with the Arizona death penalty statute Jeffers was sentenced to death. On direct review of his conviction and sentence, the Arizona Supreme Court, vacated Jeffers's death sentence and remanded for resentencing. At the second sentencing hearing, the trial court again found two aggravating circumstances beyond a reasonable doubt: that Jeffers had created a grave risk of death to another person (Van Der Veer) in the commission of the murder and that Jeffers committed the murder in an especially heinous, cruel, and depraved manner. The court found no mitigating factors, and thereupon resentenced Jeffers to death. On direct appeal, the Arizona Supreme Court affirmed the convictions and sentences.

Jeffers was executed by lethal injection in Arizona on September 13th, 1995. He had no visitors on his final day and made offensive hand signals from the gurney accompanied by a stream of expletives directed at the prison officials.

# RUBEN M. JOHNSON

Born April 26th 1979 – sentenced to death December 23rd, 2003.

On November 7th, 2000, Ruben Johnson and Jarvis Ross, both members of the Lindo Park Crips Gang (the LPC), committed a robbery at the Affordable Massage business in Phoenix. They committed the robbery at the behest of Johnson's friend, Cheryl Newberry. Newberry drove Johnson and Ross to the Affordable Massage location. Johnson and Ross then entered the massage parlour through a back door and confronted Stephanie Smith and Russell Biondo. Johnson and Ross stole Biondo's wallet and pager and Smith's cell phone and left the massage parlour separately. Johnson escaped, but police officers captured Ross after a short chase. Smith and Biondo both identified Ross as one of the robbers.

Soon after the robbery, Johnson learned from his friend Phyllis Hansen, a clerk at the Maryvale Justice Court, that Ross's preliminary hearing was scheduled for November 15th, 2000, and that the victims were going to testify at the preliminary hearing. Newberry later testified that Johnson and two other men came to her home in an SUV and made her reveal the location of Stephanie Smith's residence under threat of violence to her family.

Johnson and Quindell Carter, a fellow gang member, arrived at Smith's home shortly after one o'clock on the morning of November 15th, 2000. Smith was in a bedroom reading a story to her four-

268

year-old son, Jordan. ☐ Leonard Justice and Mike Solo were also at her home visiting. Solo heard a dog barking behind the house and went into the backyard to investigate. ☐ When he got outside, a black male put a gun to his head, threatened to kill him, and asked who else was in the house. The gunman first pushed Solo into the house through the back sliding glass door and then told him to leave the house. Solo hurried to his car and drove away. Leonard Justice looked out the back window of the house, saw what was happening, and called 911 on his cell phone. He then went into Jordan's bedroom and handed Smith the phone so she could give the dispatcher the address. After handing the phone back to Justice, Smith left the bedroom. Justice followed her, and they both saw Johnson come through the arcadia door. Justice then ran into the bathroom, while Smith ran into Jordan's bedroom. Johnson walked into Jordan's bedroom and shot Smith in the head, killing her. Arriving officers apprehended Quindell Carter after a short chase, but Johnson evaded the officers.

Two days later, Johnson visited Phyllis Hansen at her home. Hansen testified that Johnson showed her a newspaper article about the murder and told her that he was the unnamed suspect mentioned in the story. Hansen also testified that Johnson stated he killed Smith because Smith was going to testify against "his cuz or one of his homies." Hansen later went to the police and turned over papers Johnson had left at her home. One of those papers had Johnson's fingerprint on it and contained Russell Biondo's name and date of birth written in Johnson's handwriting. Johnson was arrested.

On December 22nd, 2003, Ruben M. Johnson was sentenced on four counts. Count 1, sentenced to death for the First Degree Murder of Stephanie Smith Committed on November 15th, 2000 to prevent her from testifying against Jarvis Ross, the co-defendant. Count 2 Assisting a Criminal Syndicate/Criminal Street Gang, sentenced to 17 years. Count 3 First Degree Burglary, sentenced to 24 years. On November 15th, 2000, Ruben M. Johnson acting as a member of the Lindo Park Crips entered the home of Stephanie Smith illegally. Count 4, Armed Robbery On November 7th, 2000, Ruben M. Johnson along with co-defendant Jarvis Ross robbed the Affordable Massage Parlor using weapons to threaten Stephanie Smith and Russell Biondo, occupants of the business. Johnson's appeals are ongoing.

# BARRY LEE JONES

Born August 26th 1958 – sentenced to death July 6th, 1995. Released

In 1995 Barry Lee Jones was sentenced in Prima County Superior Court to death after being found guilty of fatally assaulting Rachel Gray, who was the 4-year-old daughter of his girlfriend. He had been on death row since July 1995, according to prison records and walked free in June 2023, age 64

. Jones became the first Arizona death row inmate to walk free since Debra Milke in 2015 and the fifth exonerated since 2000.

On May 2nd, 1994, 4-year-old Rachel Gray died after being taken to the hospital with internal injuries. At the time, John Howard of the Pima County Medical Examiner's Office explained that Rachel died from internal bleeding because of a blow to her stomach.

Rachel had been living with Jones and her mother, Angela Gray, in Tucson. Police arrested Jones later that day.

The state built its case on the fact that Rachel was in Jones' care all day and that he would have been the only one who could have caused the injuries.

The case went to trial in April 1995, and Jones was found guilty of first-degree murder, sex with a minor, endangerment, and causing physical harm to a minor. He was sentenced to death.

Jones appealed his case, and the Arizona Court of Appeals affirmed the conviction. He then appealed the case to the federal court, where a new investigation 20 years later revealed that neighbouring boys had hit Rachel in the stomach with a metal bar a day or two before her death.

Detectives believed this caused her internal bleeding.

These findings, in part, swayed a federal judge and eventually led the Arizona attorney general to persuade Pima County prosecutors to offer the plea deal and vacate the murder conviction.

Statements from the Arizona Attorney General's Office and Pima County Attorney's Office described the chain of events that led to their agreement to vacate his death sentence.

*"After almost 30 years on death row for a crime he did not commit, Barry Jones is finally coming home,"* Cary Sandman, a federal public defender whose office has represented Jones for more than 20 years, said in a statement. *"Mr. Jones spent nearly three decades on Arizona's death row despite compelling evidence that he was innocent of charges that he had fatally assaulted Rachel Gray."*

In 2018, a federal district court judge ordered that Jones' convictions were to be vacated based on the compelling medical evidence that it was not Jones who caused Rachel Gray's injuries. A unanimous panel of the 9th U.S. Circuit Court of Appeals affirmed that order.

But the U.S. Supreme Court ignored its own precedent and sais Federal Courts had no power to even consider the case.

Despite the high court decision, the state of Arizona was able to reconsider the new evidence. After review, the attorney general agreed that Jones' conviction and death sentence should be vacated and asked the Pima County Superior Court to vacate them both.

As a result, according to a news release from the Pima County Attorney's Office, Jones agreed to plead guilty to second-degree murder because he neglected to take Rachel Gray to the hospital the night before she died, despite seeing how sick she was from an unknown fatal injury,

Pima County Superior Court Judge Kyle Bryson spelled out the details in a June 15th court order.

*"On or about May 1st to 2nd, 1994, under circumstances manifesting extreme indifference to human life, Barry Lee Jones recklessly engaged in conduct which created a grave risk of death and thereby caused the death of Rachel Gray, when he failed to seek or contributed to the failure to seek medical care for Rachel Gray,"* the court ruled.

*"The court has imposed a sentence of 25 calendar years with credit for time served,"* the order stated, adding that Jones *"is now eligible for release from prison. It is therefore ordered that the Arizona Department of Corrections, Re-entry and Rehabilitation release forthwith."*

Jones was in custody at the Arizona State Prison Complex–Eyman in Florence, according to prison records. Officials there declined comment.

Jones was kept on death row because of 2022 U.S. Supreme Court decision in Shinn v. Ramirez case. In that case, the high court said federal courts had no power to consider Jones' case despite the evidence that proved he was wrongfully convicted and denied a "constitutionally just trial," Sandman said in the news release.

At Jones' trial in 1995, his court-appointed lawyer failed to conduct an investigation into whether Rachel Gray died as a result of an injury she sustained while in Jones' care, the news release stated. The release stated Rachel Gray sustained her injuries when she was not in his care, but the jury never heard any of that evidence. It convicted him and recommended he be sentenced to death.

Jones' case had relied on a limited time period in which an eyewitness saw Jones hit Rachel. But there were other medical experts who were never interviewed who contested the facts and argued that other people also could have struck the girl. Jones' court-appointed lawyer, who didn't meet the state's qualifications to represent capital defendants, never interviewed witnesses who could have exonerated him. Neither did his lawyers in his post-conviction appeal.

Jones filed for federal court review to challenge his conviction and sentence, citing ineffective counsel. Two Federal Courts decided that because Jones' state-appointed attorneys failed to do their jobs, he either deserved a new trial or the state needed to release him.

But in a 6-3 ruling last year, the U.S. Supreme Court decided that federal judges can't determine the guilt of people for state crimes, even if there is evidence proving their innocence.

Justice Clarence Thomas wrote the majority opinion stating that federal courts only should act to review state procedures and whether they were applied correctly when finding someone guilty.

The state had argued that the federal court violated the 1996 Antiterrorism and Effective Death Penalty Act law by listening to evidence and then determining — based on that evidence — the outcome of the state's previous trials. That law limited the ability of people sentenced to death to argue new evidence in federal court.

In the high court case, Jones and another Arizona death row inmate citing ineffective counsel, David Martinez Ramirez, relied on a 2012 ruling, Martinez v. Ryan. That case decided that federal judges could allow the argument that people had poor representation in post-conviction appeals.

Before that, death row inmates in Arizona alleging poor counsel had little chance of getting their cases heard in federal court. That's because legal representation in post-conviction review is not a constitutional right, unlike in direct appeals for capital defendants.

Federal courts only stepped in when states misinterpreted laws, evidence, or violated constitutional rights. However, the Martinez ruling changed that by deciding that U.S. district and circuit courts could review cases if prisoners could prove they had an incompetent lawyer.

Despite the Martinez ruling, the U.S. Supreme Court in its 2022 opinion shot down Jones' chances at being released or retried.

Thomas wrote that it would be unseemly in the U.S. dual system of government for a federal district court to upset a state court conviction without giving an opportunity to the state courts to correct a constitutional violation.

Justice Sonia Sotomayor called the majority's decision "perverse" and "illogical." She described Arizona's post-conviction relief process as an "impediment" to people who wanted to prove their innocence.

Dale Baich, adjunct professor at Arizona State University's Sandra Day O'Connor College of Law, represented numerous capital defendants and witnessed 15 executions as a former federal public defender in Arizona. He called the state's death penalty system "byzantine," leaving little room for the substance of a case to determine the outcome.

"In Barry Jones's case, the U.S. Supreme Court placed form over substance and avoided dealing with the merits of his proof of innocence," he said. "In the end, the attorney general and county attorney recognized the injustice of keeping an innocent man on death row and agreed to right this wrong."

Andrew Sowards, a retired criminal defence investigator from the Federal Public Defender Office, worked on the case. He said that in more than 20 years, he had never been more convinced of someone's innocence.

Sowards launched a GoFundMe page to help support Jones now that he has been released after three decades. "Had he had a fair trial his innocence would have been easily proved. Yet his trial lawyers did no investigation into the case and were unprepared to defend Barry's life," he wrote on the donation site.

# DANNY LEE JONES

Born August 24th, 1964 – sentenced to death
December 9th, 1993.

In February 1992, Danny Lee Jones moved to
Bullhead City, Arizona, and resumed a friendship with
Robert Weaver. At this time, Weaver, his wife Jackie,
and their 7-year-old daughter, Tisha, were living in
Bullhead City with Robert's grandmother, Katherine
Gumina. As of March 1992, Jones was unemployed and
was planning to leave Bullhead City.

On the night of March 26th, 1992, Jones and
Weaver were talking in the garage of Ms. Gumina's
residence. Weaver frequently entertained his friends in
the garage, and during these times, he often discussed
his gun collection. The two men were sitting on inverted
buckets on the left side of the garage, and Ms. Gumina's
car was parked on the right side of the garage. Both
Jones and Weaver had been drinking throughout the day
and had used crystal methamphetamine either that day
and the day before.

At approximately 8:00 p.m., Russell Dechert, a
friend of Weaver, drove to the Gumina residence and
took both Jones and Weaver to a local bar and to watch
a nearby fire. Dechert then drove the pair back to the
Gumina residence at approximately 8:20 p.m. and left,
telling them that he would return to the Gumina
residence around 9:00 p.m.

Although there is no clear evidence of the
sequence of the homicides that night, the scenario
posited to the jury was as follows. After Dechert left,

Jones closed the garage door and struck Weaver on the head at least three times with a baseball bat. Weaver fell to the ground where he remained unconscious and bleeding for approximately 10 to 15 minutes. Jones then entered the living room of the Gumina residence where Ms. Gumina was watching television and Tisha Weaver was colouring in a workbook. Jones struck Ms. Gumina on the head at least once with the baseball bat, and she fell to the floor in the living room.

Tisha apparently witnessed the attack on Ms. Gumina and ran from the living room into the master bedroom and hid under the bed. Jones found Tisha and dragged her out from under the bed. During the struggle, Tisha pulled a black braided bracelet off Jone's wrist. He then struck Tisha in the head at least once with the baseball bat, placed a pillow over her face and suffocated her, or strangled her, or both.

Jones then emptied a nearby gun cabinet containing Weaver's gun collection, located the keys to Ms. Gumina's car, and loaded the guns and the bat into the car. At some point during this time, Weaver regained consciousness, and, in an attempt to flee, moved between the garage door and Ms. Gumina's car, leaving a bloody hand print smeared across the length of the garage door and blood on the side of the car. He then climbed on top of a work bench on the east side of the garage, leaving blood along the east wall. Jones saw him and  struck him at least two additional times in the head with the baseball bat, and, as Weaver fell to the ground, Jones struck him on the head at least once more.

A few minutes before 9:00 pm., Dechert returned to the Gumina residence and noticed that the garage door, which previously had been wide open, was closed. Dechert went to the front door and knocked. Through an etched glass window in the front door, he saw the silhouette of a person locking the front door on the inside and walking into the master bedroom. Dechert then looked through a clear glass portion of the window and saw Jones walk out of the master bedroom. He heard Jones say loudly, "I will get it," as if he were talking to another person in the house. Jones then opened the front door, closing it immediately behind him, walked out onto the porch, and told Dechert that Weaver and Jackie had left and would return in about 30 minutes. Dechert noticed that Jones was nervous, breathing hard, and perspiring. Although Dechert felt that something was wrong, he left the Gumina residence. As he was leaving he heard the door shut as if Jones went back into the house. Shortly thereafter, Jones left the Gumina residence in Ms. Gumina's car.

At approximately 9:10 pm., Jackie Weaver returned home from work. When she opened the garage door, she found Robert Weaver lying unconscious on the garage floor. Jackie ran inside the house and found Ms. Gumina lying on the living room floor and her daughter Tisha lying under the bed in the master bedroom. She then called the police, who on arrival determined that Tisha and Robert Weaver were dead and that Katherine Gumina was alive but unconscious. The medical examiner later concluded that Robert Weaver's death was caused by multiple contusions and lacerations of the central nervous system caused by multiple traumatic skull injuries. The cause of Tisha's death was the same, but also included possible asphyxiation.

After leaving the Gumina residence, Jones picked up his clothes from a friend's apartment where he had been staying and drove to a Bullhead City hotel. At some point before reaching the hotel, he threw the baseball bat out the car window. Jones parked the car at the hotel and hailed a taxi cab to drive him to Las Vegas, Nevada. The police eventually recovered Ms. Gumina's car and found a pink baseball cap and a note, which were identified at the later trial as belonging to Jones.

When he arrived in Las Vegas, he gave the cab driver one of Weaver's guns to pay for the fare and checked into a hotel. The next day Jones met Marcia and Gary Vint and arranged to pay rent to sleep on the couch in their apartment. While at the apartment, he sold most of the remaining guns from Weaver's collection. The police ultimately recovered several of the guns; two witnesses from Las Vegas testified that Jones sold them the guns, and Jackie Weaver identified the guns as Robert Weaver's property.

A few days later, the Vints learned that Jones was a suspect in the Bullhead City murders. By then, he was staying at another apartment the Vints had rented, although his belongings were still at the original apartment. The Vints called the Las Vegas police, who arrested Jones and took possession of his belongings.

The state charged Jones with two counts of premeditated first degree murder and one count of attempted premeditated first degree murder. Although Katherine Gumina ultimately died as a result of the injuries Jones inflicted, the state chose not to amend the indictment. Jones pleaded not guilty to all of the charges. At his trial in August, 1993, he testified that he killed Robert Weaver in self-defence, that he struck Katherine Gumina reflexively and without criminal intent because she startled him, and that another person killed Tisha Weaver. The jury found defendant guilty of all three counts on September 13th, 1993 and he was sentenced to death on December 9th, 1993.

Danny Lee Jones appeals are ongoing and include claims of mental instability brought about by sexual abuse as a child by his grandfather; exposure to chrome, his mother worked in a chrome plating factory; a traumatic breach birth; abuse by two step fathers; substantial drug use as a child etc..

# ROBERT GLEN JONES

Born Xmas Day, 1969 – executed by lethal injection in Arizona October 23rd, 2013.

Jones was born on Christmas day, 1969 in Tyler, Texas. He was kicked out of his mother's home at the age of 15 when he dropped out of school and began using cocaine and methamphetamine.

On 30th May 1996 Jones, with an accomplice, Scott Nordstrom, went to the Moon Smoke Shop in Tucson whilst Scott's brother David kept watch outside. They followed customer Chip O'Dell into the shop and Jones immediately shot him in the head from behind killing him. One employee escaped and two others were shot at by Jones. One was not hit and the other survived being shot. Nordstrom then shot another employee twice in the head, execution style having made him lay on the floor face down. Money was stolen which was shared with the lookout, David Nordstrom.

Two weeks later, on 13th June, the pair went to the Fire Fighter's Union Hall in Tucson. Jones executed three customers with shots to the head after forcing them to bend forward and put their heads on the bar. The bartender was shot and killed by Nordstrom after she was unable to open the safe. Cash believed to be approximately $1,300 was stolen from the till.

The pair killed one other person, on 23rd August when they went to the home of Richard Roels in Phoenix. He was found bound with duct tape and shot in the head. His bank cards had been stolen.

Phoenix police tracked the use of the credit cards shortly after the final murder. The couple had bought pizzas and a pair of cowboy boots. They then tried to buy ammunition at a gun store but the shop worker became suspicious, called the police and provided them with CCTV photos of the pair.

The police sent the photos to local hotels and one called in identifying the offenders as staying at their motel near Interstate 17.

Police tracked them as they left the hotel and a chase followed with the police helicopter tracking Jones and another accomplice, Stephen Coats. Following the thefts of several cars they split up and Jones hot-wired a Porsche which he crashed. Jones was eventually arrested and was found to be wearing a watch belonging to Richard Roels.

The link to the Tuscon murders didn't happen immediately. David Nordstrom, the lookout/getaway driver, who was already on parole and wearing an electronic tag was persuaded by his girlfriend to hand himself in and told police that Jones and Nordstrom were responsible for the killings. He testified against them for all charges against him being dropped.

Jones maintained the first 6 murders were carried out by Nordstrom and it was a case of mistaken identity, however he pleaded guilty to Richard Roel's murder.

Jones received six death sentences. The post trial appeal at the Arizona Supreme Court on June 15th, 2000 affirmed the sentences. On 23rd October 2013, he was executed by lethal injection.

At the execution the doctors struggled to find a viable vein to insert the IVs in. After almost an hour they opted to inject him via the femoral artery in his leg after Jones joked that with all his years of injecting dope, he could find his own vein if they freed his hands.

# RICHARD LEWIS JORDAN

Born October 21st, 1930 – executed by asphyxiation–gas in Arizona November 22nd, 1958.

Phyllis Thompson, a twenty-three year old single girl, whose home was in Lyons, Colorado, but who had worked elsewhere as a stenographer and secretary, was returning to her home from a vacation in California and arrived in Tucson, Arizona on the 24th of May, 1954. She had with her a note to the manager of the Club Esquire from the manager's brother, who lived in Denver, Colorado and whom she had met whilst on holiday.

She went to the Club Esquire and gave the note to the manager's wife at approximately 8:00pm on May 24th, 1954. The manager's wife was on duty at the time and introduced Phyllis to Richard Jordan, a club member who was in the Club. Phyllis remained at the Club Esquire until approximately 9:00 or 9:30 pm. and whilst there drank one or more soft drinks with Jordan who was having beer. She and Jordan then left and went to the Tropical Inn, another tavern in the east section of Tucson where they remained until approximately 11:00pm. They then returned to the Club Esquire and remained there until approximately 11:45pm when they left together. That was the last time Phyllis was seen alive.

At approximately 4:30pm the next day, May 25th, 1954, her lifeless body was found approximately six or seven miles north east of Tucson.

Her body was approximately sixty feet into the desert from the Indian Ruins Road near Tucson. She was completely naked except for the right shoe. There were sixteen stab wounds in the chest area, four of which had penetrated the heart and caused her death. Her face was mutilated by twelve slashes, evidently made by a knife. Her clothing was found approximately eight hundred and sixty feet north and on the opposite side of the road from where she was found.

There was evidence to the effect that her brassiere strap had been cut. Sheriff's officers found tyre tracks on and off the roadway opposite the point where her clothing was found and opposite the point where her body was found. Plaster casts were made of two sets of foot prints which led from the car tracks to the place where her body was found and those footprints had the same measurements as Jordan's right shoe and Phyllis's bare foot. There was a hole in the sole of Jordan's right shoe which also appeared in the plaster casts taken at the crime scene. There was evidence of a struggle near Phyllis 's body in that the terrain was torn up and the scrub laid flat.

After taking witness statements from staff at the Club Esquire linking Phyllis with Jordan, he was arrested early in the morning on May 26th, 1954. At the time of his arrest a knife was obtained from the glove compartment of his car. There was blood on this knife, which on examination proved to be of the same type and RH factor as Phyllis's blood. There was blood on his clothing and gloves, which were found in his dirty clothes hamper at this home. The blood on his clothing and gloves was also of the same type and RH factor as Phylli's. There was also some blood on the right hand side of the front seat of Jordan's car that was the same type and RH factor as Phyllis's blood.

Jordan orally admitted having killed Phyllis, but refused to put his admission in writing. He did sign a written statement, which amongst other things, alleged that he might or might not have killed Phyllis, that he had been on the Indian Ruins Road with her and that he blacked out and did not remember what happened. Phyllis's fountain pen was found in his car, her overnight bag and purse were found near Jordan's home where they had apparently been thrown from a car. Jordan admitted in the Written Statement to having disposed of them on his way back from the Indian Ruins Road.

On August 23rd 1954, trial was held in Superior Court, No. 1, and the jury returned a verdict of Guilty of first degree murder with the penalty of death. The case was appealed to Arizona Supreme Court and reversed and a new trial was ordered. In compliance with the Supreme Court decision Jordan was tried again on October 6th, 1956 and the jury again found him guilty of first degree murder and assessed a penalty of death. He was sentenced to death on December 18th, 1956. A Stay of execution was denied and Jordan was executed on November 22nd, 1958.

# GEORGE RUSSELL KAYER

Born August 20th, 1954 – sentenced to death July 17th, 1997

On December 3rd, 1994, two couples searching for Christmas trees on a dirt road in Yavapai County discovered a body which was later identified as Delbert Haas. Haas had been shot twice, evidenced by entry bullet wounds located roughly behind each ear. On December 12th, 1994, Yavapai County Detective Danny Martin received a phone call from Las Vegas police officer Larry Ross. Ross told Martin that a woman named Lisa Kester had approached a security guard at the Pioneer Hotel in Las Vegas and said that her boyfriend, George Kayer, had killed a man in Arizona. Kester said a warrant had been issued for Kayer's arrest in relation to a different crime, a fact Las Vegas police officers later confirmed.

Kester had given Las Vegas police officers the gun she said was used to kill Haas, and she had led the officers to credit cards belonging to Haas that were found inside a white van in the hotel parking lot. Kester appeared agitated to the police officers and security guards she was with and said she had not come forward sooner because she feared Kayer would kill her, too. She asked to be placed in the witness protection program. She described Kayer's physical appearance to the officers and agreed to go with an officer to the police station.

A combination of Pioneer Hotel security guards and Las Vegas police officers soon spotted Kayer leaving the hotel, they arrested him and took him to the police station for questioning. Kester had already been arrested for carrying a concealed weapon. Detectives Martin and Roger Williamson from Yavapai flew to Las Vegas on December 13th to interrogate Kester and Kayer.

Kester gave a complete account of events that she said led to Delbert Haas' death. Kayer, in contrast, spoke briefly with the detectives before invoking his right to have an attorney present.

Kester's statements to Detectives Martin and Williamson formed the basis of the State's prosecution of Kayer. She said that he continually bragged about a gambling system that he had invented to defeat the Las Vegas casinos. However, neither Kayer nor Kester ever had enough money with which to gamble. Kayer was a travelling salesman of sorts, selling T-shirts, jewellery, and knick-knacks. His only other income came from defrauding the government of benefits through fake identities that both he and Kester created.

Kayser learned that Haas recently received money from a large insurance settlement. Kester and Kayser visited Haas at his house near Cordes Lakes late in November 1994. Kester said that Kayser had convinced Haas to come gambling with them. On November 30th, 1994, Kayser, Kester, and Haas left for Laughlin, Nevada in Kayser's van. They stayed in the same hotel room in Laughlin, and after the first night of gambling, Kayser claimed to have "won big." Using his system. It was a lie. Haas agreed to loan Kayser about $100 of his insurance money so that Kayser could further utilize his gambling system. Kayser's gambling system proved unsuccessful, and he lost all the money Haas had given him but told Haas again that he had won big but that someone had stolen his winnings. Kester asked Kayser what they were going to do now that they were out of money and Kayser said he was going to rob Haas. When Kester asked how Kayser was going to get away with robbing someone he knew, Kayser said, "I guess I'll just have to kill him afterwards." The three left Laughlin to return to Arizona on December 2nd, 1994. On the road all three, but mostly Haas, consumed alcohol. Kayser and Haas argued continually over how Kayser was going to repay Haas. The van made several stops for bathroom    breaks and to purchase snacks. At one of these stops, Kayser took a gun that he stored under the seat of the van and put it in his belt. Kayser asked Kester if she was "going to be all right with this." Kester said she would need a warning before Kayser killed Haas if that was what he was going to do.  Kaser took a route through back roads that he claimed would be a shortcut back to Haas' house. While on one such road, Kayser stopped the van near Camp Wood Road in Yavapai County. At this stop, Kester said Haas exited the van and began urinating behind it. Kester started to climb out of the van as well, but Kayser    motioned to her with the gun and pushed her back inside. The van had windows in the rear and on each side through which Kester viewed what occurred next. Kayser walked quietly up to Haas from behind while he was urinating, trained the gun at Haas' head at point-blank range, and shot him behind the ear. Kayser then dragged Haas' body off the side of the road into the bushes where the body was eventually found. Kayser returned to the car carrying Haas' wallet, watch, and jewellery. Kayser and Kester began to drive away in the van when Kayser realized that he had forgotten to take Haas's house keys. He turned the van around and returned to the murder scene. Kester and Kayser both looked for the body; Kester spotted it and then returned to the van. Kayser returned to the van too, and asked for the gun, saying that Haas did not appear to be dead. Kester said Kayser then approached Haas' body and that she heard a gunshot. Kester and Kayser then drove to Haas's home. Kayser entered the house and stole several guns, a camera, and other of Haas's personal property. He attempted unsuccessfully to find Haas's bank PIN number in order to access His bank accounts. Kayser and Kester sold Haas's guns and jewellery at pawn shops and flea markets over the course of the next week, usually under the aliases of David Flynn and Sharon Hughes. Kayser and Kester then went to Las Vegas where Kayser used the proceeds from selling these items to test his gambling system once again and to pay for a room at the Pioneer Hotel. At this time, Kester was beginning to think Kayser might kill her as she was the only witness to Haas's murder and she approached the Pioneer Hotel security guard and reported Kayser's crime.

On December 29th, 1994 both Kester and Kayser were charged with premeditated first degree murder plus subsidiary charges and the following February the state of Arizona filed a notice that it would be seeking the death penalty against both of them.

Kester agreed to testify against Kayser in return for a significantly less sentence. The trial was delayed for a year when Kayser asked for a new attorney   just days before the start date and it finally started in March1997.

Kayser's whole defence was based on his claim that Kester was the killer not him. The jury weren't fooled and found Kayser guilty of first degree murder and on July 15th, 1997 he was sentenced to death. His appeals continue.

# THOMAS ARNOLD KEMP

Born June 2nd 1948 – executed by lethal injection April 25th, 2012.

On July 11th, 1992, at approximately 11:15 pm, Hector Juarez awoke when his fiancé, Jamie, returned home from work to their shared unit at the Promontory Apartments in Tucson. A short time later, Juarez left to buy something to eat. Jamie assumed he went to a nearby Jack-in-the-Box at the corner of Oracle and River Roads. He never returned.

At around midnight, Jamie became concerned that Juarez had not come home and began to look for him. She found both her car and his car in the parking lot. Her car, the one Juarez was driving, was unlocked, smelled of fast food, and had insurance papers laying on the roof. After checking with Juarez's brother and a friend, Jamie called the police.

Three days before Juarez was abducted, Jeffery Logan, an escapee from a California parole farm, arrived in Tucson and met with Thomas Kemp. On Friday, July 10th, Logan went with Kemp to a pawn shop and helped him buy a .380 semi-automatic handgun. Kemp and Logan spent the next night driving around Tucson. Between 11:15 pm. and midnight, Kemp and Logan abducted Juarez from the parking area of his complex. At midnight, Kemp used Juarez's ATM card and successfully withdrew approximately $200. He then drove Juarez out to the Silverbell Mine area near Marana. Kemp walked Juarez 50 to 70 feet away from the truck, forced him to undress, and shot him in the head twice. Kemp then made two unsuccessful attempts to use Juarez's ATM card in Tucson. The ATM machine kept the card after the second attempt. Kemp and Logan painted Kemp's truck, drove it to Flagstaff, and sold it. They bought another .380 semi-automatic handgun with the proceeds.

While in Flagstaff, Kemp and Logan met a couple travelling from California to Kansas. At some point they kidnapped the couple and forced them to drive to Durango, Colorado, where Kemp forced the man to undress. He then sexually assaulted him. Later, Kemp, Logan, and the couple drove to Denver. Two weeks after Juarez was abducted from Tucson, the couple escaped. For reasons that remain unclear Logan left Kemp, contacted the Tucson police about the murder of Juarez, and was arrested in Denver.

With Logan's help, the police discovered Juarez's body. Later that day, the police arrested Kemp at a homeless shelter in Tucson. He was carrying the handgun purchased in Flagstaff and a pair of handcuffs. After having been read his rights, Kemp answered some questions before he asked for a lawyer. Kemp admitted that he purchased a handgun with Logan on July 10th. He said that on the day of the abduction and homicide of Juarez he was "cruising" though apartment complexes, and that there was a very good possibility he was at the Promontory Apartments. When the police confronted him with the ATM photographs, he initially denied being the man in the picture. After having been told Logan was in custody, and having again been shown the photographs, Kemp admitted the murder.

While awaiting trial, Kemp on two separate occasions made admissions to prison officials. He asked for protective custody because the person he killed was Hispanic and the Hispanics in the jail were after him because they thought the crime was racially motivated and the whites would not protect him.

Logan's and Kemp's trials were carried out individually. Logan was tried first, convicted, and sentenced to life imprisonment for the murder under an assumed name to protect him from Hispanic revenge.

A jury found Kemp guilty on all counts. The court found three statutory aggravating factors: a prior conviction of a felony involving the use or threat of violence against a person, the murder was committed with the expectation of pecuniary gain, and the murder was committed in an especially heinous, cruel or depraved manner. The court did not find any mitigating circumstances and sentenced Kemp to death. Twenty years later a defiant Kemp, now 63, was executed by lethal injection after refusing to argue for clemency

# ALVIE COPELAND KILES

Born May 21st, 1961 – sentenced to death June 13th, 2006.

In January 1989 Alvie Kiles moved in with Valerie Gunnell and her two daughters, one aged 9 months the other five years. Valerie and Kiles soon began arguing about Kiles stealing her food stamps to sell to support his cocaine habit. On February 9th, 1989, Deirdre Johnson, who lived next door to Valerie, saw Kiles outside the apartment working on his car. Early the next day, Johnson saw Kiles back his car into a parking space at the apartment. Later that morning Valerie's mother knocked on the door of the apartment, but got no answer.

Larry Hawkins saw Kiles outside his apartment that morning in Valerie's car. Valerie's step-father also saw Kiles driving her car that day. Later, Deirdre Johnson noticed Kiles struggling to lift a trash bag over the fence behind the apartment. He dropped the bag, which emitted a "loud thud sound" when it landed.

That afternoon, Kale Johnson saw Kiles sitting in Valerie's car at a Yuma park. Kiles told Johnson, "I killed that girl." Kiles admitted to Johnson that "I killed the kids too" because they were "crying and hollering and screaming." He told Johnson that he had used something he took from the car to commit the murders. Kiles also told Johnson that he had disposed of the children's bodies in the Colorado River.

Johnson did not believe Kiles, so Kiles took Johnson to Valerie's apartment where Johnson saw

Valerie's body lying on the floor. There was a puddle of blood on the floor and blood "all over the walls and the ceilings." Johnson attempted to leave the apartment, but Kiles hit him with a broom handle. Johnson managed to get out and went to the police the next day.

Kiles admitted killing Valerie and the children to other people as well as Johnson. Kiles told Larry Hawkins that he had killed Valerie and her children. He explained that he and Valerie had argued over food stamps that Kiles had taken to sell to buy cocaine. Kiles told Hawkins that Valerie had slapped him twice, once after he had told her not to. Kiles then went to his car and retrieved a tyre jack, which he used to strike Valerie at least twice. Hawkins stated that Kiles told him that Valerie had "regained consciousness" after the initial blow and asked Kiles, "Why did you do this?" Kiles told Hawkins that he had killed the children "because . . . they had seen him." Hawkins did not inform the police but wrote a letter to Yuma Silent Witness describing Kiles' admissions.

Kiles also admitted to Jesse Solomon, a family friend, and to his own mother, Imojean Kiles, that he had killed Valerie with the jack. He further told his mother that he had "taken care of the children because they could talk," and had "dumped" their bodies in a canal.

The Yuma police went to Valerie's apartment on February 11th, 1989 after Kale Johnson had talked to them. They found the apartment in "disarray" with cartons of eggs on the floor and a lamp overturned. An officer saw blood spatters in a bedroom, signs of a struggle, blood on the bed, and something "wrapped up in a blanket" in the hall. It was Valerie's body.

Further investigation at the apartment revealed blood smeared on the bathroom floor "as if somebody had tried to wipe it up." The bathroom smelled of cleanser and police found a pile of blood stained towels.

In Valerie's bedroom, the bed was covered in papers and money and there was clothing all over the floor. A blood-soaked pillow and a piece of a car jack with her hair and blood on it were also found. In the children's bedroom, two "very large pools of blood" were found on the bed. Blood spatter was found on the walls, drapes, ceiling, and door of the west bedroom. A blood spatter expert testified that at least fourteen blows were delivered in the children's room. In the northwest corner of the living room, a blood-stained ottoman and a bone fragment were also found. Blood had soaked into the carpeting. Blood spatter and blood stains were found in the living room. A chair in the living room had stains that indicated someone had lost a lot of blood. A large bone fragment and blood spatter was found near the south wall. In addition, blood smears were found on the front door of the apartment. Blood spatter and smears were found in the kitchen-dining area as well.

Valerie died from multiple blunt force trauma to the head with multiple scalp lacerations, skull fractures, and a brain laceration. She had a broken arm, which medical testimony identified as a defensive wound. The body of Valerie's youngest child was later found in a canal in Mexico. She died of blunt force trauma to the skull with extensive skull fractures and a brain laceration. The older child was never found. Her blood, however, was detected on the mattress cover in the apartment.

Kiles was sentenced to death on three counts of first degree murder and two of child abuse. The sentence was affirmed on direct appeal. Kiles appealed the decision stating his counsel gave him ineffective assistance and the Superior Court vacated the sentences and sent him for a second trial in 2000. At that trial on June 13th, 2006, the jury again found him guilty and a death sentence was handed down. The Arizona Supreme Court upheld the verdict.

Kiles' appeals run on and at this time he is sitting on death row.

# ERIC JOHN KING

Born September 30th, 1963 – executed by lethal injection in Arizona March 29th, 2011.

Shortly after midnight on December 27th, 1989, a black male, brandishing a pistol, robbed the Short Stop convenience market at 48th Street and Broadway in Phoenix. During the course of the robbery, both the store clerk, 46 year old Ron Barman, and security guard, 61 year old Richard Butts, were shot and killed.

The robbery was captured on two time-lapse video cameras. The videotape was admitted into evidence at the later trial of Eric King and showed the robber pointing the gun at the clerk and that clerk moving backward and then falling to the floor as the robber left the store. Photographs developed from the videotape depict a black male wearing a dark sweater with a band of light coloured, diamond-shaped markings across the chest and arms. No one else was present in the store at the time of the robbery.

At approximately midnight that same night, Frank Madden drove to the Country Kitchen restaurant parking lot, which is behind the Short Stop on the north side, where he was to meet his date. As he drove past the Short Stop toward the restaurant, he saw two black men walking in the parking lot. The men were a little over 6 feet tall and one of them wore a blue or black and white sweater with "some kind of pattern like pyramids"; the other man wore a "green sweatshirt."

Madden and his girlfriend discovered that the restaurant they intended to eat at was closed. As they were talking, they heard gunshots and immediately drove over to the Short Stop. When Madden got out of his car and walked toward the front of the store, he saw the security guard, with an empty gun holster, lying on the ground. At the same time, the black man with the dark sweater, who Madden had seen earlier at the Country Kitchen parking lot, was also walking toward the store.

Madden heard the guard moaning and saw blood on the right side of his stomach. Madden phoned 911. While Madden was on the phone, the man with the dark sweater went over to the security guard, pulled out a white cloth, and wiped the guard's holster and belt. After Madden saw him, the man in the dark sweater left the scene. In an identity parade a few days later Madden could not positively identify King as the man he saw that night, but he testified that the man he saw had "high cheekbones" like King's, and that King looked very familiar, and the only difference was that the man he saw had facial hair and was not as nicely dressed as King was at the identity parade.

Around midnight of the night of the murders, Kevin Harris and his friend David Dils were driving through the intersection of 48th Street and Broadway when they too heard the gunshots. Harris was looking in the direction of the Short Stop and saw two black men running away from the store; one of the men held a gun in his hand. Harris and Dils drove into a nearby parking lot, got out of the car, and approached the store. Harris saw the security guard lying on the ground and Madden using the phone to call 911. Dils checked the guard's pulse and found none. They then entered the store and saw the clerk behind the counter; he had been shot in the right shoulder and stomach and was holding a telephone yelling into the receiver. Dils and Harris assisted the clerk until the fire department arrived.

Shortly after the shootings, Nolan Thomas, his son Derek, and Greg Hecky pulled into the Short Stop. Just as Nolan parked his car, Derek directed his dad's attention to the security guard lying on the ground. Nolan looked over and saw a black man with a moustache and goatee, wearing a black sweater with a white "logo" bending over the security guard. Like Madden, he saw the man wipe off the guard's empty holster with a white rag and then run off.

About that time, Phoenix Police Sergeant Richard Switzer received a radio call to go to the Short Stop. The call included a description of the suspects. While driving east on Broadway, he saw two black males walking west on Broadway across 44th Place. Sgt. Switzer made a U-turn and drove toward the men to determine whether they fitted the suspects' descriptions. Sgt. Switzer shined a spotlight on the two men, got out of his car, and walked toward them. Despite Sgt. Switzer's order for them to "halt" one of the men, wearing a blue sweater with white markings on the upper sleeve, fled the scene running south. The man who stopped identified himself as Michael Jones. After being asked about the man who ran away, Jones told Sgt. Switzer that he had just met the man and did not know him. At trial, Sgt. Switzer testified that he remembered the man he saw with Jones that night as being slightly taller than Jones, who was 6 feet 1 inches tall.

Later that night, Nekita Renee Hill and her friend Joann Smith walked to Smith's house. Ms. Smith lived in the area of 48th Street and Broadway, and her house was within walking distance of the Short Stop. During their walk, they noticed helicopters flying overhead. As they approached Smith's house, Hill saw King walking toward a dumpster. She saw him throw a light-coloured, thin plastic bag into the dumpster. Police later retrieved the bag which contained a gun and a dark sweater with a white diamond pattern that Hill had seen King wearing earlier that night.

Hill knew King, who was a childhood friend of her boyfriend Jones. King had frequently visited Jones at Smith's house while Hill was there. Sometime later, Hill saw a picture on television that she recognized as King. When she saw King's picture, she called the police.

Both King and Jones were arrested on December 28th, 1989, in connection with the robbery and murders. Michael Jones, who had been to the Short Stop a couple of times the evening of the murders, admitted at trial that he was at the Short Stop when the robbery and murders occurred. He testified that he and King had gone to the Short Stop to buy wine and that he had remained outside while King went inside the store. Jones said that while he was waiting outside, he heard gunshots. On hearing the shots, he turned toward the store and saw King leaving the store with a gun in his hand and the security guard lying on the ground in front of the store. Jones was later released and no charges were filed against him.

Jones testified at King's trial in August 1990 that earlier in the evening he had seen the security guard with a large gun in his holster, a gun that was either a .44 or a .357 magnum. Although he said that he had not seen King touch the guard, he testified, without objection, that he believed King got the gun from the security guard.

At trial, Jones testified that the next time that he saw King was several days after the murder when they both had been arrested, King's hair was shorter and he had shaved off his beard and moustache. He further testified that King, at the trial, looked like he did when he was arrested. After viewing one of the photographs made from the surveillance camera tapes, Jones testified that the person depicted in the photograph "looks a lot like" King and that "it seems like" King.

At trial, Hill was a reluctant witness, admitting that she did not want to be involved with the trial and that she was testifying only under threat of arrest. Hill testified that King and Jones had gone to the Short Stop in the "middle of the night" on the night of the murders and that she had wanted to go with them but her mom would not babysit for her. When shown a copy of the picture that was broadcast over the television, she admitted that the picture prompted her call to the police. She also admitted telling the police that the person depicted in the picture was Eric King. She tried recanting her earlier identification, however, by testifying that the person depicted in the picture did not look like King. Hill did testify that King had a beard and a moustache and that his hair was longer and wilder looking at the time of the murders.

King did not testify at trial, and the only witness who he called was Sgt. Switzer, who essentially restated his earlier testimony concerning the height of the man who ran away when he stopped Jones. King argued that the state failed to meet its burden of proof by attacking the credibility of the state's two key witnesses (Jones and Hill) and by focusing the court's attention on his height of 5 feet 8 inches as compared to testimony of two witnesses that the person with Jones was over 6 feet tall. The jury unanimously convicted King of two counts of premeditated first-degree murder and one count of armed robbery.

King did not speak on his own behalf at the sentencing hearing. In fact, he left in the middle of the hearing, telling the judge that he did not want to be there because, 'I thought I had a right to be proven not guilty. Like I said I did not commit the crime. No evidence, no effect. You already heard the case. I know the situation. You will give me the death penalty or life. I feel either way you go I lose and I want to leave.'

He was sentenced on 3rd August 1991 to death for each of the two first-degree murder convictions and to a consecutive, aggravated term of 21 years on the armed robbery conviction. King was also ordered to pay restitution of $72.84. At the time of the murders King had just been released from prison after serving 7 years for kidnapping and brutal rape.

Court documents show King had a troubled childhood. Born in a taxi on the way to the hospital in Phoenix, King was one of 12 siblings whose alcoholic, abusive and mentally disturbed father died of a heart attack when King was 11. Records also say King's mother struggled to provide for the children, who were so hungry at times that they tried to catch crawdads in irrigation canals and frequently were without electricity.

King reported to a prison psychiatrist that he had heard voices on and off during his entire life, and suffered from anxiety and insomnia. His son, 20-year-old Eric Harrison, saw King for the first time at the clemency hearing and asked the board to spare his father. "This is the first time I've ever seen my dad, ever in life, and I know I love him," Harrison said. "That's my dad. He gave me life. Just don't take him."

The U.S. Supreme Court refused to consider the case for a Stay of execution as did the Arizona Board of Executive Clemency. Eric King was executed by lethal injection on March 29th, 2011.

# DAVID BENJAMIN KNIGHT

Born July 8th, 1904 – executed by asphyxiation-gas in Arizona on September 3rd, 1937.

Around the first day of December, 1935, the Benjamin Knight, and a woman by the name of Vesta Baker, and Vesta Baker's two children, came to Maricopa County looking for work. They secured a job picking cotton at the Simmons' ranch southwest of Coldwater, Arizona, and on the south side of the Gila River.

Knight remained at the Simmons, ranch for a short while before leaving the area and leaving Vesta Baker and her two children at the ranch. Knight went to Yuma, Arizona, and returned to a ranch near Buckeye, where he got a job as a cotton picker. At that ranch Knight met J C Kalb. Kalb and Knight picked cotton together for a few days, and decided to go to California together. Kalb had an old Studebaker coach, a model from about 1925 or 1926. Knight had a Pontiac coupe.

When Knight and Kalb decided to go to California, Knight sold his car to a second hand dealer, and Kalb and Knight went to Venice, California, in Kalb's car. They stayed in Venice at Knight's brother's house for two or three days and then decided to return to Arizona. Knight and Kalb arrived at Coldwater, Arizona, on December 23rd, 1935.

Knight then borrowed Kalb's car and left Kalb at Coldwater whilst he went to the Simmons' ranch to see Vesta Baker. He stayed at the ranch a short while, and he and Vesta Baker agreed that he would come back to the ranch and stay there, and that Kalb could also stay. Kalb and Knight went to the Simmons' ranch on December 24th and stayed there until December 26th, when Knight, Vesta Baker, the two children, and Kalb moved to an auto court in the city of Phoenix.

They spent the night of December 26th in the auto court and on the morning of December 27th, Kalb and Knight left in Kalb's car saying they were going to find work. Knight returned alone about 8.00 or 9:00 o'clock that night. He asked Vesta Baker if Kalb had returned, and was told by Vesta Baker that she had not seen him since he left with Knight that morning.

Later, in custody, Knight made a statement to the County Attorney and the Sheriff of Maricopa County in which he told them that he and Kalb went to the lettuce sheds near Phoenix looking for work on the morning of December 27th and that they then went to Coldwater about noon of that day and stayed around until sundown on the evening of the 27th. Whilst they were around Coldwater, Knight and Kalb decided to go to the Simmons' ranch and steal a wood saw that was attached to a tractor. They crossed the Gila River and parked their car behind a thicket some distance from the Simmons' ranch and took some pliers, a hammer and wrenches to the tractor and attempted to remove the wood saw. They found that it was too heavy to handle and abandoned the idea of taking the saw and when they were walking back from the Simmons ranch to the car, Kalb suggested that they rob Randley's Convenience store near Coldwater. They then got into an argument about robbing the store, and Kalb struck Knight with a wrench. Knight took a hammer out of his pocket and hit Kalb with it several times. Kalb fell to the ground in the road where they were walking and Knight then dragged Kalb's body into the thicket by the side of the road and then went to Kalb' s car parked nearby, took a cotton sack out of the boot and returned to the thicket where he went through Kalb's pockets, took his purse and a can of tobacco and put Kalb in the cotton sack. At the time he put Kalb in the cotton sack Kalb was still living. Knight then dragged Kalb's body through the thicket down to the river bank near Kalb's car and put five or six big rocks in the sack with the body.

Knight changed his mind about throwing the body in the river and took the rocks out of the sack, put the body in the car and drove across the river and out into the desert between the river and Coldwater where he turned off the road and threw the body into a pile of brush before driving on towards Phoenix.

Knight stated that he threw a sun visor that Kalb had been wearing away in the desert and that he drove to the lettuce sheds near Tolleson. He then took a coat Kalb had been wearing and wiped up the blood off the floor of the car. Prior to the time he got to the lettuce sheds, he threw the floor mat out of the car because it was bloody and then drove on home and took the contents of Kalb's purse, some 15 or 20c and a small quantity of gold dust and put them in his own purse. He burned the papers and cards that were in Kalb's purse, and then threw the purse under the cabin where he and Vesta Baker were living. He stayed in the cabin that night,the 27th. The next day he and Vesta Baker drove to Chandler, Arizona intending to sell Kalb's car but he changed his mind and returned to the auto court in Phoenix where he and Vesta Baker packed up their things, and together with Vesta Baker's two children they set out for California. Kalb had a suit case with some clothing in it and they both went through the suit case and discarded the worn out and useless clothes and possessions putting them in another old suit case. They then put Kalb's suit case and the rest of his belongings that were any good in the car, and took them with them.

At Gila Bend they threw away the old suit case containing the worthless articles and drove without stopping until they crossed the line into California where they stopped on the edge of the road and spent the night in the car. The next day they drove to Knight's brother's house in Venice and arrived there in the dark on the night of the 29th. Just before they reached Knight's brothers' house, Knight told Vesta Baker and her two children to tell his brother that Kalb had come to California with them and that he had got a lift on a truck in Los Angeles and had gone to Watsonville.

This was done because Knight's brother knew the car belonged to Kalb. Knight parked the car in the alley near his brother's house and stayed there for two to three days and then rented a private garage where he stored the car. He then took the battery out of the car and removed the tyres from the two front wheels intending to sell them, but later changed his mind and dumped them down an alley; the evidence given by the Los Angeles officers showed that the car was found at the place Knight said he had left it, and that the tyres and battery had been removed, and that the front wheels had been turned as far as they could be turned, and that the steering gear had been locked so that the car could not be taken out of the garage without breaking the steering gear.

Knight further stated that after he had stored the car, he removed the title paper from the car, and when he got back to his brother's house, he tore the title paper up and flushed it down the toilet. On the 29th of December Kalb's body was found in the pile a brush where Knight had left it. An examination showed that he had been hit very hard with a blunt instrument to the back of the head and another blow in the left temple. All papers or means of identification of the body had been removed and the two hip pockets of Kalb's trousers were turned inside out.

A few days later the body was identified as J C Kalb by finger prints and a few days after that two employees of the Simmons ranch were walking down the road which Kalb and Knight had followed in going to and from the tractor they were going to steal, when they noticed scuffs in the road where something had been dragged across the road and into a thicket. They followed the drag marks and found two large pools of blood in the thicket, a pair of pliers and a wrench which bore a personal tool mark identical with marks on the remainder of Knight's tools. At the place where the blood stains, wrench and pliers were found there was also the butt of a smoked cigarette. On the bank of the river nearby was a pile of rocks that had been piled up, which was identified later by Knight as being the rocks he had put in the sack with Kalb's body and later removed.

After the two employees who found this place, where the killing occurred, told the police, they were taken to the morgue and identified Kalb's body as the man who had come to and left the Simmons' ranch with Knight. Knight was arrested after having been traced to Venice where he at first stated he had came to California in a Ford truck with a man by the name of Wilson and that he had arrived in Venice before Christmas. He later changed his story and admitted that he drove Kalb' s car to California and claimed that on the morning of the 27th December Kalb had left the lettuce sheds near Tolleson with another man, and that night the man that Kalb left with returned to the sheds and told him that Kalb had gone to California and for Knight to take the car to California and leave the car on Town Avenue between 5th and 6th Streets for Kalb. He said that the next morning he again met the same man, and he again told him to take the car to California, and leave it at the place stated and that if he did not do so he would get in trouble as Kalb would say he stole it. He then drove the car to California, and left it as directed, and told the police that he had not seen Kalb or the car since.

Knight was returned to Phoenix, and again made a similar statement to the officers, but later he changed his story and admitted that he had killed Kalb and had disposed of the body in the desert.

In his confession, Knight claimed that he only took 15 or 20c and about half a can of tobacco and a small quantity of gold dust off the deceased Kalb. Evidence from a witness named Bradley showed that the Knight and Kalb were in Bradley's store the evening of the day of the killing and that at that time Kalb made a purchase in the store and paid for it with a one dollar bill. Bradley testified that Kalb had five or six bills at the time, but that he did not know the denomination of the bills. Further evidence showed that when Knight and Kalb together with Vesta Baker and the two children went to the auto court to rent the cabins the owner of the court asked how many people would occupy the cabin and Knight had said that Knight, his wife, two children and Knight's brother in law would all move in, but that the brother in law would only be there for a day or two.

The evidence showed that Kalb was not Knight's brother in law. The evidence further showed that rain had fallen a few hours before the killing, and that the marks where the body had been dragged across the road and into the thicket were plainly visible, but that there were no signs of a fight or struggle in the road. Neither could the officers find any blood or blood stains in the road from where the body was dragged, but they did find two large blood stains in the thicket about 8 or 10 feet from the road.

It was the theory of the State that Kalb was hit in the temple while he was in the road and was later hit in the back of the head after he was taken into the thicket. This theory was arrived at from the evidence of the witness and a doctor who testified that there would be little haemorrhage from an injury to the temple, but that there would be considerable haemorrhage from a blow to the back of the head.

Knight was found guilty of first degree murder and sentenced to death which was affirmed at his statutory appeal. He was executed by asphyxiation-gas in Arizona on September 3rd, 1937.

# KARL HINZE LaGRAND & WALTER BURNHART LaGRAND

Karl- born October 20th, 1963 – executed by lethal injection in Arizona February 24th, 1999.

Walter- born January 26th, 1962 – executed by lethal gas in Arizona March 3rd, 1999.

Walter LaGrand and Karl LaGrand were both convicted of first-degree murder, attempted murder in the first degree, attempted armed robbery and two counts of kidnapping on February 17th, 1984.

They decided to rob the Valley National Bank in Marana, Arizona, on January 7th, 1982.

That morning Walter and Karl drove from Tucson, where they lived, to Marana intending to rob the bank. They arrived in Marana sometime before 8:00 a.m. Because at that early hour the bank was closed and empty the LaGrands drove around Marana to pass the time. They eventually drove to the El Taco restaurant next to the bank.

Ronald Schunk, manager of El Taco, testified that he arrived at work at 7:50 a.m. The moment he arrived, a car with two men inside drove up to the El Taco. Schunk described the car as white with a chocolate-coloured top. The car's driver, identified by Schunk as Walter LaGrand, asked Schunk what time the El Taco opened. Schunk replied, 'Nine o'clock" The LaGrands then left.

Dawn Lopez arrived for work at the bank at approximately 8:00 a.m. When she arrived she noticed three vehicles parked in the parking lot, a motor home, a

315

truck belonging to the bank manager, Ken Hartsock, and a car which she did not recognize but which she described as white or off-white with a brown top.

Because Lopez believed that Hartsock might be conducting an early business meeting with a client and want some privacy she left the parking lot and drove around Marana for several minutes. She returned to the bank and noticed Hartsock standing by the bank door with another man whom she did not recognize. Lopez parked her car and walked toward the bank entrance where Hartsock was standing. She noticed him go inside with the man.

As she passed the LaGrands' car Walter emerged from it and asked her what time the bank opened. Lopez replied, 'Ten o'clock.' and continued walking and went into the bank. When she entered the bank she saw Hartsock standing by the vault with Karl LaGrand. Karl was wearing a coat and tie and carrying a briefcase.

Karl told her to sit down and opened his jacket to reveal a gun, which was later found by the police to be a toy pistol. Walter then came through the bank entrance and stood by the vault. Lopez testified that Walter then said, 'If he can't open it this time, let's just waste them and leave.' Hartsock was unable to open the vault because he had only one-half of the vault combination.

The LaGrands then pushed Lopez and Hartsock into Hartsock's office where they bound their hands together with black electrical tape. Walter accused Hartsock of lying and put a letter opener to his throat, threatening to kill him if he was not telling the truth. Lopez and Hartsock then were gagged with bandannas.

Wilma Rogers, another bank employee, had arrived at the bank at approximately 8:10 a.m. Upon arriving Rogers noticed two strange vehicles in the parking lot and, fearing that something might be amiss, wrote down the license plate numbers of the two vehicles.

She then went to a nearby grocery store and telephoned the bank. Lopez answered the phone after her gag was removed but her hands remained tied. Karl held the receiver to Lopez' ear and listened to the conversation. Lopez answered the phone. Rogers asked for Hartsock but Lopez denied that he was there, which struck Rogers as odd because she had seen his truck in the bank parking lot.

Rogers then told Lopez that her car headlights were still on, as indeed they were. Rogers told Lopez that if she did not go out to turn her headlights off, then she would call the sheriff. A few minutes later Rogers asked someone else to call the bank and they were also told that Hartsock was not there. Rogers then called the Sheriff's office.

After the first telephone call the LaGrands decided to have Lopez turn off her headlights. Her hands were freed and she was told to go turn off the lights but was warned that 'If you try to go or if you try to leave, we'll just shoot him and leave. We're just going to kill him and leave.' Lopez went to her car and turned off the lights.

Upon her return to the bank her hands were retied. Hartsock was still bound and gagged in the same chair. Lopez was seated in a chair, and turned toward a corner of the room. Lopez testified that soon thereafter she heard sounds of a struggle.

Fearing that Hartsock was being hurt, Lopez stood up, broke the tape around her hands and turned to help him. Lopez testified that for a few seconds she saw Hartsock struggling with the two men. Karl was behind Hartsock holding him by the shoulders while Walter was in front.

According to Lopez, Walter then came toward her and began stabbing her. Lopez fell to the floor, where she could see only the scuffling of feet and Hartsock lying face down on the floor. She then heard someone twice say, 'Just make sure he's dead.'

The LaGrands left the bank and returned to Tucson. Lopez was able to call for help. When law enforcement and medical personnel arrived at the bank Hartsock was dead. He had been stabbed 24 times. Lopez, who had also been stabbed multiple times, was taken to University Hospital in Tucson.

Law enforcement personnel quickly identified the LaGrands as suspects and by 3:15 p.m., police had traced the license plate number to a white and brown vehicle owned by the father of Walter LeGrand's girl friend, Karen Libby. The apartment where the LaGrands were staying with Karen Libby was placed under surveillance.

Shortly after Walter, Karl and Karen Libby left the apartment and began driving. They were followed and soon pulled over. Walter and Karl were then arrested and the car was searched. Karen Libby's apartment was also searched and a steak knife similar to one found at the bank was seized. Karl's fingerprints were found at the bank. A briefcase containing a toy gun, black electrical tape, a red bandanna, and other objects was found beneath a bush and turned over to the police.

When questioned. Walter made no statements, but Karl confessed to the crimes in two different statements. He stated that he had stabbed Hartsock and Lopez, but that Walter had not stabbed anyone and that Walter had been out of the room at the time.

Following a jury trial in January 1984, both were convicted on all charges. After considering mitigating and aggravating circumstances the judge sentenced both defendants to death on December 14th, 1984. The Arizona Supreme Court affirmed the convictions and sentences at the statutory appeal. The Supreme Court of the United States denied a review. The LeGrands then set their appeals in motion.

The LeGrands were front page news in Germany as well as the USA as their mother was a German national and had married a US Serviceman and moved to the United States. They were the first German nationals to be executed in the USA since WW2 when several POWs were hanged. The German Embassy's attempts to stop the executions were refused by the US Solicitor General. Germany did not have a death penalty in 1984 and does not have one now. The German Embassy complained that they had not been informed about the trial and convictions.

Karl was executed by lethal injection on February 24th, 1999 and his brother Walter by lethal gas (his own request) on March 3rd, 1999 and he remains the last person executed by gas in the United States. Both executions took place in Florence State Prison.

# KENNETH JEREMY LAIRD

Born March 21st, 1975 – sentenced to death April 15th, 1994, commuted to life in prison without parole March 1st, 2005.

Seventeen year old Jeremy Laird had a mental fixation of owning a 4x4 truck. In late August 1992 he boasted to his friends that he was going to get a blue Toyota 4x4 truck 'very soon'.

On September 2nd he rode his bike from his home in North Phoenix to the home of Wanda Starnes, 37, in Tatum Ranch. He had been to Wanda's home a month before helping his stepfather tarmac the yard. Wanda had a blue Toyota 4x4.

At 2.30pm Wanda's neighbour, Anthony Sabatino noticed Laird at Wanda's door and asked if he needed any help. Laird told him that his car had broken down. Sabatino let Laird use his mobile to call a garage but apparently Laird couldn't get an answer from the number he dialled a left. Sabatino noticed Laird still in the area later that day at around 5.30pm as did another resident, Deborah Gregor, who noticed him looking over Wanda's fence into her yard.

At 7pm Wanda left her house in her blue Toyota 4x4 truck to start her shift at the local hospital as a cardiac nurse. When she had gone Laird broke into her house and during the evening he called several friends to tell them he was moving home to Tatum Ranch. He called another friend at 6am the next morning to say he couldn't drive her to school that day as usual.

Wanda's truck was seen arriving home and pulling into her garage at 9am that morning by a contractor working nearby. He assumed she was returning from the night shift. That was the last time she was seen alive.

Inside her home Laird was waiting and attacked her with some ferocity. Wanda fought back and her hands showed defensive wounds and cuts. Laird managed to subdue her and hog tied and gagged her before locking her in the bathroom and sealing the door to block any sound with clothes from a wardrobe in the bedroom. Medical examination of the body at the autopsy showed Wanda had been strangled sometime between returning home from work and 6am the morning of the following day, September 4th. Laird had slept most of the previous day as Wanda lay in the bathroom and early on September 4th decided to finish her off by forcing a screwdriver through the ropes tied around her neck and turning it to tighten the rope and strangle her. He then caved in her skull with a heavy object. Laird carried the body to the Toyota 4x4 and drove into the desert where he left her under some vegetation.

Laird spent the next week driving around in the Toyota and forging cheques on Wanda's account whilst living in her house.

Two days after she disappeared he was driving in N Phoenix and got into an argument with some other youths that ended in a fight on the street. Local residents called the police and pointed out the Toyota which drove bye as they were talking to the officers. The police called it in and were told there was a crime bulletin out on the car in connection with a murder. They caught up with Laird and arrested him.

At the police station he gave them a cock and bull story about finding the Toyota abandoned in the desert near Wanda's body when he was out cycling and took it and moved into her house as 'she wouldn't need either anymore.'

Laird was a juvenile but was tried as an adult in December 1993 for murder, kidnapping, burglary and theft plus four counts of forgery (cheques) and robbery. He was found guilty on all counts and on April 15th, 1994 sentenced to death plus consecutive prison sentences of 97 years in total.

Laird's appeals exhausted quite quickly by U.S.A. standards and his date for execution was set for January 17th, 2001. On the day a Stay of Execution was issued by the U.S. District Court. The overarching reason being that 'Arizona doesn't execute juveniles' and laird was a juvenile (under 18) at the time of Wanda Starnes's murder. Laird was sent for re-sentencing.

The death sentence was commuted to life in prison without parole on March 1st, 2005.

# CHRISTOPHER LAMAR

Born November 15th, 1971 – sentenced to death June 1st, 2001

In April 1996, Christopher George Theodore Lamar met and became involved with Myla Hogan. While the two were dating, Hogan lived in a house on 81st Avenue in Peoria, Arizona, with several other people including Mary Keovorabouth, Ouday, Tim Panmany, Vincent Macchirella, Richard Valdez, and Abraham Hermosillo.

On May 11th, 1996, Ronald Jones left his house around 1:00 p.m., telling Alicia Sosa, his live-in girlfriend, that he planned to deliver documents to a loan company to secure a loan for a car. At some point, Myla Hogan called Jones's pager to invite him to lunch. Hogan and Jones had dated and knew one another through Keovorabouth. Jones picked Hogan up at the house on 81st Avenue, and the two ate lunch together.

When Hogan and Jones returned to the house on 81st Avenue, Keovorabouth, Hermosillo, Macchirella, Valdez, Panmany, and Lamar were all present. Prior to May 11th, the group had devised a plan to kidnap and rob Jones. The purpose of the plan was twofold, to steal Jones's money and possessions so they could pay the rent they owed and to "rough him up a little bit" so he would stop spending time with Hogan which annoyed Lamar.

Lamar and the others were waiting for Jones when Hogan and Jones returned to the house. When Lamar confronted Jones about his relationship with

Hogan, Jones responded that he did not know of Hogan's involvement with Lamar. Lamar then punched Jones who fell to the floor. Macchirella pointed a gun at him and at Lamar's direction Hermosillo fetched duct tape and bound Jones's hands and ankles.

Lamar and Macchirella then moved Jones into a bedroom and took his possessions, including his shoes, jewellery, fifty dollars, and some crack cocaine. Jones cried and pleaded for his life, offering to write a cheque for the outstanding rent if they released him. Lamar demanded the gun from Macchirella, explaining that he had "done this before." The group then led Jones upstairs and held him captive while everyone watched television and took turns guarding him with the gun. □

When it became dark, Lamar and the others led Jones downstairs and forced him into the front passenger seat of his own car. Lamar directed Macchirella to drive to Lamar's and Hermosillo's old neighbourhood near 35th Avenue and Broadway Road. Hermosillo, Panmany, and Valdez followed in a stolen truck but made a stop along the way for burgers and lagged behind. Lamar sat behind Jones in the car and at one point held the gun to Jones's head and pulled the trigger, but the gun did not fire. Jones and pleaded for his life when he heard the click of the gun.

Eventually, Lamar directed Macchirella to stop the car. Macchirella pulled the car to the side of the road near a vacant lot and the three men left the vehicle and walked to the back. At Lamar's direction, Macchirella opened the trunk. Lamar then shot Jones. At the later trial, the medical examiner testified that Jones suffered two gunshot wounds to the head. Macchirella testified that as he and Lamar picked Jones up and placed him in the trunk, Jones made "gurgling" sounds, as if he were choking on his own blood.

Hermosillo, Panmany, and Valdez had stopped nearby at Hermosillo's grandmother's house when they heard the gunshots. When they arrived at the scene and asked what had happened, Lamar responded by opening the trunk and patting Jones's back.

The group decided to move Jones's car and bury his body. The car would not start, so they pushed it to a parking lot. Someone fetched a shovel, and, at Lamar's direction, Macchirella dug a grave. Lamar, Hermosillo, Panmany, and Valdez then dragged Jones's body to the grave, pushed him into the hole, and covered it with dirt and brush. Some of the group removed a cellular telephone, a radio, a CD player, a toolbox, and a tool belt from Jones's car. They then set the car on fire.

At some time during the night, Macchirella called the house in Peoria from Jones's cellular telephone, telling Keovorabouth they had made a mistake in killing Jones. Lamar chastised him for using the phone, which could connect them to Jones.

Everyone then went to a party in Lamar's and Hermosillo's old neighbourhood. At the party, Lamar saw his cousin Frances Lamar. Frances later testified that she noticed some blood on Lamar's shoes. Lamar asked Frances for a ride to Mesa, and while they were driving she saw him throw a shoe out of the car window. Lamar returned to the party and he, Macchirella, Hermosillo, Panmany, and Valdez drove back to Peoria in Jone's stolen truck. ☐They abandoned the truck in a nearby parking lot and walked back to the house on 81st Avenue.

Hogan later testified that after the group returned to the house she asked Lamar where they had been and he responded, "Don't ask." Hogan described Lamar as looking very white, as if he had seen a ghost.

According to Hermosillo, when they returned to the house, both Lamar and Macchirella accused each other of shooting Jones, but both eventually claimed to have shot Jones. Hermosillo testified that Lamar also described the size of the holes that the bullets made in Jones's head.

In September 1996, Silent Witness received a tip, apparently from Lamar's cousin Frances, that the police could find a body buried in a vacant lot near 43rd Avenue and Weir. Later, Hogan, Frances, and Frances's sister Marie spoke with Maricopa County Sheriff Detective John Strang. After interviewing the women, the police searched a gravel pit near 43rd Avenue and Weir and located a body, later identified through dental x-rays as Ronald Jones.

The police then executed a search warrant at the apartment of Debra Lamar, Lamar's aunt, where Lamar and Hogan often stayed. In a trash dumpster behind the apartment, the police discovered a tool belt, wrapped in a diaper. Debra admitted that she found the tool belt in the pantry, where Lamar kept his belongings, and that she threw the belt into the dumpster. The police also found a toolbox on a shelf located in the rear of the kitchen.

The police did not test the toolbox or the tools found in it for fingerprints. ☐ Alicia Sosa testified, however, that she recognized some of the tools as belonging to Jones and also identified handwriting on a note found in the toolbox as her own.

In February 1997, a grand jury indicted Lamar for the first degree murder and kidnapping of Ronald Jones. In October 1999, Lamar moved to represent himself but withdrew his motion when the trial judge denied his request for a continuance.

On December 10, 1999, a jury convicted Lamar of kidnapping and first degree murder on both premeditated and felony murder..After considering the aggravating and mitigating circumstances, the trial court sentenced Lamar to death. The Supreme Court of Arizona upheld the guilty verdict in July 2003. His appeals roll on.

# JOE LEONARD LAMBRIGHT & ROBERT DOUGLAS SMITH

Joe Lambright, born September 3rd, 1947 – sentenced to death May 27th, 1982. Commuted to life in prison 2007.

Robert Smith, born December 8th, 1948 – sentenced to death May 27th, 1982.

In early 1980, Joseph Leonard Lambright, 33, Robert Douglas Smith, 32, and Kathy Foreman began a cross country driving trip from Texas, to Florida, and then on to California, stopping in Arizona. Foreman was Lambright's lover who frequently engaged in sexual intercourse with Lambright in Smith's presence. The trio stopped outside Tucson and camped for the night. Smith became angry when he observed Lambright and Foreman once again having sex. He complained that Lambright, unlike Smith, had all the sex he wanted and that it was not easy to find someone.

The following day, the three drove into Tucson and went to a restaurant. Smith again spoke about wanting a woman, and Lambright spoke about wanting to "kill somebody just to see if he could do it." Lambright then told Foreman that they were going to go find someone for Smith.

After driving around town for quite a while, the trio saw a young woman hitchhiking near the University of Arizona campus. Twenty-nine year old Sandy Kay Owen explained to them that she was trying to get to the food stamp office. They drove Owen to the food stamp office and parked behind the building. Lambright jumped into the back seat with Owen and told her to "shut up and be quiet and she wouldn't get hurt." Smith moved to the driver seat and headed toward the freeway.

At some point during the drive towards California, Lambright began driving, with Smith in the back seat with Owen. Smith had sex with Owen in the back seat on the freeway, heading northwest. Owen asked if they would let her go.

The group later left the freeway and proceeded on a dirt road in a mountainous area of Pinal County. They left the car at the end of the dirt road and travelled on foot to a level area on a mountain. At the level area, Lambright and Foreman again had intercourse and Smith again had sex with Sandy Owen.

For some reason unknown Smith began choking Sandy and she collapsed to the ground. Lambright said that she had to be killed so that she could not report their crimes. He took Foreman's knife and began stabbing Owen in the torso and chest, twisting the knife around inside her. Smith and Foreman each held one of her arms, as the victim tried to resist. Smith attempted to break her neck by twisting her head, but was unsuccessful. Lambright, and possibly Foreman, then began cutting into Owen's neck. Sandy Owen was still alive and was trying to lift herself up on one arm. At that point, Lambright threw a large rock at Sandy's head, yelling, 'Die, bitch.'

The trio took some jewellery from Owen's body and then covered it with rocks before heading toward San Diego. In the car they played a song on tape entitled 'We are the Champions.' In San Diego, they pawned

Owen's ring before driving on to Anaheim, Las Vegas and finally back to Texas.

The case went cold until about a year later, law enforcement received a Silent Witness tip about the crime and the three were separately questioned and the whole affair came out and Sandy Owen's decomposed body was recovered. All three admitted the kidnapping offence and blamed each other for the murder in their statements to the police. Foreman was granted immunity from prosecution for her testimony against Lambright and Smith, who were returned to Arizona for prosecution.

Lambright and Smith were tried separately in March 1982 before separate juries. Both were found guilty of first degree murder and kidnapping plus other offences. Both were sentenced to death in May 1982.

Both launched appeals through their separate attorneys citing a history of mental problems, past suicide attempts, family abuse in broken homes and anything else they could make a case for including ineffective lawyers.

Lambright's death sentence has been reviewed and changed to life in prison he is now 77. Smith, now 76, still sits on death row.

# JEFFREY TIMOTHY LANDRIGAN

Born March 14th, 1960 – executed by lethal injection in Arizona October 26th, 2010.

A straightforward case of murder but the killer's family history is of interest.

In early November of 1989, Jeffrey Landrigan, 29, was incarcerated in an Oklahoma Department of Corrections Facility. He was serving a term of 20 years imprisonment for the murder of his 'best friend,' Greg Brown who he had stabbed to death in 1982, and he had been in prison since then. While in custody, Landrigan had not been a model prisoner. He had an argument with another prison inmate and repeatedly stabbed him, a crime for which Landrigan was convicted in March of 1986.

On November 10th, 1989, Landrigan escaped from custody in Oklahoma, and soon surfaced in Phoenix, Arizona. Within a month of arriving there he had met his next victim, Chester Dean Dyer, a homosexual man who often tried to pick up other men by showing a wad of money. On December 13th, 1989, Landrigan went to Dyer's apartment where the two of them drank beer, and had sex. They got on so well that Dyer called another friend of his to tell him about it, and even asked that friend if he could get Landrigan a job. The friend then spoke with Landrigan about that possibility.

Then something went very wrong and Landrigan killed Dyer by strangling and stabbing him. Dyer's body was found two days later and the Arizona Supreme Court described the murder scene in the following way:

Dyer was fully clothed, face down on his bed, with a pool of blood at his head. An electrical cord hung around his neck. There were facial lacerations and puncture wounds on the body. A half-eaten sandwich and a small screwdriver lay beside it. Blood smears were found in the kitchen and bathroom. Partial bloody shoeprints were on the tile floor. An ace of hearts, from a deck of cards depicting naked men in sexual poses, was carefully propped up on Dyer's back, and the rest of the deck was strewn across the bed. The apartment had been ransacked, and there were drops of blood on the bedding, the kitchen sink and the bathroom counter top.

Landrigan was soon picked up and told police that he and another man were in Dyer's that night and although he had hit Dyer after he made sexual advances the other man killed him. He was prosecuted for first degree murder and other crimes, convicted in a jury trial and sentenced to death by the trial judge who found aggravating circumstances, but insufficient mitigating circumstances to outweigh them. She pinioned that although the crime was not out of the ordinary as first degree murders go, Landrigan was. As she put it:

'to be somewhat of an exceptional human being. It appears that Mr. Landrigan is a person who has no scruples and no regard for human life and human beings and the right to live and enjoy life to the best of their ability, whatever their chosen lifestyle might be. Mr. Landrigan appears to be an amoral person.'

This seems to be a family trait. He was abandoned by his parents into care when born. His birth father, who he never met, died on death row in Kansas. His grandfather was shot dead by police whilst robbing a store.

Landrigan was executed by lethal injection in Arizona on October 26th, 2010 age 50.

# CHAD ALAN LEE

Born September 26th, 1972 sentenced to death March 24th, 1994.

On April 6, 1992, Chad Lee, 20 , and David Hunt, 14, called Pizza Hut from a pay phone and placed an order to be delivered to an empty house. When delivery driver Linda Reynolds arrived with the pizza order, Lee and Hunt confronted her with a rifle, forced her to remove her shorts and shirt, and abducted her. Lee drove his Pontiac LeMans into the desert with Reynolds, and Hunt drove Reynolds' car.

Lee removed the stereo from Reynolds' car and then destroyed the car by smashing the windows and various parts with a baseball bat, puncturing the tyres, and disabling the engine by cutting hoses and spark plug wires. ☐ Reynolds watched as one of the two shot a bullet through the hood of her car. ☐Lee later testified he destroyed Reynolds' car so that she could not escape.

Reynolds was forced to remove her pantyhose, socks, and shoes and to walk barefoot with Hunt into the desert north of her car where he raped her. ☐Hunt then walked Reynolds back toward her car where Lee forced Reynolds to perform oral sex on him.

After finding Reynolds' bank card in her wallet, Lee drove her and Hunt to Reynolds' bank to withdraw money from an ATM (automated teller machine). Lee gave Reynolds his flannel shirt to wear, walked her to the ATM, and forced her to withdraw twenty dollars. Lee and Hunt then drove Reynolds back to the desert north of where they had destroyed her car where

Reynolds managed to momentarily escape, but Hunt found her and forced her back to the car. When she returned, her face and lips were bloody.

Lee claimed that he and Hunt argued in front of Reynolds about whether to release her. Lee testified that Hunt was opposed to releasing her because she would be able to identify them. Lee stated that as he was escorting Reynolds away from Hunt, he, Lee, shot her in the head in a scuffle as she attempted to take the gun from him. Lee testified that he then ran back to the car, got a knife, went back to Reynolds, and stabbed her twice in the left side of her chest to stop her suffering. Lee then returned to his car and drove away with Hunt.

On April 7th, 1992, Lee pawned Reynolds' wedding ring, gold ring, and car stereo for a total of $170. He filled out a sales slip and used his driver's license as identification. A bad move.

Shortly after midnight on April 16th, 1992, nine days after the Reynolds murder, Lee called for a cab from a pay telephone at a convenience store. □ David Lacey's cab was dispatched, and he picked up Lee. Hunt, who had waited near the convenience store, drove Lee's car to the location where he and Lee had planned to rob a taxi. When Lacey stopped the cab and turned around to get paid, Lee pulled out his revolver and demanded money. Lee claimed that Lacey turned around and attempted to grab the gun. Lee then fired off nine shots, four of which hit Lacey. Lee took forty dollars from Lacey's pockets and dumped his body by the side of the road. With Hunt following, Lee drove the cab to a dirt road where he shot the cab's windows and tyres and rifled through its contents. Lee's cigarette lighter and a single bloody fingerprint on a receipt were later found in the abandoned cab.

On April 27th, 1992 at 01.00 am Lee went into the AM-PM store on 19th Avenue Phoenix intending to rob it whilst Hunt waited in the car He threatened the clerk, Harold Drury with a gun and demanded money. He took the entire cash drawer and shot Drury several times He dropped his pistol in a trash dumpster and fled. They drove out of town and broke the cash drawer on the road into several pieces before taking the money and throwing it into a dry creek.

After hearing news reports that police had found the same distinctive shoeprints at both the Reynolds and Lacey crime scenes, Lee drove to a forest north of Prescott and burned the shoes he had worn during both murders. At the same time he burned and buried two .22 calibre rifles including one that he used to shoot Reynolds. Lee left the knife he used to stab Reynolds stuck into a tree at the same location.

Police began their investigation of Linda Reynolds' disappearance the evening of April 6th, 1992, at her last delivery site and found her body on April 7th. They obtained videotape from the ATM she had been forced to withdraw money from that showed a Pontiac LeMans with Reynolds sitting in the front passenger seat and also showed her at the ATM with Lee standing next to her.

A patrol officer who responded to the Lacey crime scene noticed that the shoeprints found matched a shoeprint he had seen on a flyer containing information about the Reynolds murder. Subsequently, the Phoenix Police Department, investigating the Reynolds murder, and the Maricopa County Sheriff's Department, investigating the Lacey murder, began a joint investigation because of striking similarities between the two crimes.

Pizza Hut provided police with information about past orders that included Hawaiian pizza with pepperoni similar to the last order delivered by Linda Reynolds and an unusual combination. One such order had been placed from the home of David Hunt's stepmother. On May 1st, 1992, Hunt's stepmother told police that Hunt and Lee had ordered Hawaiian pizza in the past and that she recognized Lee's photograph in the newspaper. She gave police Hunt's father's address where police found him, his father, and Lee. Lee and Hunt agreed to provide police a sample of their fingerprints and did so that day. A few hours later, Lee, Hunt, and their girlfriends left town in Lee's car.

On May 3rd, 1992, at 4:00 p.m., Lee, Hunt, and their girlfriends were stopped by police in Oak Creek Canyon in connection with an armed robbery in Flagstaff. Lee was advised of his rights and transported to the Flagstaff Police Department. That evening he was advised of his rights again and signed a waiver form.

Later that day, a palm print found on Linda Reynolds' car was identified as belonging to Hunt. While attempting to alert law enforcement officers to detain Lee's car, police learned that it had been impounded in Flagstaff. □ Detectives from the Phoenix Police Department and the Maricopa County Sheriff's Department drove to Flagstaff to interview Lee and Hunt. On the way, the detectives received information that the bloody fingerprint found on the receipt in Lacey's cab matched Lee's print.

The detectives interviewed the girlfriends, then Hunt, and then Lee. In Lee's interview, which began at 2:45 a.m., May 4th, after he was again read his rights, he confessed to robbing and murdering Reynolds and Lacey and told the detectives how and where he had disposed of the weapons. He even offered to assist police officers in locating the weapons he used to murder Reynolds.

On May 5th, 1992, a Phoenix Police detective met with Lee at the Coconino County Jail and again advised him of his rights. Lee agreed to talk and then accompanied the police officers, directing them to the campsite where he had hidden a single-shot, sawn-off .22 calibre rifle and a semi-automatic .22 calibre rifle and left the knife in a nearby tree. Lee told the officers that he used the knife to stab Reynolds and the single-action rifle to shoot her. He further confessed in detail about his involvement in both murders to the Phoenix Police detective and later to two other officers during transport back to Coconino County Jail.

On May 6th, 1992, a Maricopa County Sheriff's Department detective re-interviewed Lee about the Lacey murder and robbery because the tape recorder had not functioned properly during the prior interview. On tape, Lee again waived his rights and retold how he planned the robbery and shot Lacey to death. He then admitted the AM-PM murder of Harold Drury and Hunt took the officers to recover the broken cash till which had both their fingerprints on it.

Finally, Lee testified at his trial and admitted that he made the pizza order, destroyed Reynolds' car, shot and stabbed Reynolds, and pawned her rings and stereo. Lee also admitted that he called the cab and shot Lacey in the head. Furthermore, he testified at his trial that all statements he made to police officers were of his own free will, that he was advised of his rights, and that he told officers he understood his rights.

The Maricopa County Grand Jury charged Lee with the following offenses:

(1) as to Linda Reynolds, first degree murder, kidnapping, two counts of sexual assault (sexual intercourse and oral sexual contact), armed robbery, and theft;

(2) as to David Lacey, first degree murder and armed robbery.

(3) as to Harold Drury (Lee II), first degree murder and armed robbery.

Lee filed multiple pre-trial motions including motions to appoint second counsel and to close the court proceedings to the media, both of which were denied. He also filed a motion to suppress his statements, alleging that they were involuntary. Following a suppression hearing, the trial court denied defendant's motion, finding that he had been advised of his rights on at least five separate occasions by different police officers, that he understood his rights on each of those occasions, and that he knowingly, intelligently, and voluntarily waived those rights. The trial court also found that his statements were made knowingly and voluntarily and were not the result of police misconduct.

On March 24th, 1994, a jury found Lee guilty of all charged offenses related to Reynolds and Lacey. Jurors unanimously found Lee guilty of the premeditated and felony murder of Reynolds, and they unanimously found defendant guilty of the felony murder of Lacey.

After a sentencing hearing, the trial court sentenced Lee to consecutive, aggravated terms of imprisonment totalling 101 years for the non-capital convictions. For each of the murders, Lee was sentenced to death on June 23rd, 1994. His appeals still continue as he sits on death row. David Hunt was given two life sentences and spared the death penalty because of his young age. A further life sentence was added after he took part in a murder that occurred in prison.

# DARRELL ESTON LEE

Born June 6th1957 – sentenced to death March 8th, 1993.☐

A pretty straightforward murder case with very little paperwork available for research.

On December 5th 1991, Darrell Lee, 34, and his girlfriend Karen Thompson kidnapped John Calvin at knife point in his car in Phoenix to rob him of money to buy drugs with. Calvin had no money on him and the pair escorted him to an ATM and forced him to withdraw money promising to release him if he did. Instead of releasing him they tied him up and dumped him beside a dirt track out of town and left him there.

However, they had a change of mind and a short time later returned and put him into the car's boot before driving from Phoenix to La Paz county.

Once there they pulled into a track and Lee attached a hose to the car exhaust and tried to force it into Calvin's mouth to poison and kill him. Calvin resisted and made a run for it but Lee caught him and then tried to strangle him with a belt which didn't work either so Karen Thompson killed him by beating his head with a large rock.

I have no other information other than their trial was held separately on November 10th, 1992 and both found guilty and sentenced on March 8th, 1993. Lee was sentenced to death as I would assume was Thompson. It would appear appeals were granted and both still sit on death row.

# J.C.LEVICE

Born August 26th, 1920 – executed in Arizona January 8th, 1943
## See under **GRADY B. COLE**

# LAWRENCE KEITH LIBBERTON

Born February 26th, 1961 – sentenced to death October 25th, 1982. Last known appeal in 2011 citing the ineffective assistance of counsel at the sentencing phase of his original trial. Still on death row age 64.
## See under **STEVEN CRAIG JAMES**

# SAMUEL VILLEGAS LOPEZ

Born June 30th, 1962 – executed by lethal injection in Arizona June 27th, 2012.

On October 29th, 1986, sometime around 11:00 a.m., a Phoenix police officer made a 'check welfare' call at the apartment residence of 59 year old Estefana Holmes. The check was in response to a call from Holmes's fellow employees expressing concern that the consistently prompt worker inexplicably failed to arrive at work that day. On approaching the apartment, officers noticed a broken window next to the front door.

Entering the apartment, they discovered the partially nude body of Holmes. Overturned and broken furnishings in the blood-splattered apartment indicated that a tremendous struggle took place prior to the murder. A scarf had been stuffed into Holmes's mouth, and she had been blindfolded with her own pyjama pants. An autopsy revealed that her throat had been slashed, and she had been stabbed twenty-three times in her left breast and upper chest and three times in her lower abdomen. Seminal fluid was found in both her vagina and anus.

Samuel Lopez had been seen in the neighbourhood the night of the crime. He was also seen in the early morning after the murder walking down the street, soaking wet, as if he had recently showered himself. Several days after the murder the police were questioning Lopez about an unrelated matter when he mentioned something about a woman who had been stabbed and whose throat had been slashed. The information that Holmes's throat had been slashed had never been released to the public. Realizing that only the murderer would know of the slashing, the police focused their investigation on Lopez. A check of his fingerprints matched those found at the victim's apartment and his blood group matched the semen blood group obtained from the victim's body.

Lopez went to trial on April 16th, 1987. On the 27th April he was convicted of first degree murder, kidnapping, sexual assault, and burglary. He was sentenced to death on June 25th, 1987 for the murder of Estafana Holmes and to aggravated, consecutive terms of twenty-one years for each of the other convictions.

After his appeals had failed and clemency denied he was executed in Arizona on June 27th, 2012 after 25 years on death row.

Lopez had written in his affidavit to the clemency board that 'what happened to Ms. Holmes was so horrible and so wrong. I've always been sorry for what she went through that night and for what her family have gone through ever since.' Lopez did not know Holmes, who was described by her family as hard-working, loving and deeply religious. Nearly a dozen of her family members, some of whom planned to witness the execution, pleaded with the clemency board to dismiss the clemency appeal and allow the execution to proceed.

Sarah Bryant, one of Holmes' sisters said, 'Let me ask you, Mr. Lopez, did our sister plead for her life as you stabbed her two dozen times? Did she beg you not to rape her? Did she plead with you to spare her life as you almost decapitated her? Did she? Nothing will bring her back, but you should pay for it.'

# JARED LEE LOUGHNER

Born September 10th, 1988 – sentenced to 7 consecutive life sentences plus 140 years in prison without parole on November 8th, 2012.

Jared Loughner was arrested for the January 8th, 2011 mass shooting in Tucson which led to him being charged with 19 charges of murder and attempted murder.

In the months leading up to the shooting, Loughner's parents became increasingly alarmed at their son's behaviour; at one point, they resorted to disabling his car every night in order to keep him at home. On another occasion, his father confiscated his shotgun and both parents urged him to get psychiatric help. Loughner also became obsessed with controlling what he perceived to be lucid dreams.

The shooting took place on January 8th, 2011, at a Safeway supermarket in La Toscana Village mall in Casas Adobes where the United States Representative from Arizona, Gabrielle Giffords, was holding a constituent meeting called 'Congress on Your Corner'. Giffords had set up a table outside the store and about 20 to 30 people were gathered around her when 22 year old Loughner suddenly drew a pistol and shot Giffords from close range in the head. The shooting was caught on video by a store security camera, but has never been released to the public.

Loughner then started to fire apparently randomly at other members of the crowd. He was armed with a Glock 19 semi-automatic pistol with four magazines.

Two were capable of holding 33 rounds each. A nearby store employee said he heard '15 to 20 gunshots'. Loughner stopped to reload, but dropped the loaded magazine from his pocket onto the sidewalk, from where bystander Patricia Maisch grabbed it. Another bystander, Roger Salzgeber, clubbed the back of Loughner's head with a folding chair, injuring his elbow in the process. Loughner was tackled to the ground by Bill Badger, a 74-year-old retired United States Army Colonel who had also been shot himself. Loughner was further subdued by Maisch, Salzgeber and bystander Joseph Zamudio. Zamudio was a concealed weapon (CCW) permit holder, and had a weapon on his person, but arrived after the shooting had stopped and did not draw his firearm. Thirty-one shell casings were found at the scene.

The first call from the scene to emergency services was received at 10:11 am. While waiting for help to arrive, Giffords's intern Daniel Hernandez Jr. applied pressure to the gunshot wound on her forehead, and made sure she did not choke on her own blood. Hernández, and local paramedic Aaron Rogers are credited with saving Giffords's life. David and Nancy Bowman, a married doctor and nurse couple who were shopping in the store, immediately set up triage and attended to nine-year-old Christina-Taylor Green.

Police arrived on the scene at 10:15 am., with paramedics arriving at 10:16 am. Badger observed the assailant attempting to discard a small bag containing money and identification, which was recovered by the officers. Following the shooting, the police shut down roads surrounding the shopping centre until late in the day. The intersection was cordoned off and most of the businesses in the shopping centre were closed throughout the weekend during the initial investigation. The Safeway store reopened a week later, with a makeshift memorial erected near the front of the store.

Five people died at the scene, including Chief Judge John Roll and Giffords's community outreach director Gabe Zimmerman. Several of the injured were taken to University Medical Centre in Tucson. Christina-Taylor Green was later pronounced dead on arrival at the hospital.

When Loughner's parents arrived at their home, unaware of the shootings, they found police tape and police cars around their house. Their neighbour Wayne Smith said Loughner's mother 'almost passed out right there', while his father sat in the road and cried. Smith described the family as 'devastated', feeling guilty, and wondering 'where did they fail?' Loughner's parents released a statement three days later expressing remorse for the victims and saying, 'We don't understand why this happened.'

Loughner was charged in Federal Court with one count of attempted assassination of a member of Congress, two counts of murder of a federal employee (Giffords' aide and Judge Roll), and two counts of attempting to murder a federal employee, based on his injury of two of Giffords' aides. He was indicted on three of the charges on January 19th, 2011.

Loughner was held without bail in the Federal Correctional Institution at Phoenix, kept isolated from other inmates 23 hours a day and allowed out of his cell for one hour a day to shower and exercise. On February 24th, 2011, he was transferred to the United States Penitentiary in Tucson.

On August 7th, 2012, Judge Burns found Loughner competent to stand trial based on medical evaluations. Loughner pleaded guilty to 19 counts at the hearing, these guilty pleas spared him the death penalty and automatically waived his right to appeal.

On November 8th, 2012, Loughner appeared in front of U.S. District Court Judge Larry Alan Burns in a court in Tucson. He was sentenced to serve seven consecutive life terms plus 140 years in prison without parole Even though he was convicted and sentenced in Federal Court, there was still a possibility that Loughner could be tried for murder and other crimes in an Arizona court. Pima County Attorney Barbara LaWall declared later that afternoon that she would not prosecute Jared Loughner on behalf of the State of Arizona. LaWall explained that her decision would afford the victims and their families, as well as the community in Tucson and Pima County, an opportunity to move forward with their lives. She said that, after speaking and consulting personally with each of the surviving victims and with the family members of those killed, it was clear that they would not benefit by a State prosecution. Surviving victims and family members told LaWall that they are 'completely satisfied with the federal prosecution', that 'justice has been served', and that the federal sentence is 'suitably severe'.

Loughner is currently serving his life sentence at the Federal Medical Centre, Rochester, Minnesota prison for inmates with specialized health issues.

# SHAWN PATRICK LYNCH

Born December 18th, 1961 – sentenced to death May 23rd, 2006

James Panzarella lived in a guesthouse behind his parents' Scottsdale home. On March 24th, 2001, James left his car at his brother's home and took a cab to a Scottsdale bar. He was seen at the bar with two men later identified as Mike Sehwani and Shawn Patrick Lynch. James, Sehwani, and Lynch went to James's guesthouse early in the morning of March 25th.

At around 5:00 a.m., an escort service received a call from Sehwani and dispatched an escort and her bodyguard to the guesthouse. The bodyguard collected a \$175 fee from James. The escort and Sehwani went into a bedroom while James and Lynch talked with the bodyguard in the kitchen. Sehwani wrote two cheques from James's cheque book to the escort totalling \$300. The bodyguard and escort left around 6:00a.m. At about 7:15a.m. Lynch and Sehwani went to a local supermarket where Sehwani bought cigarettes with James's American Express card. Ten minutes later, the card was reported as lost and invalidated. Later that morning, Sehwani accompanied by Lynch, unsuccessfully attempted to use the card at a department store. Around noon, Sehwani used James's Bank One credit card at a restaurant. This credit card was also used twice that day at a convenience store. That afternoon Lynch and Sehwani checked into a motel. Lynch registered in his name and paid with cash, Sehwani used James's credit card to rent movies. That evening, Lynch and Sehwani checked into another motel, again registering in Lynch's name and paying cash. On the afternoon of March 25th, James was found bound to a metal chair in the guesthouse kitchen. His throat was slit and blood had made a puddle on the tile floor. The guesthouse was in disarray. In a bedroom, police found a large hunting knife. In the kitchen, they found a knife block with a knife missing. American Express receipts from the March 25th supermarket and convenience store purchases were also found in the guesthouse. Early in the morning of March 26th, James's Bank One debit card was used to withdraw cash from an ATM. Another attempted withdrawal later was unsuccessful. The debit card was also used later that morning to buy clothing and Everlast shoes, and at least twice elsewhere that same day.

Police arrested Lynch and Sehwani that afternoon as they entered a truck in the motel parking lot. Sehwani wore white Everlast sneakers and had James's credit cards and cheques in his wallet. Book matches from the convenience store and the keys to James's car were in the truck. A black sweater with James's blood on it was behind the seats. A .45 calibre pistol belonging to James was later found in the motel room. Blood on Lynch's shoes tested positive for James's DNA. Lynch and Sehwani were charged with first degree murder (both felony and premeditated), armed robbery, burglary, and kidnapping. Lynch went to trial first. The jury found him guilty on all counts, but could not reach a unanimous verdict on premeditated murder. In the aggravation phase of the trial, the jury could not agree on whether the murder was committed in expectation of pecuniary gain. The jury made separate findings that the murder was both especially heinous and cruel, but could not decide whether the murder was also especially depraved. In the penalty phase, the jury could not reach a unanimous verdict so a second jury was empanelled. The second jury then unanimously determined that Lynch should be sentenced to death for the murder.

His death sentence was overturned in 2016 by the U.S. Supreme Court judging that Lynch should have been allowed to tell jurors that he would not be eligible for parole if sentenced to a prison term of natural life or of at least 25 years. This may have brought him one of those terms as the verdict rather than death. The case goes on with the Maricopa County Attorney disputing this.

**END**

Arizona Killers M to Z follows in volume 3 of the American Killers series.

Thank you for buying this book. To keep up with my new releases and other information on my talks, what book festivals I am attending and other useless information about me please become a friend on my Barry Faulkner Facebook page. I don't have a website, not enough time, but all my books are on my Barry Faulkner Amazon page together with the first pages of each as a taster. You can also order them at your local library or book shop if they don't have them already.

## DCS Palmer books (crime fiction)

Future Riches
The Felt Tip Murders
Killer is Calling
Poetic Justice
Loot
I'm With The Band
Burning Ambition
Take Away Terror
Ministry of Death
The Bodybuilder
Succession
The Black Rose
Laptops Can Kill
Screen 4
Underneath The Arches

## Ben Nevis and the Gold Digger Series (PE thrillers)

Turkish Delight
National Treasure
Chinese Takeaway
Double Trouble

The Pyramid

**True Crime Series**
London Crime 1930s-2021
UK Killers Vol. 1. A to E. 1900-1921
UK Killers Vol. 2. F to M. 1900- 2021
UK Killers Vol. 3. N to Z  1900-2021
USA Killers Vol. 1. Alabama
USA KillersVol.2.Arizona Ato L

-------------------------

**Others**
Bidder Beware  (Comedy crime)
Fred Karno   (biography)

Printed in Great Britain
by Amazon

46362527R00198